ELIZABET

Hermione Lee grew up in London, was educated at Oxford, began her academic career as a lecturer in Williamsburg, Virginia and at Liverpool, and taught at the University of York from 1977, where she was Professor of English until her recent appointment to the Goldsmiths' Chair of English Literature and Fellow of New College at the University of Oxford. She is well known as a writer, reviewer and broadcaster. From 1982 to 1986 she presented Channel Four's first books programme, Book Four. Her publications include a critical study of the novels of Virginia Woolf, a book on Philip Roth, a biography of Willa Cather, a popular two-volume anthology of short stories by women writers, *The Secret Self*, and numerous editions, of Bowen, Woolf, Stevie Smith, Welty, Wharton, Kipling and others. Her biography of Virginia Woolf (winner of the British Academy Rose Mary Crawshay Award) was published in 1996 and was greeted with great acclaim. It was chosen as a *New York Times Book Review* Best Book of the Year, and short-listed for the W. H. Smith Prize, the Duff Cooper Prize, the James Tait Black Memorial Prize, and the National Book Critics Circle Award for Biography in the USA. *Elizabeth Bowen* was first published in 1981 and revised in 1999 for Bowen's centenary.

ALSO BY HERMIONE LEE

The Novels of Virginia Woolf
Philip Roth
Willa Cather: A Life Saved Up
Virginia Woolf

Editor

Stevie Smith: A Selection
The Hogarth Letters
The Mulberry Tree: Writings of Elizabeth Bowen
The Secret Self: Short Stories by Women
The Short Stories of Willa Cather
Elizabeth Bowen: *Bowen's Court and Seven Winters*
Virginia Woolf: *A Room of One's Own and Three Guineas,*
To the Lighthouse, The Years

Hermione Lee

ELIZABETH BOWEN

VINTAGE

For John Barnard

Published by Vintage 1999

2 4 6 8 10 9 7 5 3 1

First published in Great Britain in 1981
by Vision Press Ltd and Barnes & Noble Books

Vintage
Random House, 20 Vauxhall Bridge Road, London SW1V 2SA

Random House Australia (Pty) Limited
20 Alfred Street, Milsons Point, Sydney
New South Wales 2061, Australia

Random House New Zealand Limited
18 Poland Road, Glenfield,
Auckland 10, New Zealand

Random House South Africa (Pty) Limited
Endulini, 5A Jubilee Road, Parktown 2193, South Africa

Random House UK Limited Reg. No. 954009

A CIP catalogue record for this book
is available from the British Library

ISBN 0 09 927715 8

Papers used by Random House UK Ltd are natural,
recyclable products made from wood grown in
sustainable forests. The manufacturing processes
conform to the environmental regulations of the
country of origin.

Typeset by Deltatype Ltd, Birkenhead, Merseyside
Printed and bound in Great Britain by
Cox & Wyman Ltd, Reading, Berks.

CONTENTS

I

RE-READING BOWEN

Easy to be wise after the event. For the writer, writing is
eventful: one might say it is in itself eventfulness . . . One may
not exactly know what one has (finally) written till one has
finished it, and then only after a term of time. Then begins a
view of the whole, a more perceptive or comprehensive vision;
but too late. However, fortunately for authors they are seldom
prey to regret. They seldom look back, for they are usually
engaged upon something else.

ELIZABETH BOWEN IS one of the greatest writers of
fiction in this language and in this century. She wrote ten
novels, at least five of which are masterpieces: strange,
original, vivid, exciting and intelligent. She is a very fine
short-story writer, a brilliant technician of the form, a
dazzling evoker of mood and place. Her stories are beauti-
fully controlled and intensely haunting. She also wrote three
books about her Irish history and a number of essays about
childhood, school, reading, social behaviour, war and Anglo-
Ireland, which make fresh, funny and alluring versions of
autobiography.

She began publishing young, in her twenties, and by her
thirties she was well known, much praised and much in
demand. In 1942, it was said of her that 'since Virginia
Woolf's death, she is coming more and more to be regarded
as the outstanding woman novelist of her generation'.[1] Since
her own death in 1973, her novels and stories have continued
to be in print; she has a strong following, particularly in the
United States and Ireland; she goes on being read.

1

Yet when I wrote this book about her eighteen years ago, she had become (certainly in England) a marginalised and undervalued figure. She was certainly not part of any academic canon (unless as an example of an Anglo-Irish tradition). She was never placed alongside Virginia Woolf or Katherine Mansfield – or, for that matter, Evelyn Waugh or Graham Greene – as one of the 'important' writers of the century. She tended to be seen as an interesting secondary figure, sidelined in the space reserved for small, likeable talents like L. P. Hartley or William Plomer, or her contemporary misfits and eccentrics, Ivy Compton-Burnett or Henry Green. She was often treated as minor because female, because writing about girls growing up, love affairs and women's lives – like Rosamond Lehmann or Jean Rhys.

In 1981 it was hard for me to find a publisher, or an audience, for a book on her work. There hadn't been a great deal written on her before that: one British Council pamphlet by Jocelyn Brooke, in 1952; Victoria Glendinning's biography, in 1977; a few articles, and four full-length American studies of her work in the years between 1961 and 1975. I began and ended my book by claiming that she deserved a higher estimation, a bigger and different reputation: that she had been undervalued and mis-read.

I wanted, in this book, to make clear what a significant, dramatic, interesting historical narrative her fictions make. I was anxious to rescue her from being identified 'only' with personal and emotional concerns. I didn't want her to be diminished as a woman's novelist, inhabiting only private spaces. One way of doing this was to give her her rightful place in literary history, to look at the reading and the influences that lay behind her writing. I set out to map her relationship to more than one fictional family: to Flaubert and James and the well-made, deeply observed, minutely crafted novel; to Forster and the English tradition of fiction as a formal vehicle for self-awareness; to Woolf's exploration of inner lives – often women's lives – in tension against the political pressures of a changing world; and to something more grotesque, extravagant and unstable, the Anglo-Irish tradition of social comedy and ghost stories.

I wanted too to make sense of the most noticeable feature of her writing – which puts off some readers – her highly formal, contrived, oblique, often elusive style. I needed to show that her manners were not just mannerisms, and to read 'style' as an essential part of what she has to say about civilisation and society.

So this book argues, as I still maintain, that Bowen's emotional plots are about more than the deaths of individual hearts or private worlds of love, but make a critique of the English and Anglo-Irish middle classes of the inter-war and post-1940s years. Bowen's intense, witty, evocative treatment of personal behaviour and feeling is also an analysis of a 'disinherited' society. She makes a modern critique – a dramatic and disturbing one – of what she sees as a period of loss and diminishment, a society which she views, ironically, as dislocated and uneasy, cracked across with treachery and bad faith. What's most extraordinary (and often very disconcerting) about her work is that she applies supremely stylish and crafty fictional methods to a treatment of chaotic, unmanageable, even incommunicable experience.

This reading of Bowen still seems to me plausible and interesting, and a useful starting point for her new readers. Apart from adding some biographical material for those who don't know Bowen's story, and revising or getting rid of the sentences I couldn't bear to read again, I have left the book much as it was. But, since 1981, a great deal has changed: in the work done on Bowen, in the wider area of feminist criticism and writing about women, and in my own writing and thinking. Working on Virginia Woolf's biography, and developing an interest in different kinds of 'life-writing', has made me less embarrassed, as a critic, about crossing between the personal and the fictional. Critical writing by and about women now moves much more freely between different approaches: cultural and gender studies, autobiography, historical analysis. Fiction writers have taken to confession like ducks to water; biographers let fictional manoeuvres trickle into their 'factual' enterprises. I am much less anxious about saying 'I' when I write. And I don't any longer think it a weak position to write about the 'merely' personal in women's writing.

I would be more interested now, for instance, in reading the sense of displacement and dispossession in Bowen as expressions of personal traumas and anxieties rather than as historical commentary. I think there is more to be said about sex in Bowen – repression, danger, ambivalence. I would want to give more space to the complicated feelings about mothers – intimacy with, loss of, resistance to – in Bowen's fiction. And I would feel free to spend more time than I did, without having to make excuses for it, on her brilliant use of trivia, of domestic and social detail, on *things* in Bowen: clothes, furniture, decor, the cinema, travel, meals, drinks, shopping, suburbs.

Some of this work has been done in the last eighteen years: it's a pleasure to see how much has been written about her since this book first came out. Now, in her centenary year, there have been several academic conferences on Bowen, and since 1992 there's been a Bowen 'Newsletter'. Six more books have been written on her and many essays (some collected into a volume of 'modern critical views' of Bowen in 1987). *The Heat of the Day* was made into a film for television, with a script by Harold Pinter, starring Patricia Hodge. Victoria Glendinning's biography was paperbacked in 1985. A film is being made of *The Last September*, with a script by John Banville, and there is a BBC *Bookmark* programme on Bowen. The novels are currently all being reissued with new introductions. New versions of Bowen have come into being, some of which she might not have recognised herself, but all of them increasing the attention she's given and the sense of her value.

These re-readings of Bowen come out of two main (and thriving) areas of academic work, which occasionally overlap: Anglo-Irish studies and feminist approaches to the novel. As an Anglo-Irish writer, her rediscovery has been part of a great

wave of new writing about Irish literary history. In Seamus
Deane's massive (and controversial) *Field Day Anthology of
Irish Writing* (1991), and in books such as Roy Foster's
*Paddy & Mr Punch: Connections in Irish and English
History* (1993), W. J. McCormack's *Dissolute Characters:
Irish Literary History through Balzac, Sheridan Le Fanu,
Yeats and Bowen* (1993), Declan Kiberd's *Inventing Ireland:
The Literature of the Modern Nation* (1995), and Eibhear
Walshe's edition of essays on *Sex, Nation and Dissent in Irish
Writing* (1997), Bowen takes central place in the ambivalent,
awkward, difficult history of connections between Ireland
and England.

These new readings of Irish literary history are extremely
various and often strongly opposed to each other. They may
look again at the whole canon of Irish writing and at how
'canonisation' works as 'a system of ratification and authority'.[2] Some make sceptical analyses of how patriotic or
nationalist bias has shaped the cultural concept of Irishness;[3]
others choose to apply 'models of postcoloniality'[4] to Irish
cultural studies. But whether these books are examining exile
and the memory of the homeland, the links between high art
and popular culture, women's histories, multi-culturalism,
censorship, the 'counter-discourses'[5] of feminism and lesbian-
ism, or the invention of fictional characters in relation to
political ideology and national identity,[6] they all make use of
Bowen as a crucial and significant figure.

Linked to the re-reading of Bowen, at an interesting
tangent, has been the late valuation given to the writing of
her cousin Hubert Butler (1900–91) by writers as diversely
influential as Roy Foster, Neil Ascherson and Josef Brodsky.
Butler (who was the brother-in-law of Bowen's favourite
cousin, Noreen Butler, née Colley) was, with his wife Peggy, a
good friend of Bowen's. He lived for most of his life in his
family house, Maidenhall, in County Kilkenny. (When I
visited him there in 1980, I saw the family portraits from
Bowen's Court hanging in his dining-room.) A Protestant
Republican, Butler committed himself to lifelong work as a
local and Anglo-Irish historian. But his travels in the 1930s

and 1940s in Eastern Europe, especially in Yugoslavia, gave him a wider focus on Irish affairs, and led to some remarkable essays. He wrote clear-sightedly on the terrible history of Serbo-Croatian conflict (for which he gave the Catholic Church its full share of blame, a position which made him very unpopular at home). His essays ranged from acute literary studies of Russian, European and Irish writers, to arguments over regional identity, secularism and religion, demagoguery, cultural pluralism and the disaster of Partition. They only began to be published in the 1980s, but by the time of his death at the age of ninety-one he had become a widely admired writer.

Butler's material often overlapped with Bowen's in his treatment of the withdrawal of a whole historical class, the Anglo-Irish Protestant Ascendancy landlords, from vigour and effectiveness.[7] His half-critical, half-nostalgic accounts of the fate of the 'descendancy' in twentieth-century Ireland and his stories of 'Big House' life in its period of demise have a great deal in common with Bowen's *The Last September*, her essay on 'The Big House', and what Butler called 'that wonderful book of social and family history', *Bowen's Court*. He was review editor for a time of Sean O'Faolain's periodical *The Bell*, to which Bowen contributed. ('The Big House' was published there.) And he bore witness, in the first volume of his essays, *Escape from the Anthill*, to her own ambivalence towards Ireland. He made a speech about her in 1979, when a memorial tablet was set up to her in Farahy Church, where she was buried. Here he spoke of her as 'closely linked to a way of life, a class, a community, that is quickly disappearing'. He said that she 'had to forge an Irish literary personality for herself', and that, though 'knowing the debt she owed to England', she felt 'passionately Irish and often explored what this Irish feeling was'.[8] Yet, three years earlier, writing about her contributions to *The Bell* and her gallant upkeep of Bowen's Court, he said that in the later years of her life she turned against Ireland. 'When I last met her in County Kilkenny, just before her own death, she spoke of Ireland with such bitterness that I have tried to persuade myself that it was her last illness that was speaking and not her utter disillusionment.'[9] Roy Foster, who talked to Peggy Butler about that conversation in 1990, commented, 'In 1972 she astounded [them] by the vehemence with which she said, "I *hate* Ireland."'[10]

That very expression of disaffection, Foster says, makes Bowen part of 'a tradition distinctively if uncomfortably Irish'. And it's that distinctive and uncomfortable Irishness – what her friend Sean O'Faolain called her 'heart-cloven and split-minded' state[11] – which has dominated the recent accounts of Bowen by historians of Anglo-Irish culture. 'Ambivalence' has always been a key word in accounts of Anglo-Irishness, but it has been applied to Bowen more and more intensively. It's not often that her Anglo-Irishness is described in the unmixed terms that the Irish writer Patricia Craig uses, when she talks of the 'robustness and decorum conferred on Elizabeth by her upbringing and temperament'.[12] More often her Anglo-Irishness is seen to produce, as in *The Last September*, a writing of 'elegy and crisis'.[13] 'Her real themes', says Roy Foster, 'are dispossession, double-crossing, cruelty, betrayal.'[14]

In common with other Irish writers, such as Sean O'Faolain, Frank O'Connor and Liam O'Flaherty, her language is described (by the critic John Hildebidle) as one of 'disillusionment' and 'loneliness', expressing 'a radical detachment'. That detachment, he says, isn't only a sense of being an outsider or displaced person: it gets into all her fictional versions of love (a violent, dangerous collision), of insecure and unreliable homes, and of the self, which in her fiction is always unstable. Her novels and stories convey 'a perilous feeling of non-existence'.[15] This feeling of 'non-existence', argues one of Bowen's keenest advocates, W. J. McCormack, is typical of Anglo-Irish self-alienation. The 'instability of language' in her novels (especially *The Heat of the Day*), the fascination with treachery, the indeterminate sense of identity in her work, reflect, he says, the bad faith and insecurity of a whole class.[16] And Declan Kiberd, in his post-colonial reading of Irish literature, says that all Bowen's writing comes out of a search for 'an assured sense of identity': 'She wrote not so much to record as to invent a self, a self which lived on the hyphen between "Anglo" and "Irish".'[17]

This re-reading of a Janus-faced Bowen, caught between two countries, and betraying through the stylishness of her work a deep uncertainty about identity, focuses most dramatically on her wartime activities. And it is an extraordinary story. Here is an Irish writer with a Big House in County Cork and an Anglo-Irish family whose roots in Ireland go back to the seventeenth century, who has chosen to live and work mainly in England and to marry an Englishman, but to write very often about Ireland and to keep her Irish house. In wartime she is mostly in London, supporting the English war effort and (like many English people) responding to air raids and bombings with stoic fortitude. But she is also spending a good deal of time in Dublin, since she has offered her services to the Ministry of Information, and is writing them reports on Irish neutrality and the mood in Ireland towards England, Germany and the war. This is secret work, which her Irish friends don't know she is engaged in. And out of this comes her wartime novel, *The Heat of the Day*, a novel about treachery and betrayal – of love and of a country.

In these secret reports, there is much that is critical of Ireland. She sees 'self-interest' as the basis of neutrality. She dislikes the parochialism, the 'claustrophobia and restlessness', the 'stagnation' which she sees in Dublin as a result of neutrality. She is scornful of the 'swivellers' in Ireland who are hostile to the British war effort and of the individuals who seem to her to have a morbid attraction to fascism. She is alert to the pernicious dangers of Catholic anti-Communism and anti-semitism in wartime Ireland. Yet, for all this, she understands Ireland's position and sees that 'Eire' (as she always calls it) has 'invested her self-respect' in neutrality. It is 'Eire's first *free* self-assertion'. And, with characteristic objectivity and irony, she comments on the mutual mistrust between the two countries: 'I could wish that the English kept history in mind more, that the Irish kept it in mind less.'[18]

These reports were quoted at length by Robert Fisk in his

book on Irish neutrality, *In Time of War*, published in 1983. Since then they have been made much use of in re-readings of Bowen. A very useful book by an American academic, Heather Bryant Jordan, full of well-researched detail, reads Bowen as essentially a writer of war, registering the violent shifts in her world that arose from the First World War, the Troubles and the Civil War in Ireland, and the Second World War. Jordan takes as her cue an (unpublished) radio play of 1949, looking back to 1918, in which the narrator says, 'I can't imagine myself without a war.' She sees Bowen's wartime activities as intensifying her 'split' Anglo-Irish vision, and *The Heat of the Day* as the novel which attempted to settle some of these 'ambiguities'. And she concludes by seeing Bowen as a writer who took 'more risks than she might otherwise have done' because her subjects were, necessarily, war and betrayal.[19]

The Irish approach to Bowen as a writer of divided loyalties, obsessed with betrayal, is confirmed by the details of her wartime activities. (Certainly they support McCormack's view that *The Heat of the Day* is as much about Irish neutrality as it is about England in wartime. They make sense, too, of the curious fact that Bowen made her treacherous lover, Robert Kelway, a Nazi rather than a Communist spy and sympathiser. Her encounters in neutral Ireland with anti-British, pro-fascist feeling may have lain behind this. McCormack calls it 'an Irish trace' in the novel.)[20] Foster sees Bowen herself, in wartime, as a 'kind of spy'.[21]

Spies and traitors have to keep up a front. So too did the Anglo-Irish, a 'race' (as she called them) characterised by observant detachment. Declan Kiberd finds it unsurprising, then, that Bowen 'became an expert analyst of the death of the heart'. 'Imperviousness . . . to feeling' was her Anglo-Irish subject. And, like the Anglo-Irish, what she constructed around the blockage of feeling was 'an assumed style'. Kiberd evolves from this an idea of the Anglo-Irish writer as dandy, playing a role, maintaining with strenuous energy a nonchalant front, like Oscar Wilde. Dandies are 'the final, decadent flowering' of the tribe, who can play any part except themselves, and who perform on a dangerous edge, since if you live by style alone 'the performance is always liable to break down'.[22]

The link to Wilde raises the issue of sexual as well as tribal ambivalence. Feminist approaches to Bowen have tended not to be so interested in her Irish context. But it's interesting when the two readings overlap, as when Irish women critics point out that Bowen shows women as 'the impotent victims of war ... confined and repressed in public life',[23] or that with the collapse of real power in the Big House, the vacuum is filled, in her novels, with violently manipulative female characters who represent a 'distorted expression' of that power.[24] The troubling uneasiness in Bowen's treatment of sexual relationships can be seen, too, as in part the product of a repressive Irish history. Eibhear Walshe's book, in particular, looks at Bowen in the Irish context of 'post-colonial censorship' and 'a deep-seated cultural fear of same-sex desire'.[25]

It's hard to turn Bowen into a committed feminist, given her own rejection of such terms ('I am not, and never shall be, a feminist'),[26] her impatience with Virginia Woolf's political arguments over women's suppression,[27] and the avoidance of polemical feminism in her fiction. And although she writes with great feeling, subtlety and interest about women's relationships, it's difficult, too, to claim her as a lesbian writer, given the facts of her life, her satirical attitude to the only lesbian writer, May Sarton, known to have fallen in love with her, and the strongly heterosexist plots of most of her novels. Attempts to force her into a narrowly defined lesbian programme look over-prescriptive to me. Renée Hoogland, in a 1991 thesis on 'Feminist Critical Theory and the Case of Elizabeth Bowen', published in 1994 as part of a 'Lesbian Life and Literature' series, argues for a re-reading of Bowen in only one permissible – hitherto impermissible – way. Writing from a post-structuralist and lesbian-feminist perspective, Hoogland claims that Bowen has been marginalised because she failed 'to meet the requirements of dominant (male) literary movements'. She reads her novels as 'incisive critiques of patriarchal ideology'. So *The Last September* is about 'the gendered operations of ideological discourses', and *The Heat of the Day* is seen as 'problematising the gender-inflected issue of narrativisation at several intersecting textual levels'. Bowen's women characters are subjected to the masculine plot of 'the phallogocentric dominant ideology'. 'It is obvious', Hoogland concludes, 'that the issue of lesbian sexuality surfaces in most of her texts.' To neglect or negate these issues is to stand accused of homophobia.[28]

This seems a flattening, intractable model for Bowen's slippery and complex fictions. A more flexible, less authoritarian application of a lesbian-feminist perspective to Bowen might be more interesting. If feminism is allowed to cover a woman writer's treatment of sexuality, sexual politics, love, marriage, and a passionate desire for some way of life for women beyond conventional and expected roles, then Bowen is a feminist indeed. Patricia Coughlan argues, in 'Women and Desire in the Work of Elizabeth Bowen', that we might want to take the model proposed by Adrienne Rich of 'woman-to-woman interaction . . . and other kinds of attachment between women' as existing within a 'lesbian continuum'. Same-sex desire may be, but need not be, on the agenda. In which case Bowen's intense treatments of 'female bonding', of 'women's mutual attraction', of mother-daughter attachments and of 'the interpenetration of desire and friendship in women's relationships' could allow for Bowen's work to be defined as a form of lesbian writing.[29]

Other feminist critics of Bowen have, similarly, prioritised the attention to women's lives in Bowen's work. Her interest in female friendships, Diane Swanson says, breaks her out of the 'traditional fictional plot of "compulsory heterosexuality"'.[30] Harriet Chessman argues that female figures in Bowen have no language that works for them, are inarticulate or silent, 'inherently outside the discourse, unless they turn traitors and defect to the other side'.[31] Phyllis Lassner, in a short psychoanalytical feminist book on Bowen, places her

11

treatment of women's roles at the centre of her work. Her crucial subject, Lassner says, is the 'formation of female character against the literary and social traditions which has been responsible for its development'. As part of this project, Bowen dwells on 'the nature and place of women's sexuality', the 'bonds between children and mothers', and the 'emotional paralysis' of women constricted within 'domestic and maternal roles'. To approach Bowen as part of a 'patriarchal tradition' of writing is to diminish her, since 'her work serves to question and revise the ideological and social assumptions of all tradition'.[32]

These re-readings of Bowen present her, rightly, as a subversive writer with a passionate interest in women's lives, even if, for the purposes of argument, they have to underplay the social comedy, the unpredictable lack of formulae, and the surprising, ambushing oddness of much of her work, which doesn't lend itself to fixed agendas.

That oddness is brought out in a collaborative book on Bowen by two young male British academics, Andrew Bennett and Nicholas Royle, who have no doubt at all of Bowen's supreme importance as a writer for our times who 'is only now beginning to be recognised': 'She is emerging as a significant figure within several key areas of contemporary study and interest: twentieth-century women's writing, Anglo-Irish and minority literatures, writers of the Thirties and Forties, postcolonialism and postmodernism.' She seems to them an utterly original and extremely disturbing writer who requires a new kind of post-Derridan critical language of deconstruction to be made sense of. So they go as far as can be from seeing Bowen in historical, cultural or realist terms. Their book is called *Elizabeth Bowen and the Dissolution of the Novel: Still Lives*, because Bowen, they say, embodies 'the dissolution of the twentieth-century novel'. Her novels dissolve reality, distinctions between life and death, 'personal identity, patriarchy, social conventions and language itself'. They are about states of abeyance and immobility, catatonia and 'thought-stoppage'; dreaming, hauntings, trance and convulsions; the deferment and disruption of time; traumas, secrets, mourning and dread. Identity in Bowen is always 'riven by constant invasion, intrusion, transgression'. Her fictions are 'uncannily dramatic'; everyone is playing a multiplicity of parts; no identity is stable or single. Above all, her texts are constantly reminding us of themselves as 'writing and textuality'.[33] These readings lead them to place great weight on (and to make very illuminating readings of) the last two novels.

As a counterweight to this challenging and inventive new reading of Bowen, I am happy to bring back into print my version of a more political, realist, socially observant and self-consciously controlled Bowen. But the work of Bennett and Royle shows us, too, what is compelling in her: her wild originality, her strangeness, her dangers, her shadowy uncertainties. All the recent critics of Bowen, however different their methods, agree that she is a voice like no other. A hundred years since her birth, and over a quarter of a century since her death, there is much more to be said about her. She is, more than ever before, a writer to be re-read and a writer who can never be forgotten.

2

ONLY CHILDREN

> Each of these houses, with its intense, centripetal life, is
> isolated by something very much more lasting than the
> physical fact of space: the isolation is innate; it is an affair of
> origin. It is possible that Anglo-Irish people, like only children,
> do not know how much they miss. Their existences, like those
> of only children, are singular, independent and secretive.

WHEN ELIZABETH BOWEN was very young, her 'endemic
pride' in her own country arose from a childhood confusion
between two words, 'Ireland' and 'island'. 'It seemed fine to
live in a country that was a prototype. England, for instance,
was "an ireland" (or, a sub-Ireland) – an imitation.'[1] This
misunderstanding was typical of her blithe, youthful chauvinism, which she drily recorded in her two autobiographies,
Bowen's Court (1942) and *Seven Winters* (1942). As the only
child of middle-class Protestant Unionists, her father a lawyer
and her mother the offspring of a considerable Anglo-Irish
family, the Colleys, 'Bitha' Bowen had no idea that Protes-
tants were a minority. She was brought up, in Dublin in the
winters and at Bowen's Court in the summers, among
families like her own who seemed to exist comfortably on
'unquestioned rules.'[2] No one was shy, or vulgar, or Catholic,
and everyone had a brass plate with his name on the door.
Her first view of London, 'street after street of triste
anonymity', confirmed her sense of Dublin's grandeur and
exclusiveness. 'All the important people live in Dublin, near
me.'[3]

Elizabeth Bowen's ironic memory of her childhood confidence partly mocks the short-sightedness of a vanished élite. There is some similarity of tone in the way she writes about herself as a child and in the way she writes about her Anglo-Irish ancestors. But even at a very early age, she also felt the ambivalence which is just as typical of her forebears, and which would dominate her literary treatment of them. She never records a simple response to being Anglo-Irish, either as a child or later. Though Dublin seemed grand to her, it also seemed oppressive and gloomy. As an adult she describes it as exhaling melancholy, 'the sense of an obliterated purpose . . . an anti-climactic, possibly endless pause hangs over her large squares, long light streets and darkening Georgian façades.'[4] As a child she detected 'a malign temper at work' in the Georgian area just north of her house in Herbert Place. 'Perhaps a child smells history without knowing it – I did not *know* I looked at the tomb of fashion.'[5]

She was born on 7 June 1899, in Herbert Place, Dublin, an only child, nine years after her parents' marriage. Her mother Florence, charming and vague, was anxiously devoted to her; her father Henry, who had left the Bar for the Land Commission, was abstracted by overwork.

For her first seven years 'Bitha' Bowen had an idyllic and protected Protestant childhood. But when she was seven, her father had a violent breakdown – diagnosed as 'anaemia of the brain'. Bowen's Court became a melancholy place for her, and that feeling would always linger on.

> Repetitive eighteenth-century interiors with their rational proportions and faultless mouldings . . . said nothing to my imagination . . . I found them 'sad', associating them perhaps with my father's illness.[6]

The summer her father's illness was diagnosed, 1906, was also the summer 'Bitha' Bowen learned, very late, to read – and developed the stammer she would have all her life. The shock of the father's illness was followed by separation. Doctors recommended that Henry should live apart from his wife and daughter, so Florence and Bitha left to live in

England, with the help and support of Florence's network of Colley relations. They lived in Kent, moving between Folkestone, Hythe and other coastal towns, living together very closely and intimately. This move to Kent at the age of seven was in some ways liberating. She felt her imagination set free by English villa architecture and English history; at the same time she was 'semi-sceptical'[7] about this abnormal, unclassical country, and developed further a belligerent pride in her Irish origin. In short, Elizabeth Bowen's early childhood gave rise to a particularly acute form of the Anglo-Irish split between confidence and ambivalence, the sense of dislocation and alienness, intensified in her case by a 'cleft between my heredity and my environment'.[8]

Her relationship to Ireland continued to be that, if not exactly of an absentee, then certainly of a part-timer. Henry's illness was cured, but when Bowen was twelve her mother developed cancer. She died in 1912: so Bowen lost her mother at the age of thirteen (the same age as Virginia Woolf). She stayed at school in England, being looked after by her aunt, Laura Colley, going to school at Harpenden Hall in Hertfordshire and later, in wartime, to Downe House in Kent. She entered school in a state of shock and of 'total bereavement'.[9]

After her mother's death, Bowen's teenage years, during the First World War, were spent between boarding school in England and Bowen's Court with her father. In 1914 she was a teenager going to County Cork dances and teas; her response to the outbreak of war was: 'Then can't we go to the garden party?'[10] Schooling ended in 1917; in spite of the war, and then the Troubles, social life at Bowen's Court, where her father was living with his second wife, continued. Elizabeth fell in love, briefly, with a British soldier.[11] She was away, on holiday in Italy, when the houses near Bowen's Court were burned down in 1921.

The discontinuous relationship with Ireland continued into adult life. Bowen went to art school in London for two terms when she was twenty, and then started to write stories. She moved into her Great-aunt Edith's house in town, and began to 'haunt' literary London.[12] She had her first story published,

with the help of Rose Macaulay, and her first volume of
stories, *Encounters*, came out in 1923, when she was twenty-
four. And in 1923 she also married the thirty-year-old Alan
Cameron, who had been wounded and gassed in the war and
had just become Assistant Secretary for Education in North-
amptonshire.

The marriage to Alan Cameron meant that Bowen would
never live permanently in Ireland. His work kept them in
England, first in Northampton, then Oxford, then London,
where they moved in 1935.

Between 1930, the year of her father's death, when she
inherited Bowen's Court, and 1952, when Alan Cameron
died, there were long holidays and house parties in Ireland,
though not during the war years, when travel between Ireland
and England was restricted. Both her books about Bowen's
Court were written from a distance, in place and time. *The
Last September* was written in Headington, in 1928, about
County Cork in 1920: 'Ireland seemed immensely distant
from Oxford ... another world.'[13] *Bowen's Court*, which
takes the history of the house and family up to 1914, was
started in the summer of 1939 and finished in December
1941. After Alan Cameron's retirement, the couple planned
to live at Bowen's Court. But he died later the same year, and
though Elizabeth Bowen tried to keep up the house, she
found it financially impossible. In 1959 it was sold to a local
farmer, who gave the impression that he intended to live in
the house; but soon after the purchase he demolished it and
cut down most of the timber.

Elizabeth Bowen recognised the effects on her work of a
very early transplantation, of the trauma of her father's
illness, and most of all of her mother's sudden death when
she was thirteen. These shocks underlay all her writing, which
she always described as peculiarly Anglo-Irish – for instance,
in the theatrical quality of her imagination ('To most of the
rest of the world we are semi-strangers, for whom existence
has something of the trance-like quality of a spectacle'[14]) and
the sensationalism of her characters. Permanence is always at
risk in her novels and stories. They are full of deracinated

people, lovers without a home and dispossessed children trying to impose their will on an alien world.

The pattern of Elizabeth Bowen's life gave her a clear view of the history and the temperament of the Anglo-Irish, and allowed her to write about her family with the sharpness provided by distance. Her early visits to Europe alerted her to the non-continental feel of Dublin, and the lack of a European tradition in Ireland so alienating, she felt, to Europeanised foreigners.[15] (She was anxious to assert her European sympathies, setting her early novels in France and Italy, developing an interest in French literature, particularly Proust and Flaubert, and later writing a book about Rome.) Yet she also had the close feeling for her part of Ireland which comes from childhood familiarity. There is always a nostalgic note in her treatment of Ireland, whether in the rather brisk, gaudy account of pre-Union Dublin, in *The Shelbourne*, or in the suspended atmosphere of the Irish visit in *The House in Paris*. The two novels set in Ireland, *The Last September* and *A World of Love* feel retrospective. *The Last September* is deliberately set back in a vanished era; *A World of Love* deals with the legacy of the past. And they are both novels about young girls. Ireland, in several of the stories and in *The Heat of the Day*, belongs to inexperience and immaturity. It is the young, heart-whole Roderick, and not his disabused mother Stella, who will put the Irish home to proper use in *The Heat of the Day*. But innocence is not necessarily comforting. In one brilliant story, 'Her Table Spread', Anglo-Irish innocence is distorted into an embarrassing retardedness. In another story, 'Sunday Afternoon', a young girl in wartime Anglo-Irish society bitterly resents the sheltered, delayed quality of her life.

Bowen's feeling about Ireland is summed up in the story 'The Happy Autumn Fields' which dates from 1944 and so comes out of writing *Bowen's Court* in wartime London, and out of the bombing of her London house. (There are Victorian diary entries in *Bowen's Court* which inspired 'The Happy Autumn Fields'.) A sophisticated woman in wartime London, her house bombed, finds a cache of letters and documents about a Victorian Anglo-Irish family. (The setting is not specified, but is meant to be County Cork.[16]) Locked in the tawdry violence of the modern world, the woman tries to project herself back into the lost youth of Henrietta and Sarah and into the house they inhabited with such apparent security.

That reaching back out of an uncongenial landscape towards an apparition of tranquillity, is typical of her use of Irish material. Her nostalgia for Big House life before the Treaty is also a nostalgia for her own youth. When she came to revise *Bowen's Court* for the second edition of 1964, she left the description of the house with which the book begins, in the present tense, though the house no longer existed. 'There is a sort of perpetuity about livingness,' she concludes. She's not only thinking about her own lost youth, but about a whole way of life, of a class which reached its peak in the latter part of the eighteenth century, found itself in decline thereafter and was by the 1920s an isolated minority cut off from the country it had once dominated. That decline led to a kind of wistful repining among the Anglo-Irish which continued for years, for instance in the *Journal of the Butler Society*, where Hubert Butler laments the Anglo-Irish betrayal of its own traditions:

> I am sorry that so few Anglo-Irish emigrés interest themselves now in what is happening in the land of their fathers . . . Every year the Anglo-Irish make less and less acknowledged impact on what is happening here.[17]

Elizabeth Bowen was wary of Anglo-Irish 'repining': 'In my own day, I hear a good deal too much of it.'[18] It's important not to exaggerate the quality of wistfulness in her Irish work, for it is mixed with a satirical coolness about a diminished class and society. The social relations between British soldiers and Anglo-Irish gentry in County Cork during the Troubles, which she describes fondly in *Bowen's Court* as 'dashing and sentimental', are portrayed in *The Last September* with a caustic eye as much as with gentle nostalgia. There is a hazy, enchanted feel to the courtship of Lois and Gerald in the novel, but there's also a witty representation of social patterns, reminiscent of the relationship between the officers and the local bourgeoisie in *Pride and Prejudice*. *Bowen's Court* is not a self-indulgent retrospective, but a rational account of Irish politics from a localised Anglo-Irish viewpoint. Some of her ancestors may be a little romanticised, but no excuses are made for certain Anglo-Irish forms of behaviour, and nothing is blurred.

The relationship between the two Bowen's Court books suggests the kind of double vision which the Anglo-Irish writer seems obliged, by history and temperament, to possess. *Bowen's Court* describes the peculiarities, the failings and achievements, of one Anglo-Irish family in its relation to history. It begins with the Cromwellian settlement and ends in 1914, intercutting the story of the Bowen family with sections of general history. Though there is a preference for the late eighteenth century, when the Protestant Ascendancy was in its prime, and a particular fondness for the Victorian life of Bowen's Court, the book does attempt an impartial survey, sympathetic but critical, of her family as the representatives of a class. But the pre-existence of *The Last September* sheds an ironic light on the later book. In the novel, the class and the tradition which *Bowen's Court* describes so carefully have become ineffectual and redundant within Ireland. We're shown their absurdity, their isolation, their lack of an active position, their helplessly conflicting loyalties. Grandeur has become snobbery, fanaticism has dwindled to eccentricity. The two books, taken together, show the difficulty for Anglo-Irish writers in presenting objectively, without regret, the history of their houses. Retrospection, 'repining', always had to be balanced with some kind of ironic distancing.

That tone of mixed regret and parody is typically Anglo-Irish. But there are other qualities in Elizabeth Bowen's work which put her in that tradition in spite of her English themes and affinities. In *Pictures and Conversations* she projects her own book about Elizabeth Bowen and says that it will begin with 'Origins. My own: Anglo-Ireland and its peculiarities. The infiltration – I believe? – of at least some of these peculiarities into my books. This documented by the Jonah Barrington memoirs, Le Fanu and Edgeworth novels, and others.'[19] This acknowledgement of influence doesn't only refer to the importance of individual works, such as Sheridan Le Fanu's *Uncle Silas*. The implication of 'and others' is a debt to a literary atmosphere found in all kinds of writers. 'And others' might be expanded, from references in *Bowen's Court*, *The Shelbourne*, and elsewhere, to include the novels of Charles Lever and of Lady Morgan (*Wild Irish Girl*), of George Moore (particularly, for *The Shelbourne*, *A Drama in Muslin*) and of Somerville and Ross. In addition to Barrington's *Personal Sketches of His Own Time*, she drew on many other Anglo-Irish memoir and essay writers: Aubrey de Vere ('poet-landlord, Catholic by conversion'[20]); J. D. Herbert, author of *Irish Varieties* (1836), which is a gentlemanly exercise in post-Union nostalgia; Dorothea Herbert, whose eighteenth-century *Retrospections* give a vivid girlish picture of Anglo-Irish social life; and several local works, such as Maurice Healy's *The Old Munster Circuit* (1939), a lively account of the legal world in the Bowen's Court area. And she was interested in English versions of Ireland, such as Arthur Young's *A Tour in Ireland* (1780) and Trollope's Irish novels.

But how much were the Anglo-Irish works simply used as background reading, and how much did she share some of their characteristics? Elizabeth Bowen doesn't *have* to be read as an 'Anglo-Irish' writer. You could place her instead with Forster and Virginia Woolf, or in company with a group of English contemporaries – L. P. Hartley, Henry Green, Rosamond Lehmann. Some of her best novels, *To the North*, *The House in Paris*, and *The Death of the Heart*, are not – or are only incidentally – about Ireland. She was quite as much a London literary figure as she was a member of the County Cork Protestant gentry. And the term 'Anglo-Irish', as applied to literature, is fraught with ambiguities. George Dangerfield points to the problem of definition:

Yeats and the Irish Literary Revivalists made their place in the world by deploying a literature of great distinction, flexibility and beauty: but they did not fully answer the question, 'What is Anglo-Irish?' It could be the language that was caught by Douglas Hyde's *Beside the Fire* or Lady Gregory's 'Kiltartan' – the language of the indigenous Irish, which consists of an English vocabulary superimposed upon a Gaelic syntax. Or it could be the kind of literature which Professor Daniel Corkery, in his *Synge and Anglo-Irish Literature* (Cork, 1955), that severe but significant work, excludes from his strictures – English written by men who lived in Ireland and wrote for the Irish people. Such writers would include Young Ireland's poet, Thomas Davis: they would not quite include William Butler Yeats.[21]

J. C. Beckett, in *The Anglo-Irish Tradition*, says that if the term is used simply to 'lump together' all the Irish-born writers who write in the English language, it 'can serve no useful purpose and may be dangerously misleading'.[22] He feels that a distinction should be made between works which actually have Irish themes, and works which have distinctly Anglo-Irish attitudes. The second group includes writers as diverse as Burke, Swift, Berkeley, Goldsmith and Sheridan, all 'unmistakeably and characteristically Anglo-Irish' and suggests a tradition stretching from 'Swift to Bernard Shaw'.[23] Elizabeth Bowen, in her own note on her 'Origins', says that she belongs here.

She partly qualifies as a 'typical Anglo-Irish writer' by being an absentee. *Bowen's Court* is written far away from Cork; *The Last September* is at a long remove from the young Elizabeth Bowen, in love with a British officer during the Troubles. J. C. Beckett points out that it was largely the Anglo-Irish who represented Irish life in literature, but that they very often did so as 'spectators rather than participants'. Even the Literary Revivalists presented only 'a small and unrepresentative fraction of the total Irish experience';[24] the Anglo-Irish writers found it hard to bridge the gap between themselves and the Irish people. The ambiguity of their position is reflected in their audience. Who were the Anglo-Irish writing for? Not, on the whole, for the native Irish, but for their own class (which in many cases had 'forgotten its own history'),[25] and for the English, whose attitude to Ireland in the eighteenth and nineteenth centuries was not unlike their attitude to America, as Arthur Young observes:

> To judge of Ireland by the conversation one sometimes hears in England, it would be supposed that one half of it was covered with bogs, and the other with mountains filled with Irish ready to fly at the sight of a civilized being.[26]

But Bowen points out in *Bowen's Court* that Arthur Young is himself occasionally 'tart' or unrealistic about Ireland. English spectators were bound to encounter the fatal tendency of the Irish to 'play up' to the English image of them, which was compounded of ignorance, guilt, fear and Europeanised cultural standards. The results are described in *Bowen's Court* (when she is talking about the pre-Union English policy of dividing the Anglo-Irish from the Irish).

> It was difficult for her [England] to see the native Irish as anything but aliens, and as worse, sub-human – potato-eaters, worshippers of the Pope's toe. The squalor in which the Irish lived was taken to be endemic in their mentality: it would have seemed fantastic to reform their conditions. To distract the English conscience the buffoon Paddy was to come into being – the capering simians of the Cruikshank drawings for Maxwell's *Irish Rebellion in 1798* represent him exactly. At the same time, those Anglo-Irish who had not taken to Gothic were to find in the Lever heroes agreeable prototypes in art. Propaganda was probably at its most powerful before there was any name for it. Both classes in Ireland saw themselves in this mirror: the gentry became more dashing, the lower classes more comic. We are, or can become at any moment, the most undignified race on earth – while there is a gallery we must play to it.[27]

The passage, typically witty, exact and shrewd, suggests that the Irish and the Anglo-Irish were equally prone to play up to the English image of them, and points to the unfortunate relationship between the two nations, which elsewhere she calls 'a mixture of showing off and suspicion, nearly as bad as sex'.[28] It's a relationship which invited comic treatment. One of Elizabeth Bowen's most obvious Anglo-Irish traits is the kind of humour she enjoys. The comedy of *The Last September* is reminiscent of Somerville and Ross's satires, like Sir Harold Burgrave ('You Irish are all thieves') in *The Big House of Inver* or Miss Evelyn Hope-Drummond in *The Real Charlotte*. Anglo-Irish humour is always verging on the grotesque. The tendency of the Irish to play to the gallery exaggerates the eccentricities of isolated 'Big House' life. Novel after novel includes humorous accounts of a potty old landlord, nursing his fantasies or his bottle (old Lord Dysart, for instance, in *The Real Charlotte*) or dramatic legends of wild erratic deeds by long-dead ancestors (like the duel in the waves at the start of *The Big House of Inver*), or sad stories of crazed, lonely old women hanging on to the relics of a house. The relish of the Anglo-Irish writer for macabre, grotesque figures, vigorously shown by Maria Edgeworth in *Castle Rackrent*, lent itself happily to the Gothic mode, as in Sheridan Le Fanu's work. *Uncle Silas* is sinister and ambiguous, but it also has some bizarre, uncouth comedy (in the characters of Mme de la Rougierre and Cousin Milly). The Anglo-Irish tone fused comedy and violence. This is always surfacing in Jonah Barrington's memoirs, which are full of robust anecdotes – early versions of the 'Irish Joke' – about maddened loyalists strangling their wives in bed while screaming 'You infernal Papist rebel! You United Irishman!' or 'a man decapitating himself by mistake ... indeed a *blunder* of true Hibernian character'.[29] Barrington's memoirs show how much vivid material there was for use by the Anglo-Irish novelist. J. C. Beckett may complain that his emphasis on 'the bizarre and the eccentric' has given a false picture of Anglo-Irish life, and that Edgeworth's novels are guilty of the same thing because 'what appears absurd or grotesque is always more memorable than the familiar'.[30] But you can see the temptations for the Anglo-Irish novelist. With an audience eager to believe that Ireland was funny rather than threatening, it was no wonder that Anglo-Irish writers allowed themselves to paint in sensational or grotesque colouring. Dorothea Herbert's *Retrospections* shows the kind of material that was available:

> He [Edward Eyre, a cousin of the Herberts, heir to an immense property] spent and dabbled among Usurers to the tune of one hundred thousands Pounds which kept him at law and in poverty all his Life – He had a glass coach . . . He sat dress'd from Top to Toe in a Suit of the Gayest Colour Silk or Sattin lined with Persian of a different colour – He wore Sattin Shoes . . . His Hair was dress'd like a woman . . . He sometimes carried a Muff, sometimes a Fan, and was always up to the Eyes with deepest Carmine – His Manners and Actions were as Outré as his Dress . . . We all doated on him . . . He lived in most Romantic Retirement with . . . two very large spotted spaniels of the Leopard Breed which He called Miss Dapper and Miss Kitsy and adopted as Daughters and CoHeiresses . . . Tea and Cold Water were his only Beverages and Sweetmeats or Pickles of every kind his constant food.[31]

Elizabeth Bowen inherits from this tradition a liking for the violent and the grotesque. But she also followed a pattern of standing back from the comic material: it was nothing new for an Anglo-Irish writer to go away from Ireland in order to write about it. That dislocation always left its mark. Many of Elizabeth Bowen's Irish stories contain unhappy visiting figures who have Anglicised themselves, have come back to an environment they can now objectify, but who find themselves dispossessed, alien in both worlds.

For all its objectivity, *Bowen's Court* is grounded on a pattern of political assumptions which Elizabeth Bowen shared with much of the Protestant Ascendancy. She laments, for instance, the historical fact of the Act of Union, which she regards as 'a bad deal . . . against the stated wish of the country . . . forced through an unrepresentative parliament'. She is critical of the flaw in the Anglo-Irish temperament, 'a fatal lack of connection between enthusiasm and resolution', which made them lukewarm in their support of Henry Grattan, the leader of the Patriot Party, who secured a brief independence for Ireland in 1782. And she is harsh on those

Anglo-Irish (not the Bowens) who were bought or bribed into supporting the Union. But she is reconciled to what she calls the rationalisation of Unionism in the early twentieth century, when it became divorced from the 'landlord interest'. She sympathises with her father's Liberal-Unionism, and feels that the Tory policy pointed to 'an Ireland adult and stabilized'.[32] She speaks highly of Disraeli and Balfour, and evidently finds congenial the concept of a paternalistic, gradual 'hand over' of power with England in a 'senior, advisory, kindly role'. In the tradition of Edmund Burke, she appreciates the Tory attitude to Ireland, which she takes to be an enlightened imperialism, and dislikes Gladstone's policies of disestablishment and Home Rule. Above all, she follows a well-charted Anglo-Irish path in her nostalgia for their late eighteenth-century political and social heyday, the time of Grattan's parliament and the Volunteers and of the youth of Bowen's Court, built in 1775. There were innumerable memoirs lamenting the decay of Dublin high society, the lowering of morale, the sense of lost purpose and power after the Union, harking back to 'the good olden times, when Dublin was in a flourishing state, long before the Union was projected, when the nobles and gentry lived on their estates in their native country, and when the improvement of that country was their glory and their pride.'[33]

The post-Union repining of men like Barrington and Herbert went with a strong sense of local pride, and firm ideas about the proper quality of life. Though Elizabeth Bowen is sharp about Anglo-Irish self-congratulation and self-delusion, she shares those firm ideas. *Bowen's Court* is very definitely and enjoyably a local book. The more general historical passages take their tone from events in Munster and the landlords described are, particularly, the small gentry of north-east Cork. The key historical moments in the book, such as the Cromwellian settlement or the Jacobite wars, are rendered in terms of their effect on the area. Loyalism is summed up by the Kingston family, who built a special castle at Michelstown for a visit of George IV that never came off. The 'rule of sheer fantasy' into which the Ascendancy declined in the nineteenth century is summed up by 'Big George' Kingston, who went berserk when his tenants voted against his candidate. The Troubles are described in terms of the destruction of houses and barracks around Fermoy, Mallow and Michelstown. The anti-Jacobite feeling among the Protestant Ascendancy in the 1740s is encapsulated in the Minute Book of the 'Moyallow Loyal Protestant Society', and the grandeur of eighteenth-century Ireland is contained in the vivid picture of Mallow as a lively Spa, 'the Bath of Ireland'. In Bowen's account of post-Union decline, she notes the gentry's abandonment of Mallow in favour of the real Bath.

That firm sense of locale is linked to an equally traditional appreciation of landlord–tenant relations (which finds its grotesque expression in the madness of 'Big George'). One of the most interesting passages in *Bowen's Court* is a humorous comparison of English and Irish landlords.

> The Irish and the English squire are very differently placed: the first is imposed and the second indigenous ... The English squire can, or could till quite lately, combine with the parson in dragooning the lower classes into healthy activities; exceedingly conscientious, he feels he is where he is to teach the poor what is what ... The Irish landowner, partly from laziness but also from an indifferent delicacy, does not interfere in the lives of the people round ... The greater part of them being Catholics, and he in most cases being a Protestant, they are kept from him by the barrier of a different faith ... There exists between classes, at least in the country in Ireland, a good-mannered, faintly cynical tolerance, largely founded on classes letting each other alone. There does also, in many cases, exist a lively and simple spontaneous human affection between the landed families and the Irish people round them – this is said to have roots in the foster-system, which until quite lately prevailed. In a crisis, there may always be an alliance – against outsiders, in money troubles, against the law.[34]

(She goes on to make a comparison with pre-revolutionary Russia, which points to the Chekhovian flavour of *The Last September*.) Clearly, she sees nothing wrong in itself with the fact of landlordism, mentioning in *Bowen's Court* the good relations between the Bowens and the 'country people': 'I only realize how much this is the case when I am in England, and feel lonely.'[35] There is not much difference between this and Jonah Barrington's description of his grandfather's house at Cullenaghmore where he found a 'happy reciprocity' between landlord and tenants,[36] which served him as a model all his life. That belief in a special relationship which can be 'let alone' is a recurrent theme in Anglo-Irish literature. Sometimes it takes a bizarrely self-admiring form:

> His tenants adored him, and never married a daughter without asking his consent, which he always gave, and a wedding gown besides to the girl. He was full of little oddities . . . Once when, in a fit of irritation, he had spoken roughly to some labourer, a certain formalistic relative reproached him. 'You speak to them like dogs!' His answer was: 'And don't you think they would rather be treated like dogs by me, than like gentlemen by you?'[37]

Elizabeth Bowen's assumptions about landlordism are not so remote from Aubrey de Vere's in that passage.

Her conservatism should not be simplified as snobbery. She writes wittily in *Seven Winters* about the childish confusion which arose from 'my mother's stylish contempt for rich people and my governesses' patient regard for money', her youthful chauvinism, and her squeamishness on the subject of Catholicism:

> The difference between the two religions . . . appeared to share a delicate, awkward aura with those two other differences – of sex, of class. So quickly, in a child's mind, does prudery seed itself and make growth that I remember, even, an almost sexual shyness on the subject of Roman Catholics.[38]

In her essay on her school, 'The Mulberry Tree', and in her late autobiographical sketch, 'Pictures and Conversations', she describes how that early Anglo-Irish alertness to the 'U' and the 'non-U' was overlaid by an obsession with behaviour and social standing in her English girls' schools. This complicated class-consciousness shouldn't be simplified. But she is certainly alert to vulgarity, admires classical rectitude and has a lurking admiration for what, reviewing Lord Dunsany's memoirs in 1937, she calls 'lordly' art, which avoids the bourgeois 'lack of attachments'.[39] Bowen's distaste for the *nouveau riche*, for gimcrack villas and mock-Tudor ('Waikiki' in *The Death of the Heart*, or Robert Kelway's family house in *The Heat of the Day*), seems almost startlingly vindictive to the English reader, until placed alongside, say, Edgeworth's description in *The Absentee* of the pretentious grocer's wife buying up a Big House and filling it with crass attempts at Gothic picturesque effects – 'a little *taste* of everything'.[40]

Whether or not it's fair to call Bowen a snob, she is a recognisable type of conservative. Her belief in the moral effects of property, in benevolent imperialism, in tradition, in private ownership, all point to the intellectual influence of Burke. In *The Anglo-Irish Tradition*, J. C. Beckett emphasises the influence of Burke on the nineteenth-century Anglo-Irish 'orthodoxy' of imperialism. But what Bowen has inherited is not a political opinion so much as an attitude to man's position in society:

> The desire of acquisition is always a passion of long views. Confine a man to momentary possession, and you at once cut off that laudable avarice which every wise State has cherished as one of the first principles of its greatness. Allow a man but a temporary possession, lay it down as a maxim that he never can have any other, and you immediately and infallibly turn him to temporary enjoyments; and these enjoyments are never the pleasures of labour and free industry, whose quality it is to famish the present hours, and squander all upon prospect and futurity; they are, on the contrary, those of a thoughtless, loitering, and dissipated life.[41]

> For these people – my family and their associates – the idea of power was mostly vested in property (property having been acquired by use or misuse of power in the first place). One may say that while property lasted the dangerous power-idea stayed, like a sword in its scabbard, fairly safely at rest. At least, property gave my people ... the means to exercise power in a direct, concrete and therefore limited way ...

29

> Without putting up any plea for property – unnecessary, for it
> is unlikely to be abolished – I submit that the power-loving
> temperament is more dangerous when it either prefers or is
> forced to operate in what is materially a void. We have
> everything to dread from the dispossessed.[42]

The tone is modern. It shares the unassuming suggestiveness
of, say, E. M. Forster's 'What I Believe', and cannot risk
Burke's dogmatism. But the argument is strikingly similar.
Elizabeth Bowen inherits a secularised rational conservatism
from the eighteenth-century Anglo-Irish ideal that property is
morally beneficial and that proper social behaviour is the
expression of a grand idea. In *The Shelbourne* and in *Bowen's
Court* a great point is made of the relationship between
architecture and behaviour. Martin Burke's 'acumen', in the
1820s, in revitalising a hotel that had been a row of Dublin
Georgian houses by building a bigger edifice is admired not
just for the imposing building which resulted but for the
'social idea of life' which it represented. The Shelbourne was
a monument to the keeping up of social standards in post-
Union Dublin; it sustained an admirable 'nonchalance', a
'brave acting-up' which continued into the time of the
Troubles. When she describes Easter afternoon tea being
served in the lounge during the Rising, with St Stephen's
Green under fire, she illustrates her belief that 'behaviour . . .
does really help to jack up morale'.[43]

If in *The Shelbourne* she tries too hard to turn a nineteenth-
century hotel into a symbol, in *Bowen's Court* the treatment
of the Big House as a place built to 'indicate that life ought to
be lived in a certain way'[44] is very convincing. It's often said
that the Big House in Ireland has a symbolic value,[45] that it
expresses an idea of power which, since its twentieth-century
demise, now seems ironic. But Bowen places as much
emphasis on the idea of style as on the idea of power. In fact
she argues that the eighteenth-century builders of the Big
Houses *subsumed* their drive for power into a concept of
style, which might contain and restrict them, make them
behave better. So she insists on the self-validating, self-
centred existence in the Big House, a form of egotism

comparable to a literary device: 'Like Flaubert's ideal book about nothing, it sustains itself by the inner force of its style.'[46]

Bowen is careful not to make exaggerated claims for the Big House. But she does describe Bowen's Court as a '1775 house, boldly letting in light and exultantly serious'.[47] In an essay of 1940 called 'The Big House' she pursues these moderate claims. The Big House in Ireland is, after all, not very big: 'In England they would be called "country houses", no more ... Have they been called "big" with a slight inflection – that of hostility, irony?' The 'bigness' is not of size but of style: the houses were built for 'spacious living':

> There was a true bigness, a sort of impersonality, in the manner in which the houses were conceived. After an era of greed, roughness and panic, after an era of camping in charred or desolate ruins (as my Cromwellian ancestors did certainly) these new settlers who had been imposed on Ireland began to wish to add something to life ... They began to feel, and exert, the European idea—to seek what was humanistic, classic and disciplined.
>
> It is something to subscribe to an idea, even if one cannot live up to it.[48]

Bowen's Court is about the loss of that idea. It is the story of what happens to a minority when they lose the confidence which enabled them to build as they did in the eighteenth century. It describes a 'big', impersonal, dignified concept of living – 'traditional sanctity and loveliness' – going into retreat. So *Bowen's Court* is intimately related to Bowen's fiction, all of which is concerned with how to live in a world where rootedness, acquisitions, permanence – the Burkean 'goods' – are at risk, and where a decorous idea of behaviour has degenerated into 'the dire period of Personal Life'.[49]

The 'break up' which began, for the Anglo-Irish, with the Post-Union decline of the 1820s and with Gothic encroachments into feeling, literature and architecture, is still, according to Bowen, having its effects. 'The main healthy abstract' of eighteenth-century society has been lost, and strong discipline – even 'genius' – is needed to deal with the neuroses, the fragmentation, that arise from a dependency on 'Personal Life'. It's an idea (strongly expressed in her Irish story 'Summer Night') which leads to a harsh comparison between the concept of living that produced the Big House, and the quality of modern life. This comparison dominates *Bowen's Court*, and is the most revealing expression of Bowen's conservatism.

> Education is not so important as people think. Nothing he learned, certainly, but at the same time nothing he did not learn, impaired Henry's flair for living, his innate stylishness and his love of the grand ... [he] lived in a Philistine, snobbish, limited and on the whole pretty graceless society. But he got somewhere, and lived to die in his drawing-room surrounded by hosts of children and the esteem of what looked like a lasting order. And to what did our fine feelings, our regard for the arts, our intimacies, our inspiring conversations, our wish to be clear of the bonds of sex and class and nationality, our wish to try to be fair to everyone bring us? To 1939.[50]

This looks dangerously like a crude romantic opposition between the noble innocence of the eighteenth century and the over-refinement of modern life. But *Bowen's Court* doesn't, in fact, naïvely eulogise the 'grand idea' of the Anglo-Irish Enlightenment. Elizabeth Bowen is too well aware of the burdensome legacy of the Big House for its inheritors, of the physical and financial after-effects of the grand idea, to present it as an unmitigated good. She suggests that the 'Builders' were the victim of an absurd fanaticism, an obsession with the idea of self-perpetuation and self-advertisement which could mean nothing but harm for their descendants. Speaking of the first George Moore, great-grandfather of the writer, she describes how he originally had modest plans for his home, but inevitably 'deviated' into the grand idea – thus saddling his descendants 'with that something between a *raison d'être* and a predicament – an Irish estate'.[51] Too many of the Protestant gentry in the late seventeenth century and afterwards, came, she says, to be dominated 'by a sort of Versailles fantasy' which would 'cripple their bank accounts and endanger their private lives'.[52]

When she summarises the Bowens (whom she felt became as a family 'slightly better as the Anglo-Irish in general got slightly worse'),[53] she praises the discipline which enabled them to live up to 'their too-grand idea of themselves'. But, taken in detail, the history of the Bowens shows all the problems that came from 'the Builder's' aspirations.

The Bowens were an unusual Anglo-Irish family, not only in their 'slightly better' behaviour, but because they were originally a Welsh family – ap Owen became Bowen in the sixteenth century – with a thriving branch in the Gower peninsula. So they were 'hybrid' Anglo-Irish, polite rather than loyal to England, bound to Ireland only by their passion for land. And Bowen's Court, she says, was unusual in its isolation: the Bowens were thrown back on themselves rather more than other Anglo-Irish families. Nor were they import-ant gentry, as she makes clear in her account of the unsalubrious bargaining that led to the Act of Union: 'I should like to say that the Bowens refused such crumbs, but I fear that, plainly, they were not in the way of any: they were very remote gentry, inactive in public life, not in a big way, not, in short, worth buying.' All the same, she feels entitled to praise them in some ways. They didn't abandon their land and their house. They treated the 'country people' well – particularly during the Great Famine when the Protestant landowners were so anathematised. They did not let them-selves be 'stampeded' at the time of the Union. There are repeated accounts of Bowens putting their shoulders to the wheel: Robert, a younger son of 'the Builder', whose elder brother saddled him with the management of Bowen's Court, is admired for the way he rose to his responsibility; Robert's son Henry, who inherited at the age of twenty, and who was, she imagines, a sweet-natured romantic young man who would have liked to live in Paris and go to the opera, 'devoted himself to duty with the resolution, the single-mindedness of one who has turned from everything else'. He became a local JP, made roads and kept up the house.[54]

But the Bowens also displayed the weaknesses of their class: susceptibility to obsessions, infatuation with the idea of power, a tendency 'to avoid or baulk at facts only to torment themselves with fantasies'.[55] These characteristics led to a fatal propensity for litigation, lack of realism about money matters, and occasional violent conflicts between fathers and sons. The story of the Bowens is dominated by a recurrent lawsuit which has its roots in the seventeenth century and erupts periodically and unhappily, until as late as 1843. John, the second Bowen to come to Ireland (son of the black-tempered Welsh Colonel Bowen who was given the lands around Farahy by Cromwell, in 1653) married the daughter of a rich Cromwellian called John Nicholls, who lived in Kilbolane Castle, about twenty-six miles from Farahy. Nicholls had John Bowen financially under his thumb, but when John's wife died, John got away from Kilbolane and left his three sons to be brought up by their rich grandfather. The oldest of these boys, John Bowen II (Bowen distinguishes her family generations from each other as though they were monarchs) grew up to build a house in the grounds of Kilbolane Castle. When old John Nicholls died, he was said to have left a large treasure buried in various parts of the Castle, and his grandson, the builder of Kilbolane House, filed several suits against another Nicholls relative, to try and get hold of the treasure. This was in 1690, and marked the start of the Bowens' fatal *idée fixe*:

> This obsession about the Nicholls treasure was at the root of that main Kilbolane obsession that, for generations, continued to rule the Bowens, unbalance their view of life, and, through lawsuits, lose them so much money. We do not know – it never has been established – how much treasure there *was*, in the first place. We do know that the whole of the treasure – on that scale, at least, on which the Bowens envisaged it – was not ever found. The longer it remained missing the greater its visionary proportions grew.[56]

It was not merely the possibility of an unclaimed treasure

which haunted the Bowens. It was the whole idea of the possession of Kilbolane – which was to be a much-disputed property – that became a 'hereditary obsession', because it was there, and not at Farahy, that 'the Bowens first built a house and struck a root into Ireland'.[57] Bowen says that she felt a twinge of the old obsession when she went to visit Kilbolane while writing about Bowen's Court; she would have liked to live in both places at once. This may have been a pleasantly wistful sensation, but there was nothing pleasant or wistful about the recurrence of the lawsuit, which essentially centred on the Bowens' attempts to get hold of the bits of Kilbolane Castle which had come into the possession, either of Nicholls's original tenants, neighbours of John Bowen II of Kilbolane House, or of families to whom the Bowens themselves had, later, sold or rented their parts of the castle and its buildings.

There were temperamental and financial problems enough for the Bowens without the Kilbolane lawsuits. The son of the builder of Kilbolane House, 'Henry Bowen II', managed to introduce some money into the family, as so many Anglo-Irish heirs did, by marrying a rich heiress, Jane Cole, in 1716 (whose surname was permanently absorbed into the Bowen family tree). But *his* son, 'Henry Bowen III', 'the Builder', again went to law for possession of part of Kilbolane and for the treasure – a case which dragged on from 1759 to 1764, was finally unsuccessful, and left crippling debts. In spite of this, Henry III built Bowen's Court in 1775. Though the house, which was intended as a square, could not be completed for lack of funds, though Henry died with his affairs in terrible confusion and with debts amounting to £40,000, and though he was evidently an inadequate father, many of whose children turned out badly, Bowen forgives him all this for the grand idea behind the building of the house.

Henry III's son, the discontented, dissolute 'Henry Bowen IV', who gets little sympathy from the family historian, did try to sort out the financial situation. He sold what there was of the Bowen Kilbolane property in 1790 (a sale which left unfortunate and ambiguous loopholes for litigation), and then left Bowen's Court to the care of his younger brother, the conscientious Robert. Elizabeth Bowen expresses dutiful admiration for Robert Cole Bowen's plain-living, high-minded upkeep of the house. But it was his widow and daughter who again opened the Kilbolane lawsuit, trying to claim back the property that Henry IV had got rid of, and who again lost their case, in 1843. Though this fiasco was submerged almost immediately by the terrible period of the Famine, its after-effects were far-reaching. 'Henry IV's' grandson (who was to be Elizabeth Bowen's grandfather), on whose behalf his mother and grandmother had gone to court, had to work with fanatical, ruthless discipline in order to make Bowen's Court pay. Elizabeth Bowen describes with great intensity – it is one of the most vivid parts of the book – the Victorian life of Bowen's Court, the heavy clutter of Victorian furniture, the endless breeding, the close, intimate, self-contained life of the girls (her aunts, from whose diaries she gives long evocative excerpts), and the dauntingly well-organised running of the demesne: 'This was Personal Life at its most intense.'[58]

Elizabeth Bowen's formidable grandfather, Robert, became a tragically despotic figure, and, reading between the lines, seemed to have suffered from some form of senile dementia. His relationship with his eldest son, Henry, her father, was appalling. This dated from the time when Henry brought the smallpox back to Bowen's Court from his European tour and was nursed by his mother, who died as a result – while his father in a panic of self-preservation took the rest of the children and fled from the house. Later, Henry made up his mind to become a barrister and not to spend his life as a landlord, leading to an irreconcilable conflict between father and son. Robert felt that his life's work was being betrayed. Henry, arguing for 'free will, as against predestination', was, Elizabeth Bowen suspects, secretly in revolt against what he saw as a place 'mortared together by Robert's egotism'. Robert's vindictive attempts to punish Henry (whom he couldn't disinherit, since Bowen's Court was entailed on the eldest child) by cutting down timber, selling off parts of the demesne and leaving him a pittance in his will, were an ironic form of self-punishment:

> The headlong decline of Bowen's Court seems to have been implicit in Robert's will: in the dark in which he now increasingly dwelled he planned the destruction of his life's work. To-day, his fine iron field-gates rusting off their hinges, his metalled avenues grass-grown, his roofless farm-buildings, his 'machines', that used to fill the yard with their humming, now with belts snapped, teeth rusting into the ground, make me feel a pang – on Robert's behalf. I think of the Giotto figure of *Anger*, the figure tearing, clawing its own breast.[59]

The combined effects of the obsession with Kilbolane and the family conflicts left Elizabeth Bowen as a much-burdened inheritor of Bowen's Court. Standards were kept up: like Dublin in the early nineteenth century, she was exercising the Anglo-Irish talent for 'brave acting-up'. There are many personal witnesses to this – Hubert Butler reminisced affectionately about the unstinted hospitality at Bowen's Court (and in London), and said that he was allowed no idea of how hard up Elizabeth must have been; Virginia Woolf gave a more caustic picture (which illustrates the English upper classes' inability to understand the living habits of the Anglo-Irish), in a 1934 letter to Vanessa Bell, of 'acting up' in the Big House:

> There is no architecture of any kind: all the villages are hideous; built entirely of slate in the year 1850: so Elizabeths home was merely a great stone box, but full of Italian mantlepieces and decayed 18th century furniture, and carpets all in holes – however they insisted upon keeping up a ramshackle kind of state, dressing for dinner and so on.[60]

When she sold the house in 1959, she was resisting the Bowen unwillingness to face up to reality. But there may have been some self-deception, too, in her belief that the house would not be demolished.

The history and the fate of Bowen's Court are interesting for three reasons. One is the vigour and vividness of the book of the house, *Bowen's Court*. Like a character in a novel, the house becomes important to the reader: its end is sad. Another is the fact that the decline of Bowen's Court and the loss of the 'grand idea' that lay behind it infiltrate the rest of Bowen's work, even when she is not writing about Ireland. And the third is that the story of Bowen's Court belongs to a great tradition of Anglo-Irish literature. Bowen sums up the typical fate of the Big House and its owners in her essay of 1940, 'The Big House':

> Many of these genial builders died badly in debt and left their families saddled with mansions that they could ill afford. Then, decline set in almost at once. A more modest plan of living would have made, in the end, for very much more peace: big houses that had begun in glory were soon only maintained by struggle and sacrifice . . . Husbands and wives struggled, shoulder to shoulder, to keep the estate anything like solvent . . . their children grew up *farouches*, haughty, quite ignorant of the outside world . . . The big house people were handicapped . . . by their pride, by their indignation at their decline and by their divorce from the countryside in whose heart their struggle was carried on. They would have been surprised to receive pity. I doubt, as a matter of fact, that they ever pitied themselves: they were obsessed, and to a degree exalted. They had begun as conquerors and were not disposed to let that tradition lapse. These big house people admit only one class-distinction: they instinctively 'place' a person who makes a poor mouth.
>
> It is, I think, to the credit of the big house people that they concealed their struggles with such nonchalance and for so long continued to throw about what did not really amount to much weight . . . Nowadays, what I hear most commented on is the apparent futility of the sacrifice. New democratic Ireland no longer denounces the big house, but seems to marvel at it. Why fight to maintain life in a draughty barrack, in a demesne shorn of most of its other land, a demesne in which one can hardly keep down the thistles, far from neighbours, golf links, tennis clubs, cinemas, buses, railways, shops?

The answer lies, of course, still, in an 'idea':

Life in the big house, in its circle of trees, is saturated with
character: this is, I suppose, the element of the spell. The
indefinite ghosts of the past, of the dead who lived here and
pursued this same routine of life in these walls add something,
a sort of order, a reason for living, to every minute and hour.
This is the order, the form of life, the tradition to which big
house people still sacrifice much.[61]

This connects to a great number of Anglo-Irish novels and
memoirs, right through from Maria Edgeworth's acute
descriptions of the landlords who abandoned their houses, or
Dorothea Herbert's reminiscences of her mother 'at her Wits
End many years to supply the Exigencies of a falling House
and growing family',[62] to the journals of Lady Gregory ('I
think the country would be poorer without Coole'),[63] and to
the contemporaneous novels of, for instance, Jennifer Johnston, who has written in *The Gates* and *The Old Jest* of the
decline of the Big House.

What *Bowen's Court* describes is a more moderate, less
sensational version of the tradition. In Maria Edgeworth's
novels, the 'hand-to-mouth' existence at Castle Rackrent and
Sir Condy's lovable embarrassments, the harmful absenteeism
of the Clonbronys, are images of what might have become of
the Bowens if they had been less responsible, more given to
procrastination and passivity. As it is, Elizabeth Bowen finds
some affinities between her ancestors and Edgeworth's
colourful prototypes, particularly in 'Henry IV and his wife
the Honourable Catherine Bowen', the next in line to 'the
Builder', whose 'fashionableness and high play at cards'
became a legend. Henry IV's marriage went to the bad, and
he was gripped by the 'ennui' which was such a notorious
feature of life in the Big House. (The George Moore who was
the son of the builder of Moore Hall and the grandfather of
the writer, said of his house: 'Beautiful as it is, much as I love
it, I have not always been able to exclude ennui from its
precincts.')[64] Henry was a bad landlord, a restless, dissipated
seeker of fashion, and left Bowen's Court in 1816 with, she
imagines, 'a shut heart'. He and his wife seemed to her more
like 'stock' fictional characters than the rest of her ancestors:

'They seem to belong more to Maria Edgeworth's fashion-able-moral fiction than to the Bowen past.' She also suggests that 'Henry V's' experience of Dublin may still have been a bit like Lord Colambre's in Edgeworth's *The Absentee* (1812), who was pleasantly surprised to find that his foolish absentee parents had exaggerated the post-Union decline of Dublin society.[65]

But Bowen is careful throughout *Bowen's Court* to avoid cliché, to make clear how the Bowens differed from other Big House gentry. The stock ingredients of Anglo-Irish fictions and memoirs – scenes of hunting and drinking, lawsuits, deeds of sale, demesnes falling into ruin, eccentric members of the family, marriages for money, intermarriages or inter-breeding between the gentry and the locals, agents swindling their employers or oppressing the peasants or taking over the house, absenteeism, Dublin society, and nostalgia for pre-Union life – are not all present in the Bowen family history. But quite a lot of them are. The clichés and exaggerations of Anglo-Irish life as represented in fiction repeat themselves too often for all of them to be caricature.

This overlap between history and fiction in Anglo-Irish literature shows up clearly if we compare *Bowen's Court* with a Somerville and Ross novel, *The Big House of Inver* (1925), written by Edith Somerville after Violet Martin ('Martin Ross')'s death. The novel has a more tragic version of the Anglo-Irish fall, but it does share some features of the Bowens' history. Its first chapter, which describes Mr Robert Prendeville's building of the Big House in the reign of Queen Anne, and traces the ensuing decline of the Prendeville family through isolation, 'profligacy', 'living with country women, fighting, drinking, gambling', tells a more sensational and less honourable history than that of the Bowens. But the Prendevilles' lawsuits for their property, the fanatical deter-mination of their bastard descendant 'Shibby Pindy' to resuscitate the fallen house for her half-brother, and the lingering influence of the original 'grand idea', have some-thing in common with *Bowen's Court*:

Inver House embodied one of those large gestures of the minds of the earlier Irish architects, some of which still stand to justify Ireland's claim to be considered a civilized country.[66]

Bowen's Court is similarly about the attempt to sustain that claim to civilisation. And it shares the main theme of *The Big House of Inver*, the alarming, self-destructive effects of an obsessive fantasy. The most powerful parts of the novel are those which describe Shibby's 'great idea' for the reclamation of the house; the driving theme of *Bowen's Court* is the investigation of what made the Bowens stick to their land and their house long after its original glories were sunk under a load of financial embarrassments. Both books consider the strange, spiritualising effect of place. Elizabeth Bowen is eloquent about the impossibility of being 'wholly opaque or material' in Ireland: 'Reason can never reconcile one to life: nothing allays the wants one cannot explain.'[67] *The Big House of Inver* embodies that semi-mystical state in, of all people, the ruthless and pragmatic Shibby, whose plans for the house go beyond material desires.

The Big House of Inver is very much concerned with mixed blood, with the effects of the old Prendeville gentry acting on the tough peasant stock. Inver's decay is seen most clearly by the girl whose blood is half-English and half-peasant:

She had to pass the Big House, looming large and mysterious in the dense air. She stood still at the beautiful old wrought-iron gates, that had been meant to keep inviolate the great circle of gravel in front of the hall-door, but that now hung crooked on their hinges, always open. The gravel was greened over with weeds; a goat, standing on its hind legs, was eating the ivy that grew on the area wall. Peggy looked at the house meditatively, considering it and its history. It was so dominating, and yet so appealing; so splendid, and so neglected. It could remember a past so lordly and so brilliant, and now had to endure this miserable present, forsaken, given over to desolation. It seemed to Peggy to eye her through its many windows appraisingly and censoriously, and to find her, with her rough frieze coat and skirt and her walking stick, an

41

outrage, standing on the very spot over which the silken Lady Isabella, in her coach-and-four horses had so often passed.

'It thinks that I and my people are *canaille* who have robbed it of its demesne!' Peggy thought . . . She was looking at the stone over the hall-door, that was carved with the clenched, mailed hand, and the arrogant motto, '*Je prends*!' had caught her eye.

'You can take!' she tossed the taunt to the old house, laughing, 'but you can't hold, and I and my sort can!'[68]

There are two connections here with *Bowen's Court*. One is the ineffectuality of the Anglo-Irish gentry in the twentieth century. The other is the fascination with ruined places that dominates Anglo-Irish literature. Somerville and Ross are particularly interested in the inheritors of the 'great idea'. In *The Real Charlotte* (1894) there is a self-critical, cultured, ineffectual heir, Christopher Dysart, who isn't sporting enough to be a country gentleman or dynamic enough to take up any other pursuit. He is a man born out of his time, who can't save himself from his own class or do anything to improve it, but is at the same time entirely aware of his deficiencies. Bowen feels for the members of her family who didn't want the responsibility of the Big House life, didn't know how to deal with it, and whose natural temperaments, without the claims of poverty, would have taken them elsewhere. And some of her other ancestors resemble fictional Anglo-Irish characters. Like Somerville and Ross, she appreciates the strong matriarchal influence in Anglo-Irish families. Several Bowen generations throw up one of those 'women of character'[69] who dominate events, to the extent sometimes of dragging their families to court. Somerville and Ross show what happens to this forceful strain when it is joined with peasant stock; they describe the fearsome drive for power in ageing single women like Shibby and Charlotte and the eccentric expressions of self-will in upper-class ladies like Lady Dysart.

Even more, though, than in its characterisation, *Bowen's Court* has an affinity with other Anglo-Irish literature in 'the romantic, endemic feeling for ruin'.[70] Ruins are a part of life in Bowen's area of the country. The barracks at Fermoy, once the focus of so much social life, were burnt in the Civil War and left as an empty shell overlooking the town. The castle at Michelstown built by 'Big George', scene of the garden party where the fifteen-year-old Elizabeth learned of the outbreak of war, is now 'little more than a mound'; 'grass grows where the saloons were.' 'History evaporates' from the Irish landscape, or leaves its trail of ghosts, 'lordly or humble, military or domestic', showing 'gashes of violence' or 'simply the dull slant of decline'.[71]

The feeling for ruins is everywhere in Anglo-Irish literature. Lady Gregory's Journals for the 1920s are full of descriptions of Big Houses which she knew as a child, now destroyed:

> The house – the ruin – is very sad, just the walls standing, blackened, and all the long yards silent, all the many buildings, dairy, laundry, cow-houses, coach-houses, stables, kennels, smith, sawmill and carpenters' workshops empty. Some of the roofs falling in. I am afraid the house will never be built up. Yet the road by the deer-park and the avenue most beautiful, river and hills, and the trees in their autumn foliage. All silent that had been so full of life and stir in my childhood, and never deserted until now.[72]

The decayed castles and houses, the burnt-down creameries and derelict mills of *Bowen's Court* and *The Last September* are like the derelict estate of Edgeworth's *The Absentee* ('Walks overgrown, shrubberies wild, plantations run up into bare poles; fine trees cut down'),[73] or the wreck of the House of Inver, or the disused turf quay in *The Real Charlotte*.

But this romantic interest in ruins does not (at least in one branch of Anglo-Irish literature) extend to Celtic customs and landmarks. Bowen's treatment of Ireland displays no Gaelic interest whatsoever. Her feelings for ruins is more like Arthur Young's eighteenth-century English quest for 'picturesque circumstances' than, say, Standish O'Grady's passionate reclamation of the lost Irish past. What interests her is her own civilisation's decline, and not the obliteration of a native culture by English colonisers. She is aware of this. Bowen's Court, she says, was built as 'the negation of mystical

Ireland'. It was houses like this, gentry like the Bowens, who forced Gaelic culture to 'run underground, with its ceaseless poetry of lament'. There was an entire separation between the blossoming of the Protestant Ascendancy and the language and traditions that it dominated for so long. And that separation persisted in some quarters even during and after the Irish Literary Renaissance. Elizabeth Bowen's parents, in Dublin in the 1890s, were 'untouched' by the activities of Yeats and the mystical, nationalist poet and journalist George Russell ('AE'); Elizabeth Bowen herself 'only heard of this [the Irish Revival] for the first time when I was at school in England, about 1916'.[74]

The history of the Anglo-Irish is of an ambiguous position, of a culture existing in a world from which it was, even if unconsciously, separate. Writer after writer emphasises the insensitivity of the Protestant Ascendancy to Gaelic Ireland. This is the novelist George Birmingham:

> We built our Georgian houses and some of our Dublin public buildings in a style which was spacious, dignified, and beautiful; a style to which we gave a national distinction. But there is not the smallest trace in this architecture of any Celtic feeling.[75]

When the Anglo-Irish society 'emerged' at the beginning of the eighteenth century, its tragic ambivalence was, as he says, to be 'no more Gaelic than it is English'. In decline, the Protestant Ascendancy began to feel its separateness from the country it inhabited: 'The aristocracy is no less exiled [than the Gaelic one which preceded it] though they linger in their houses and demesnes in Ireland. They are spiritual exiles who have . . . been driven forth from the life of the community.'[76] Sean O'Faolain makes the point again in *The Irish* (1947):

> They were . . . a separate enclave. They resided in Ireland. It was their country, never their nation. So that their achievements were, for the most part, so remote from the life of the native Irish (now utterly suppressed) that they ultimately became part of the English rather than the Irish cultural record.[77]

Ironically, those nineteenth-century Anglo-Irish who became passionately interested in Gaelic history were pointing 'unwittingly, to the downfall of their own tradition':

> From this cloudy but exciting concept of a golden and heroic age sprang the idea of Gaelic nationality, of an Ireland that would reject not only English power but English culture and express its independence not only in its own government but its own language.[78]

Perhaps, as George Dangerfield suggests in *The Damnable Question*, the Anglo-Irish who fostered the Irish Literary Revival, unlike most of the Irish landlords, had already seen in the Home Rule movement and the rural reforms of the 1880s 'the writing on the wall, where they could read the doom of their class'.[79] But they can hardly have guessed that a romantic interest in Cuchulain and Queen Maeve would point towards the de-Anglicising of Ireland and the Sinn Fein.

Bowen, however, remained outside the Anglo-Irish interest in Gaelic culture, whether political or purely literary. Her solution – the result of circumstances, of temperament and of education – was to live the most Anglicised kind of Anglo-Irish life, to write as much of English themes, and out of English and European influences, as of Ireland, and thus to submit, in her art as well as in her life, to the disappearance of the Ascendancy. This laid her open to challenge from Irish writers who had committed themselves to living in, and writing about, Ireland, though in the English language. Sean O'Faolain wrote to Elizabeth Bowen in 1937 (before he had read *The Last September*) urging her to write a book about Ireland. After he had read it, he wrote again suggesting that she write another book about a Bowen's Court 'that was at least aware of the Ireland outside . . . that, perhaps, regretted the division enough to admit it was there'. He wanted a book about the life of the Ascendancy '*now*'. But the gap between Regent's Park and County Cork is, he realises, too wide:

> I am writing like a fool. You will look up at the cars swishing quietly along the road in the park, and at the graceful movements of boats or people or the little trees. And this

Ireland will seem a ragged, untidy thing, like a man in a poorhouse trying to pretend he is free and rich. You will say, these people are in a mess, and I cannot be bothered; this is work for a social reformer not a novelist.[80]

The division between the Anglo-Irish and Ireland, which O'Faolain writes to her about, is a division which Bowen both expresses and embodies. She brings to consciousness a long history of unawareness. The Bowens, she says, had an 'unconscious' relation to history. They were largely oblivious of the ambivalence inherent in the possession of Bowen's Court. It was for her, the last of the Bowens, the first to live mainly away from the house and in the end to leave it to its inevitable fate, to bring into consciousness their relationship to history. What she presents as the tragedy of the Anglo-Irish is their lack of insight into the ambiguity and isolation of their position:

> If Ireland did not accept them, they did not know it – and it is in that unawareness of final rejection, unawareness of being looked out at from some secretive, opposed life, that the Anglo-Irish naïve dignity and, even, tragedy, seems to me to stand. Themselves, they felt Irish, and acted as Irishmen.[81]

That situation came to a painful climax in the Troubles and the Civil War of the 1920s. The Anglo-Irish families, enclosed in the Big Houses, aloof from the nationalist cause but already – ever since disestablishment – feeling themselves abandoned by the English, and about to be left to their fate by the Treaty of 1921, had to watch their own or their neighbours' houses burn, and to see the tenants they had known all their lives at war with the English soldiers, with whom they themselves would be taking tea or playing tennis. The demesnes became islands; the life in them went on in isolation, or else they were destroyed, as an image of the oppressive past. That period in the history of the Anglo-Irish is the subject of Elizabeth Bowen's second novel, *The Last September*, 'which of all my books is nearest my heart'.

The action takes place during 'the Troubled Times' – i.e. the roving armed conflict between the Irish Republican Army and British Forces still garrisoning Ireland. Ambushes, arrests, captures and burnings, reprisals and counter-reprisals kept the country and country people distraught and tense ... The position of such Anglo-Irish land-owning families as the Naylors, of Danielstown [the Bowen's Court of the novel] was not only ambiguous but was more nearly heart-breaking than they cared to show. Inherited loyalty (or at least, adherence) to Britain – where their sons were schooled, in whose wars their sons had for generations fought, and to which they owed their 'Ascendancy' lands and power – pulled them one way: their own temperamental Irishness the other ... [Their] ambivalent attitude to the English ... is a marked Anglo-Irish trait.[82]

For some of these families the Troubles meant the end of their Big House life. (One such victim of the times is Uncle Bill Bent in *The House in Paris*.) Bowen's Court did not burn, unlike its neighbours, Rockmills, Ballywalter, Convamore, which were destroyed in the same night;[83] but 'so often in my mind's eye did I see it burning that the terrible last event in *The Last September* is more real than anything I have lived through.'[84] It looks back on a vanished era and also on the end of her own girlhood. Elizabeth Bowen says that the book is 'at many, many removes from autobiography': when she herself, like Lois in the novel, was nineteen or twenty at Bowen's Court, she was mainly discontented and frivolous. But it is those fallow periods of time, she quotes Proust as saying, 'that most often fructify into art'.[85] Proust provides the epigraph for *The Last September*: 'Ils ont les chagrins qu'ont les vierges et les paresseux.'

Proust's paradox is that the most intense art comes out of the bits of life least responded to at the time, out of the sorrows of inaction and inexperience. This links with the book's tension between elegy and anticipation. The novel is firmly placed in the past. From its first page ('In those days, girls wore crisp white skirts') there is a deliberate emphasis on 'a former time', on the sense of this being an era that is 'done with and over'.[86] A melancholy autumnal transience hangs over the whole. Social life is carefully made to feel like a period piece. At the same time, the novel is edgy, fraught and keyed-up. Though mainly offstage, at the edge of the family's consciousness, the Troubles make constant irruptions into the narrative. There may be guns buried in the lower plantation. The patrol cars circle their boundaries after dark. Lois, walking in the shrubbery, is passed by a stranger in a trench coat, 'down from the mountains, making a short cut through their demesne'. People talk about what's happening, but in self-protective ways. The Anglo-Irish family plays it down ('Something said in the English press has given rise to an idea that this country's unsafe'), the visitors are baffled and nervy, the British soldiers use matter-of-fact understatement. As the novel continues, the sense of threat is intensified: barracks are burned, a neighbouring Big House is raided for guns, nearby troops are fired on, a local tenant on the wanted list is arrested. The two final tragedies are increasingly strongly anticipated.

The tension centres on the character of Lois, the only child. She is the nineteen-year-old orphaned niece of the Naylors, and she lives at Danielstown, entertaining visitors, having tea, going to dances with the soldiers, and visiting neighbours. Like other young women in Elizabeth Bowen's Irish stories, Lois is restless, dissatisfied with herself, longing for her sheltered youth to be over and for something to happen. Self-conscious, unformed, easily embarrassed by the personal, susceptible, eager for illusions and drama, she is one of Bowen's brilliant studies of pre-adulthood. But the character study is not a self-indulgent piece of retrospection.

Lois's state of mind is carefully aligned with the situation of the house and the family. In one, ironical way, her impatience anticipates the tragic destruction of the house. She wants a conflagration: at least it will mean change. Life in Danielstown is too slow and mannered for her; it has 'a sense of detention, of a prologue being played out too lengthily, with unnecessary stresses, a wasteful attention to detail'. Her desire to be violently precipitated into her future is granted with a vengeance: it's as though her restlessness partly *wills* the end of Danielstown. At the same time she is like the house. All round her is a war she cannot understand or share.

'How is it that in this country that ought to be full of such violent realness there seems nothing for me but clothes and what people say? I might as well be in some kind of cocoon.'

Lois's ignorance, her sheltered isolation, her restless anticipation of the future, have only got the material to hand to work on: the social life of the family, of visitors, of the British soldiers. She is, as a disenchanted older woman describes her, 'simply sick with eagerness', but nothing quite comes up to scratch. The book is full of anticlimaxes, disappointing visits, premature departures, inadequate emotions: all of which reveal to Lois, in herself and in the house, 'the discovery of a lack'.

Lois is surrounded by disenchanted characters (this is going to be one of Bowen's recurring themes) who have passed her painful stage of waiting and are getting by, living as they can, in the adult world.

The most interesting of these is Hugo Montmorency, an early version of the Jamesian spectators, wearily conscious of their own impotence, who will come back, especially in her Irish stories. Lois anticipates Maria, an impatient young girl in a fine later story, 'Sunday Afternoon' (1941), sheltered and restless among her decorous, ageing Anglo-Irish relatives, visited in wartime by the Anglicised Henry, who feels caught 'between two generations', an alien in both countries. Henry leaves the disappointed Maria at the end of the story, calling her 'Miranda' and urging her not to leave her enchanted island for the ordinary violence of the modern world. She replies, 'The trouble with you is, you're half old.'[87] Mr Montmorency, discontentedly married to a frail, affectionate older woman, his house sold, his life a mixture of 'the perception of regret' and lack of prospects, seems, as Henry does to Maria, irritatingly unsatisfactory to Lois. She particularly dislikes him for falling in love with Danielstown's most romantic visitor, Marda, a sophisticated, professional house-guest, about to make a rich London marriage, and quite cut off from Irish life. Marda seems as promising and glamorous to Lois as Mr Montmorency seems depressing; but both characters are there to pass a disenchanted verdict on the fate

49

of the 'dispossessed' or 'exiled' Anglo-Irish. Their conversation about the Troubles is the novel's most direct expression of the impotence of their kind:

> 'How far do you think this war is going to go? Will there ever be anything we can all do except not notice?'
>
> 'Don't ask *me*,' he said, but sighed sharply as though beneath the pressure of omniscience. 'A few more hundred deaths, I suppose, on our side – which is no side – rather scared, rather isolated, not expressing anything except tenacity to something that isn't there – that never was there.'

When Lois looks to other attitudes than this for guidance, she meets the comic stoicism of the older generation, refusing to admit to change or threat, or the cynicism of her irritating brainy cousin, Laurence, an Oxford undergraduate and self-appointed socialist, who goes in for an affectedly brutal version of Lois's impatience: 'This might all just as well be going on in the Balkans. I sometimes rather wish that I were a gunman' . . . 'I should like to be here when this house burns.' In contrast to this, there is the inadequately simple certainty of the 'ideal' British soldier, Gerald Lesworth, whose single-minded courtship of Lois is the opposite of Mr Montmorency's futile pursuit of Marda. Gerald is the novel's one purely romantic figure. Like Jacob in *Jacob's Room* (but without his brains), he is the perfect ideal of the English boy, handsome, inarticulate, enthusiastic, incorruptible, certain, who does not conceive of love 'as a nervous interchange, but as something absolute'. There is as much nostalgia in this characterisation as in the evocation of Danielstown. Gerald is old-fashioned: a pre-1914 type of soldier who hasn't caught up with history. He dislikes the personal elements in the job he is doing – the disconcerting relationships, for example, between wanted members of the IRA and the families where he goes to play tennis. But otherwise his attitude to the war is straightforward:

> 'Well, the situation's rotten. But right *is* right.'
>
> 'Why?'

'Well . . . from the point of view of civilization. Also you see
they don't fight clean.'

'Oh, there's no public school spirit in Ireland. But do tell me
– what do you mean by the point of view of civilization?'

'Oh – ours.'

When Gerald has been killed in an ambush, Lois sums him
up, in her mind, in his own kind of absolute terms: 'He loved
me, he believed in the British Empire.' But Gerald's death, the
climactic shock which brings the troubles home to Danielstown and precedes the burning of the house, is not the
greatest tragedy for Lois. Bowen avoids any predictable
romanticism by putting the failure of the relationship before
Gerald's death. Like everything else, Gerald is a disappointment to Lois. His love fails to break the spell of apathy in
which she is caught. Deep down, he leaves her cold.

This failure of love in Lois is the strongest image of impotence and isolation in the novel. And it's done in rather
clichéd, sensationalist language: ' "I don't understand you,"
he cried in agony . . .' ' "But what have I done? What have I
not done?" ' Bowen's lovers often speak in apocalyptic terms
like these, to underline the significance of their failures. But
the thwarted love works in *The Last September* because of
the novel's general feeling of unreality and unease. Bowen has
a great talent for suggesting a constant sense of peril. She does
it with edgy, macabre images, odd turns of phrase, sinister
details. The mannered quality of her writing is perfect for
making the reader feel nervous – as in horror stories like 'The
Cat Jumps' or 'The Demon Lover'. In *The Last September*,
disconcerting images are constantly creeping in. Lois, coming
back from her night-time encounter with the stranger in the
shrubbery, where the leaves against her bare arms were like
'tongues of dead animals', sees 'the rug dropped in the hall by
Mrs Montmorency sprawl like a body across the polish'.
Figures are seen as in a picture, or a dream. We see Lady
Naylor and Mrs Montmorency passing 'in profile, under the
west windows very close together under a green *en-tout-cas*
discussing the vice-regency of the Aberdeens', or tennis
players on the upper court 'flickering against the dark screen

of the trees like figures cut out of light green velvet'. The general oddness culminates in the dance given in the officers' huts at the back of the Clonmore barracks, when Lois encounters the alarming shell-shocked Daventry – 'not a man, hardly even a person':

> 'About our young friend –' He pulled up his chair close; she had a feeling like gates shutting. 'Tell me this –'
> But the roar of merriment, solid and swerving steadily as a waterfall past the door, splintered off in a crash. Silence came, with a hard impact. 'Thank God, *they've upset the gramophone*!' Daventry smacked his knee, remotely, as though rehearsing the gesture. His look decomposed in laughter. 'Done in,' he said, drawing life from the thought. Simultaneously, a universal shriek went up: it was smashed, finished. 'Really,' she thought, 'you laugh like Satan!'
> 'Well, well,' said Daventry, tilting his drink about, 'it's been a pleasant evening.'

Daventry (who is to break the news of Gerald's death) opens up the only true reality lying behind the transient, local history of the novel: that 'life, seen whole for a moment, was one act of apprehension, the apprehension of death.'

But though *The Last September* is a sombre and disquieting novel, it is also a sharp comedy of manners. She will combine these tones again, especially in *The Death of the Heart*. There are several set pieces which do the period immaculately: the tennis party at Danielstown, the dance in the huts, the visit to the Careys at Mount Isabel ('full-bosomed silver, hands balancing Worcester, dogs poking wistfully up from under the cloth'), the tea-time in Mrs Fogarty's drawing-room in Clonmore, (the small town based on Fermoy, near Bowen's Court). Here the soldiers sing 'The Green Eye of the Little Yellow God' and 'The Shooting of Dan McGrew', the room smells of 'wallpaper, tea and tea-cakes, polished Sam Browns' and 'the *Nuit d'Amour* on Mrs Vermont's handkerchief', and everyone feels 'very easy and very Irish'. The encroachment of the Troubles is dramatic, but it can also be absurd:

'Castle Trent was raided for arms last night. Of course they didn't find any. They think the thing was entirely amateur, nothing to do with the I.R.A. at all. They took away some boots. The Trents think one of the raiders was a gardener's cousin from Ballydarra who hates the family. He left a quite unnecessary message behind with a skull and crossbones. He sounds to me rather a silly man.'

This speech of Laurence's, half-flippant, half-excited, shows how carefully the dialogue catches the tones of the Anglo-Irish response to the Troubles. The Naylors are splendid 'types'. Sir Richard's stoic eccentricities are comical but convincing: his refusal to take the Troubles seriously, his qualms about the occupying forces ('They tell me there's a great deal of socialism now in the British Army'), his blithe expectations that colder weather will put an end to this 'ambushing and skirmishing and heyfidaddling', and his nightmares ('his friends cut him; he discovered he was a Black and Tan'). Lady Naylor's calculated spasms of absent-mindedness, and her ability to dispose of inconveniences, like a penniless young British soldier in love with her niece, give her the robustness of an Anglo-Irish Lady Bracknell. Lady Naylor has pronounced views on the English, their barbaric habits of paying morning calls and talking about their insides, the dullness and hostility of their lower classes, their peculiar geographical distribution:

'His mother, he says, lives in Surrey, and of course you do know, don't you, what Surrey is. It says nothing, absolutely; part of it is opposite the Thames Embankment. Practically nobody who lives in Surrey ever seems to have been heard of, and if one does hear of them they have never heard of anybody else who lives in Surrey. Really altogether, I think all English people very difficult to trace. They are so pleasant and civil, but I do often wonder if they are not a little shallow: for no reason at all they will pack up everything and move across six counties . . .

Like Jane Austen, Bowen knows her subject. This distinguishes Anglo-Irish upper-class snobbery very precisely from its English equivalent. Lady Naylor's relations with the British Army officers' wives are sharply done; the treatment of the wives themselves, however, suggests that Elizabeth Bowen's prejudice is on the side of the Big House. Vulgar, patronising Mrs Vermont is an early version of that kind of woman in Bowen's fiction. These caricatures of the middle class are unsympathetic, even spiteful. But, in the context of the ambivalent relations between the Anglo-Irish and the British, Mrs Vermont's outbursts are very funny: 'I never knew Tipperary was really a place till I came to Ireland' . . . 'Myself, I do like a house to be bright and homey' . . . 'What is the good of being in Ireland if one isn't a bit unconventional?'

> 'All this is terrible for you all, isn't it? I do think you're so sporting the way you just stay where you are and keep going on. Who would ever have thought of the Irish turning out so disloyal – I mean, of course, the lower classes! I remember mother saying in 1916 – you know, when that dreadful rebellion broke out – she said: "This *has* been a shock to me; I shall never feel the same about the Irish again!" You see, she had brought us all up as kiddies to be so keen on the Irish and Irish songs. I still have a little bog oak pig she brought me back from an exhibition. She always said they were the most humorous people in the world, and with hearts of gold. Though of course we had none of us ever been in Ireland.'
>
> 'Well, I hope you are pleased with us now you have come,' said Mrs Carey hospitably. 'I expect you have all been enjoying this lovely weather?'
>
> 'Oh *well* – you see we didn't come over to enjoy ourselves, did we? We came to take care of all of you – and of course, we are ever so glad to be able to do it. Not that I don't like the country; it's so picturesque with those darling mountains and the hens running in and out of the cottages just the way mother always said. But you see one can't help worrying all the time about Timmie – my husband – and all the boys; out all night sometimes with the patrols or else off in the mountains.'
>
> 'Terrible. And do you find this a tiring climate?'

Bowen plays off Mrs Carey's veiled *grande dame* manner

against English obtuseness in one of the novel's high comic points. This satire illustrates the ambivalent Anglo-Irish attitudes towards the English, and is also a form of elegy. The 'grand idea', the sense of family pride, the almost mystical apartness which are to be the factual subjects of *Bowen's Court* are shown, in the novel, as having declined into laughable eccentricities; there can now, in the 1920s, only be a comedy of the Ascendancy. Sir Richard, funny in his refusal to admit to the situation, is in the end a pathetic figure: 'He was an old man really, outside all this, and did not know what to do.' Lady Naylor, whom Lois calls 'as designing as a cardinal', is a diminished version of those powerful matriarchs in *Bowen's Court*. Her scope is reduced; her field of activity is now limited to preventing the marriage of Lois and Gerald, a piece of plotting which events render supremely redundant. *The Last September* is a witty novel, but its acknowledgement of loss prevails throughout.

As with *Bowen's Court*, the novel is dominated above all by a sense of place. To take the two books together is to see the house from different perspectives. In the first chapter of *Bowen's Court*, and throughout *The Last September*, there is a strong evocation of the lost house and its surrounding countryside, done through contrasts of light and dark. The house looks different in different weathers. In the rain it is a 'cold shell . . . streaked . . . and hollow-looking from interior darkness'. With the early or late sun shining into its expanse of glass, it appears 'riddled with light'.[88] In the autumn, it seems benign, tinged with 'a kind of expectancy'. The bare austerity, the cliff-like height of the house is always felt; inside, the big, cold, mirrored drawing-room can seem like 'an ice-palace'. But from a distance this chill, light quality is hidden. From the bright, empty countryside (a quality she always emphasises in her County Cork landscapes, in both these books and in 'The Happy Autumn Fields') the house looks secret and obscure:

> To the south, below them, the demesne trees of Danielstown
> made a dark formal square like a rug on the green country. In
> their heart like a dropped pin the grey glazed roof reflecting

the sky lightly glinted. Looking down, it seemed to Lois they lived in a forest; space of lawns blotted out in the pressure and dusk of trees. She wondered they were not smothered; then wondered still more that they were not afraid. Far from here, too, their isolation became apparent. The house seemed to be pressing down low in apprehension, hiding its face, as though it had her vision of where it was. It seemed to huddle its trees close in fright and amazement at the wide light lovely unloving country, the unwilling bosom whereon it was set . . . Fields gave back light to the sky . . . Rivers, profound in brightness, flowed over beds of grass . . . only the trees of the demesne were dark and exhaled darkness. Down among them, dusk would stream up the paths ahead, lie stagnant on lawns, would mount in the dank of garden, heightening the walls, dulling the borders as by a rain of ashes. Dusk would lie where one looked as though it were in one's eyes, as though the fountain of darkness were in one's own perception. Seen from above, the house in its pit of trees seemed a very reservoir of obscurity . . .

The countryside, with its separate, changing life, is bold, exposed, and unsympathetic. The house seems, from above, not proud and enlightened, as when one is in it, but huddled down, at risk, a separated island, 'singular, independent and secretive'.

3

THE DISINHERITED

She saw that events led nowhere, crisis was an illusion, and
that passions of momentary violent reality were struck off like
sparks from the spirit, only to die. One could precipitate
nothing. One is empowered to live fully: occasion does not
offer.

ELIZABETH BOWEN BEGAN to make her name as a
writer in the mid-1920s, after she and Alan Cameron left
Northampton for a pretty house in Old Headington, on the
edge of Oxford, where he was appointed Secretary for
Education in 1925. Once they arrived, she began to publish
energetically: three volumes of stories and three novels in the
Oxford years, between 1926 and 1934. In Oxford, Bowen
moved into new circles that suited her very well: John and
Susan Buchan, David Cecil, Maurice Bowra, Isaiah Berlin,
Cyril Connolly, John Sparrow. She and Alan went over
regularly to Bowen's Court. Her father died there in 1930
and she became the owner of the house.

In the early 1930s, she travelled widely, and began to spend
more time in London and to make new friends there: William
Plomer, Ottoline Morell and, gradually, Virginia Woolf. She
was starting to review in the *New Statesman*, the *Tatler*, the
Spectator and elsewhere. In 1923 she changed her publishers,
in England to Gollancz (she would go to Jonathan Cape after
the war, where William Plomer was her editor), in the United
States to Knopf. By the early 1930s, she had made herself into
a distinctive literary figure.

The novels on either side of *The Last September* – *The Hotel* (1927), Bowen's first novel, and *Friends and Relations* (1931) – are not as good. They show their literary debts very clearly, but they establish some key Bowen subjects (like the spiritually corrupting effect of an older woman, or the restrictiveness of the family ties). This makes them interesting preludes to her major works. They are not about Ireland and not discernibly the work of an Anglo-Irish writer. With the much better novel that followed them, *To the North* (1932), they show that to place Bowen only in the tradition of Edgeworth, Le Fanu or Somerville and Ross, is not enough. Like Joyce Cary, who wrote two novels – *Castle Corner* (1938) and *A House of Children* (1941) – out of his Anglo-Irish experience, but whose work ranges well beyond it, Bowen needs viewing from more than one perspective. The ideas and tone of *The Last September* and *Bowen's Court* are central, and permeate all her work, even when her subject is not the Anglo-Irish. But from her first volume of stories onwards, Bowen wanted, as well, to establish herself in an English, and a European, context.

It's telling though that of the three early novels *The Last September* is so much the best. Its mood and subject seem to have come naturally to her. Her English themes and settings are more obviously being 'practised' in the other early novels, and it's not until the dramatic and assured *To the North* that she masters them.

The Hotel and *Friends and Relations*, like her own awkward adolescent characters, are rather affected. Sometimes she is mannered because she is imitating: sometimes because she is self-consciously forging her own style. But in *The Hotel* her sense of herself is largely missing. Though she had already found her voice in the early short stories, *Encounters* (1923) and *Ann Lee's* (1926), the leap into a novel seems to have inhibited her. As a result the novel shows a curious mixture of debts. Its setting and story are a combination of Forster's *A Room With a View* (1908) and of Virginia Woolf's first novel, *The Voyage Out* (1915), while the style in which the characters react to each other reads like a pastiche of Henry James's dialogue.

The novel is set in a hotel full of English people on the Italian Riviera. Its central figure is a confused, passionate, intelligent girl called Sydney, who has fallen under the influence of a subtle, fundamentally unfeeling older woman, Mrs Kerr. The arrival of Mrs Kerr's effete son Roland (a similar type to Laurence in *The Last September*) leads to Sydney's being 'chucked' by her friend. Disillusioned with Mrs Kerr, who turns out to have had 'vulgar' designs on her, Sydney allows herself to become engaged to a colourless middle-aged clergyman called Milton. But a moment of danger on an excursion in the hills makes her suddenly aware that she has been acting passively, in a kind of dream; she breaks off the engagement, and the main characters leave the hotel.

The novel's comedy – silly pairs of women, husband-hunting girls, aggressive married couples, farcical picnics, failures on the tennis court – owes a lot to Woolf and Forster. In *The Voyage Out*, there is a split between the 'funny' characters and Rachel Vinrace's emotional development. The inhabitants of the hotel in South America are compared to animals in the zoo, and are grotesquely satirised. To an extent *The Hotel* makes this kind of distinction. When Sydney imagines that the front of the hotel could be taken off, revealing a doll's house of fixed, separate attitudes, she is echoing Rachel's clinical interest in the circumscribed, puppet-like lives in 'the little box-like squares'.[1] Like Rachel, Sydney is scornful of and baffled by much of the hotel's 'grown-up' life – marriages, arguments between women, the 'purposeful groping' of the husband-hunters. As in *The Voyage Out*, the hotel is an isolated microcosm of English social life from which Sydney needs to withdraw in order to understand herself – when she does this, she often sounds like Rachel: 'She was mapping out for herself a deep-down life in which emotions ceased their clashing together and friends appeared only as painted along the edge of one's quietness.' Her intense relationship with Mrs Kerr is a more sinister version of Rachel's instruction in the way of the world by her aunt, Helen. And Sydney's attempt to have the right feelings for James Milton is a bit like Rachel's struggle for unity with Terence. They have similar experiences: a picnic at which they both see another couple kissing, a walk in which they feel over-exposed to the wild countryside.

But this opposition between comedy and emotion is mixed with a more Forsterian search for truth within a comic context. Bowen draws on Forster for some of her details – a mackintosh spread at a picnic by a chaperoning lady, a casual Italian peasant directing a young man, as though providentially, towards the English 'bellissima'. And she imitates his placing of emotional 'muddle' inside a parochial, limiting world – quite different from Woolf's separation of 'real' experience from the habitual surface of life. Sydney, like Lucy Honeychurch, is in the sort of muddle which leads to disappointment and a broken engagement, rather than (as with Rachel) to withdrawal from human beings and death from fever.

The Hotel also casts a tentative eye at Proust ('He was convinced . . . that a need corresponding to his must exist in her somewhere'; 'The present, always slipping away, was ghostly, every moment spent itself in apprehension of the next') and more than an eye at Henry James. Mrs Kerr's exploitation of Sydney is an early example of a Jamesian theme in Bowen. Power wielded manipulatively by an older woman against an inexperienced girl will reappear in *The House in Paris* and *The Death of the Heart*. In the later works, Henry James will be left behind. But at this stage Mrs Kerr is too obviously a mixture of Mrs Gereth and Mme Merle, and talks a funny kind of Jamesian lingo:

'One's idea of a person', she told him, 'refuses to take certain possibilities, like a material refusing to take certain dyes. Don't you feel so? For instance: for anyone else, any woman, as angry and hurt in her pride, and as disappointed as I'm afraid Sydney's been with me lately, to have taken you up with the strong position you've given her would have been the inevitable, rather sordid, perhaps, but effective, complete little gesture. One would have looked for it, wouldn't one? and – taking the thing at its own valuation – rather applauded. One can't help applauding the score-off, the adequate pat little retaliation, all the more perhaps because, oneself, one could never achieve it.'

But sometimes Bowen's own voice emerges. These moments always have to do with the oddities of life in the hotel – the sort of thing she has already been doing well in short stories like 'Breakfast' in *Encounters* and 'The Secession' (also about a betrayal in an Italian hotel) in *Ann Lee's*. She gives the hotel setting a queasy, unnerving edge which is recognisably her own:

> The glass doors behind and beside her flashing as they opened and shut, the staircase going up and down and doubling off at angles into oblivion, and the way the lift came sliding down the shaft to wait behind the latticed gates, were all like so much expressionist scenery, emphasizing the effect she gave of being distracted, mechanical and at a standstill.

Though she is straining to be a modernist here – the first paragraph of *To the North* will get a similar effect without using the word 'expressionist' – the description works disconcertingly well. That discomfort about hotels and their inhabitants will recur. They are places for the dispossessed, people hanging on to the edges of middle-class life. In this account (the best thing in the novel) of an ageing lady's reasons for wintering abroad, *The Hotel* begins to do what Bowen does best:

> 'As winter comes on with those long evenings one begins to feel hardly human, sitting evening after evening in an empty room. One can't always be going out or visiting people or inviting people to come to one. If I shut my drawing-room door, I begin to feel restless at once; it feels so unnatural shutting oneself in with nobody. If I open it, one hears the servants laughing, or something to worry one. I am fond of reading, but I always begin to feel that books are so bad; then of course I realize, well, it's not fair, is it, to expect a book to take the place of human society? If the telephone bell rings, to hear a voice and then be cut off simply unsettles one; and if it

doesn't ring the whole evening, one begins to worry and imagine things about one's friends. Once I sat with the door open and, believe me, I could hear four different clocks ticking – I counted them – in different parts of the flat. It's not, of course, that I'm nervous, but I really begin to feel – if you'll understand my saying anything so extraordinary – as if I didn't exist. If somebody does come to the door or the telephone does ring, I'm almost surprised to find I'm still there.'

The way that she makes surface details create a sensation of vacancy and unreality, 'the discovery of a lack', is one of Bowen's greatest strengths. In *Friends and Relations*, accumulations of factual incidentals – social habits, family trees, furniture, shops – show up fear and emptiness inside a cluttered, habituated, comfortable veneer of upper-middle-class provincial family life. These early novels start a criticism of a class and a society which will continue with the Michaelis family in *The House in Paris* and the Quaynes in *The Death of the Heart*. It will culminate in *The Heat of the Day*'s theory that such habits of life produce traitors.

The title *Friends and Relations* sounds like an Ivy Compton-Burnett novel. She had published *Pastors and Masters* in 1925 and *Brothers and Sisters* in 1929 (*Men and Wives* came out in the same year as *Friends and Relations*). Bowen would describe Compton-Burnett as dealing with 'the battle for power that goes on in every unit of English middle-class life'.[2] Like a Compton-Burnett novel, *Friends and Relations* is contained within one complex family, it is concerned with a long-kept secret and it portrays the mannerisms of a class. But Bowen is not really very like Compton-Burnett. Her manner is different: the narrative style of *Friends and Relations* is elaborate, not like Compton-Burnett's laconic, deadly manner and her bleak dialogue. And Bowen's tribal conflicts are harmless by comparison with Compton-Burnett's. The family skeleton in *Friends and Relations* is a 'coincidental' connection between the husbands of two sisters. Laurel, the pretty daughter of the Studdarts, a pleasant Cheltenham family, marries handsome Edward

Tilney; Janet Studdart, the dark brooding daughter, then gets engaged to Rodney Meggatt. But Rodney's uncle and guardian, a big-game hunter called Considine Meggatt, was, it turns out, the co-respondent in Edward's mother's divorce case. The Studdart parents and daughters manage to override this embarrassment – and Considine and the world-weary Lady Elfrida Tilney are now 'good friends'. But Edward, whose childhood has been made unhappy by his mother's disgrace, is 'difficult' about the situation, and wants to protect his children from the combination of Considine and Elfrida. This continuing family delicacy is the public side of the novel's real secret. Janet has married Rodney, it transpires, knowing his relation to the Tilney family, as a way of having some connection with Edward. Janet's suppressed, and Edward's reluctant, love for each other threatens after ten years to bring the whole fabric crashing down, but doesn't have enough force to persist against the family, the world and the ominous example of the previous generation.

But this is a mild collection of family secrets and skeletons compared with, say, the incestuous curse hanging over the family in Compton-Burnett's *Brothers and Sisters*. Bowen often deals with the effects of drastic passion on the next generation. But her families are never as grotesque as Compton-Burnett's, whom she describes as advancing 'on each other's houses in groups, like bomber formations'.[3]

Other literary influences are also at work in *Friends and Relations*. There is a reference to Katherine Mansfield's 'Prelude', when the failure of the love affair is summed up by the phrase 'the aloe had not flowered'. There are traces of Virginia Woolf, as in this mother-and-child bedroom scene, which reminds me of Mrs Ramsay putting Cam to sleep in *To the Lighthouse*:

Janet turned the pillow; Hermione, her cheek to the cool new pillow, was practically asleep. Her arms loosened. Her face was close to a shining, slippery stream; she, stirring like that live thing down in the leaves that she never discovered, shook the flat bright leaves above her to someone else's astonishment. She was hidden like a corncrake, distant like a cuckoo, close like a nesting swallow under the roof. She came up once through the hollow strong stems, knocking light from the leaves to murmur: 'It's almost the next day.'

But the main debt is again to Henry James. The novel investigates compromises and repressed emotions. So it presents long series of qualified formulations, producing an evasive text which seems to resist interpretation by over-interpreting itself:

> He might never have moved her. It remained impossible for him, now as then, to tell at what point he had committed himself to failure. She undid passion . . . Having now only him, she sent him away finally. She had perhaps injured him, perhaps even vitally. Then she had persistently sought the light man in him, match for her light woman. Under her dry-eyed farewell look, her last tragic un-regret, in Paris, he had certainly desiccated.

In *Friends and Relations* she had tied her own hands (Virginia Woolf said, 'I feel you're like somebody trying to throw a lasso with a knotted rope')[4] because the novel is so much concerned with a surface life which constricts the passions. The mannerisms, through which love and pain struggle to find expression, are like the social world in which the characters are contained.

Friends and Relations 'does' Cheltenham and Knightsbridge and the Meggatt country seat in detail; it moves itself along by family meetings, which are at once the mechanism and the subject of the novel: 'For as long as we live, I suppose about fifty years, we shall all always be meeting and talking over arrangements. At least, that is how we have been brought up. You must see what families are; it's possible to be so ordinary; it's possible not to say such a lot.' As Janet says, 'there only *is* one world' for these people. The women who try to break out, like Lady Elfrida, are never free from the after-effects. Love, under these circumstances (which are those of most middle-class families of the period) appears as 'a very high kind of overruling disorder', an 'inconvenient cruelty'. Life has to be 'an affair of charm not of passion'. So

Elfrida's regrets, Janet's anguish, Laurel's fear are contained within a charming, mannered surface, and their feelings are interspersed with comic set-pieces. Theodora Hirdman is the best of these, one of Bowen's intense, horrible, self-important schoolgirls, who allows for a splendid caricature of an advanced girls' school of the time:

> The girls at Mellyfield developed very early a feeling for character. They were interested in their own personalities, which they displayed, discussed and altered ... Everyone knew ... that Jenna's insincerity arose from a nervous opposition to circumstance; that Marise to live at all would have to break down her overpowering sense of order, that Hester since she was six had ruined all her friendships by her intolerance and that Ludmilla must be ignored when she squeaked at games because of a bad heredity.
>
> So that Jenna (notoriously over-anxious to put herself in the right) resumed later to Marise: 'If we all can't bear Theodora, it must be because she's aggressive, mustn't it? I mean it isn't as if she looked so awful, or smelled or anything, or were at all common. Now I do wonder *why* she –'
>
> 'She certainly is aggressive, she can't even do her hair without banging the things on her dressing-table about as though she were cooking.'
>
> 'Perhaps she's unhappy.'
>
> 'I don't suppose she's more unhappy than we are,' said Marise with some annoyance.
>
> 'But we at least do *know* we're unhappy.'

Theodora is obsessed with Janet, and her lesbian feelings are presented as partly ludicrous and oppressive, partly as an energetic, furious resistance to convention. The novel gets suddenly much more vigorous when it deals with her. But in general both *The Hotel* and *Friends and Relations* are about the failure to rise to crisis or tragedy. A 'large non-occurrence' is a phrase used in *Friends and Relations*. Any clash of wills (more painful and extreme in later novels) is, at this point, subdued. The heroines are unable to make their feelings come to anything or to assert themselves:

> Sydney took no notice of what was being said; she did not

seem as though she had heard. She stood between Tessa and Mrs Kerr as inanimate and objective as a young girl in a story told by a man, incapable of a thought or a feeling that was not attributed to her, with no personality of her own outside their three projections upon her: Milton's fiancée, Tessa's young cousin, Mrs Kerr's protégée, lately her friend.

She [Janet] stood powerless, looking through her life, at, not regainable, her whole habit of mind. This, like a house long inhabited without feeling and vacated easily, bore in, revisited in its emptiness, an anguishing sense of her no-presence ever in the past.

The later novels are more complex and dramatic because the characters are capable of drastic actions: they have a drive for power, or an incapacity for compromise, or the absolutism of innocence.

In the next novel, *To the North*, there is a marked change of tone from *Friends and Relations*. The opening points towards something more powerful:

Towards the end of April a breath from the north blew cold down Milan platforms to meet the returning traveller. Uncertain thoughts of home filled the station restaurant where the English sat lunching uneasily, facing the clock. The Anglo-Italian express – Chiasso, Lucerne, Basle and Boulogne – leaves at 2.15: it is not a *train de luxe*. To the north there were still the plains, the lakes, the gorges of the Ticino, but, as the glass brass-barred doors of the restaurant flashed and swung, that bright circular park outside with its rushing girdle of trams was the last of Italy.

This beginning is in part deceptive: leaving Italy is not in itself going to be important, and Cecilia Summers, the 'young widow' waiting for the train, is not going to be the heroine. The tone is odd and ambiguous. It looks as if we are going to get the same sort of social narrative as in *The Hotel* and *Friends and Relations*. Cecilia is first identified by her fur coat and dressing-case; at lunch she is thrown together with a young man who has a cigarette case engraved with his name,

'Markie', an old Harrovian tie, and a grand set of acquaintances in Rome. Their brittle dialogue ('It looks like a lake.' 'Yes, doesn't it; terribly') matches the worldliness of the narrative. The England to which Cecilia returns is comfortable: this is again the world of the Studdarts and the Tilneys. Cecilia shares an elegant home in St John's Wood with Emmeline, sister of Cecilia's late husband, Henry. Emmeline runs an eccentric travel agency financed by 'some' of her own capital; Cecilia is an object of interest to the 'immaculate' Julian Tower, who has 'inherited a rather too flourishing family business of more than two hundred years' standing'. Both young women are related to Lady Waters, an English Lady Naylor, a comic character who believes in the absolute reality of her social setting. Within this affluent, solidly established context Cecilia dithers about accepting Julian, and Emmeline falls in love with Markie: but, as in *Friends and Relations*, these emotions develop while people lunch, dine, and go to parties, choose what to wear, or go shopping:

> [Julian's sister] wanted a massage after her journey, a fitting at her corsetière's, a new silver saucepan to boil milk in her bedroom, a chat with her specialist and one of those mackintosh coats she had just seen advertised for her dog. She desired to visit her hat shop, which concealed itself upstairs in Mayfair with a discretion so sinister one might expect to rap three times on a panel or be regarded narrowly through a grille.

All the same, there is a discomforting tone to the first paragraph of the novel, strongly suggesting that its material world is going to be undermined. The knowing information about the Anglo-Italian express sounds a little ominous. The season, like the travellers, is 'uncertain'. Suspended between anticipation and loss, they lunch 'uneasily', awaiting their journey to the north. They are not moving yet, but the swinging of the bright restaurant doors and the rushing of trams through the bright park – violent, repetitive images – precipitate them towards movement, and, even, with 'brass-barred' and 'girdle', towards an idea of imprisonment. That they sit 'facing the clock' even hints at the idea of a train journey as a journey out of life, into the after-world (like the horrifying taxi ride in the later story, 'The Demon Lover'). Cecilia and Markie's *blasé* dialogue is not exactly entertaining. As the train 'fled . . . with a shriek' to Lucerne, 'lashing about its passengers as though they were bound to a dragon's tail', Cecilia imagines herself in hell:

> And in an afterworld, she might deserve just such a companion: too close, glancing at her – if any shreds of form still clung to the spirit – without sympathy, with just such a cold material knowingness.

Cecilia and Markie are a punishment to one another for being what they are (we are told that 'neither had nice characters'). The image of a journey in hell is not insistent, but the language keeps bringing in cruelty and violence. 'On a long journey . . . the brain like a horrified cat leaps clawing from object to object.' The last page of the novel, Emmeline's desperate drive with Markie (whom she loves and who has betrayed her) 'to the north' and to their deaths, is prefigured in the sinister tone, the incipient violence of the first chapter.

Bowen has already used Gerald's death in *The Last September* as a symptom of the passing of innocence – of some form of betrayal, personal or national – and she will do this again with Max in *The House in Paris* and with Robert in *The Heat of the Day*. She needs to make these deaths feel inevitable, not grotesquely sensational. In *To the North*, a pattern of images leads us, with an almost classical formality, towards murder and suicide.

Emmeline, the book's heroine, is not quite of this world. She is ethereal, angelic, 'pale and clear', 'more than half transparent materially'. When Julian first meets her she is drinking iced tea, dressed in silver, and sitting in an alcove 'alarmingly flooded with white light'. She is repeatedly described as short-sighted and thus disconnected from her surroundings; 'a curious distant look, not like a woman's' is apt to come across her face in conversation. Her work at the travel agency partly gives her pragmatic, competent qualities, but also associates her with distance and aerial aloofness, suggesting that she is always on the point of no return. Before she meets Markie, she is the unawakened ice maiden, the unfallen angel: 'nothing could be as dear as the circle of reading light round her solitary pillow'.

On the other hand, Markie, as Cecilia perceives at their first meeting, is Satanic. (She notices at once that he has the 'quick-lidded eyes of an agreeable reptile'.) He marks the first appearance in Elizabeth Bowen's work of the modern anti-hero who has lost touch with the sources of faith and idealism. Reason is his God (he is a very good lawyer), and he masters the threatening implications of love and passion by reducing them to sensual needs. He dislikes any kind of discomfort. Suffering ('out of place in the rational scheme'), marriage, an over-demanding affair, nature, and machines which may be beyond his control (he can't drive, and has never flown before meeting Emmeline) all come under this head. He will abandon Emmeline because her spirituality alarms him: 'One can't live on top of the Alps,' he tells her. His fear of her clearly comes from his *not* being entirely rational and pragmatic. He is an 'uneasy moralist', a sensualist who has repressed his sensibilities. Bowen dislikes Markie's type, but she likes showing us what it feels like to be him, a damned soul:

> The edge of his mind was restless with superstition: like natives before the solid advance of imperial forces, aspiration, feeling, all sense of the immaterial had retreated in him before reason to some craggy hinterland where, having made no terms with the conqueror, they were submitted to no control and remained a menace. Like savages coming to town on a fair day to skip and chaffer . . . feeling crept out in him from some unmapped region. His brain held his smallish, over-clear view of life in its rigid circle.

Cecilia can take Markie or leave him ('All this *âme damnée* is such a bore'), but Emmeline is melted by his desire for her (Julian is even made to envy him for 'cutting so much ice').

For here Markie was: in his presence . . . this idea of pleasure as isolated, arctic, regarding its own heart only, became desolating to Emmeline as a garden whose flowers were ice. Those north lights colouring the cold flowers became her enemies; her heart warming or weakening she felt at war with herself inside this cold zone of solitude. She desired lowness and fallibility, longing to break the mirror and touch the earth.

This highly metaphorical language is more charged up than the tepid formulations of *Friends and Relations*. But there's some strain felt in the effort to load Emmeline and Markie's relationship with elemental imagery and ominous images of travel. Still, at the two points of greatest intensity in the affair, the weekend of Emmeline's seduction in Paris, and their final car drive together, this patterning of images pays off. Markie's nervousness and Emmeline's exhilaration (she is, after all, in her element) on their plane flight to Paris anticipate his sexual sensations 'of having been overshot, of having, in some final soaring flight of her exaltation, been outdistanced'. Emmeline makes a joke about the violent pace of Paris taxis being like 'the Last Ride Together'. All this points towards the powerful, catastrophic ending. Emmeline, wearing her original silver dress, drives Markie northwards, back into the element which he has defied, in order to take revenge. Her fey looks culminate in a final distractedness; while Markie struggles to bring her back to earth, she is given up to speed. The associations that have been made between her work (over which she has lost control), her passion and her unearthly innocence fall into place.

> Something gave way.
> An immense idea of departure – expresses getting steam up and crashing from termini, liners clearing the docks, the shadows of planes rising, caravans winding out into the first dip of the desert . . . possessed her spirit, now launched like a long arrow . . . Like earth shrinking and sinking, irrelevant, under the rising wings of a plane, love with its unseen plan . . . dropped to a depth below Emmeline . . . She was lost to her own identity, a confining husk.

Emmeline and Markie, characters in what is partly a comedy

of manners, have to end as tragic protagonists. The strict formality of the novel's plot – two women, two lovers, a journey to begin with and a journey to end with – undermines the characters' opportunities for free choice, like the relentless patterning of the book's images. Even when the emphasis is on the comic world (traditionally one of choice and self-improvement), freedom of will seems no more than a toy, or as Emmeline thinks, idly considering silly little Gerda Bligh's indecisiveness about her marriage, 'a mistake'. Cecilia and Julian, although less extreme and more engaging than the tragic pair, are also enfeebled by their freedom of choice:

> She nightly returned to . . . her sense of being a far too general gift to the world . . . a novel for any subscriber to take out.

> Something in him that would not bring off the simplest relationship, that could be aware of any relationship only as something to be brought off.

They dither, are indefinite, finally decide to marry; it seems to be a good thing, and they seem to have chosen it (though Bowen typically bypasses, so as to diminish, the moment of choice). But Cecilia, though constantly weighing up her choices (should she wear a rose at dinner? should she go to America?) is as much a victim as the more obviously 'driven' Emmeline. Her first husband, Emmeline's brother Henry, died soon after their marriage. Her character has hardened accordingly, her emotional stature has been lessened by the death. She is not blamed for this. But perhaps she is to blame for casually bringing Markie to Emmeline, and for remaining uninvolved. It's implied that Julian and Cecilia could have 'done something' to prevent Emmeline's tragedy, and that they will suffer from pangs of conscience. But that idea of moral responsibility is undercut by the inevitability of the events. There is the same clash of will and fate in Emmeline's relationship with Markie. Both express a belief in the will. 'She had undone herself; she was her own victim,' Markie thinks. It is the lawyer's point of view: 'Justice . . . remained Markie's cold ally.' But Emmeline agrees with this judgement: 'One does oneself in,' she says to him. Both, however, are compelled: 'She might be said to be drawn, with a force of which she was hardly aware, by what existed in Markie in spite of himself.'

Markie is a predator and Emmeline is his victim. But, like Portia in *The Death of the Heart*, she is as dangerous to the fallen adult world as it is to her. Her innocence, her immoderate 'exaltation' in love, her 'too high idea of life and himself' terrify Markie, who senses that the victim can become the avenger.

His fear leads into a histrionic passage on Tragedy which takes the novel to its furthest point from realism:

> Here figures cast unknown shadows: passion knows no crime, only its own movement; steel and the cord go with the kiss. Innocence walks with violence, violence is innocent, cold as fate; between the mistress's kiss and the blade's is a hair's-breadth only, and no disparity; every door leads to death . . . The curtain comes down, the book closes – but who is to say that this is not so?

The high, ritual tone is not a great success. But it's meant to be a major statement of the novel's meaning, the clash between tragic necessity and individual goodness and innocence.

The combination creates an unsettling of realism. Sometimes the novel's tragic formality is made explicit; sometimes, as in the opening paragraph, realism is used as a cloak. Bowen manages to make her 'extreme' character, Emmeline, plausible, by rooting her in reality. She does this partly by attaching Emmeline to Cecilia, in a 'quiet marriage' of 'domestic confidence'. Emmeline's conflict between her commitments to Cecilia and to Markie and the constant interplay of the plot between the two couples (with a suggestion of their being wrongly paired) gives Emmeline's affair an ordinary, humanised aspect. Emmeline's angelic qualities, evidence of Bowen's belief that there must be 'at least one *magnetic* character . . . capable of keying the reader up, as though he . . . were in the presence of someone he is in love with',[5] are insisted upon, but not all the time. A context of the normal is provided:

Emmeline lunched not far from Woburn Place at a shop called 'The Coffee Pot', with Peter Lewis, her partner. She read a book about Poland, he blue-pencilled manuscript; they ate poached eggs on spinach, each paid for their own lunches and did not speak to each other.

Her rare nature is placed against two kinds of minor characters. There are the predators like the meddlesome Lady Waters, and the fearsomely efficient Miss Armitage, who takes over the office. And there are the hapless muddlers who wear their hearts on their sleeve. Pauline, Julian's embarrassing niece, is a nicer-natured Theodora (a visit to her school, which is very like Theodora's makes a fine comic scene). Miss Tripp, the secretary, has a painful crush on Emmeline. Gerda is a 'child-wife' in whose marital difficulties Lady Waters takes an obviously disastrous interest. The muddlers provide clouded, imperfect versions of Emmeline's innocence; the predators stand for the hostility of the adult world.

But, as in *The Last September*, it's the places which are the richest source of the novel's power. After the burning of the Big House at the end of *The Last September*, Bowen's novels turn their attention to what is left: places for the dispossessed. Boarding houses, rented cottages, shut-up homes, empty villas, obscure shops one can never find again, parks at dusk, and, later, bombed houses – places where people have stopped living or are on their way to somewhere else – such settings (particularly in the short stories) are always at the heart of what is odd or ominous in the 'Bowen terrain'.[6] They attract people who have lost their homes or their way, such as Lady Waters's guests, 'a little party of exiles', dragged off (like the tourists in *The Hotel*) to visit a Roman villa, closed on Sundays, who 'cast round in spirit, to find nothing'. They are places for 'the disinherited', like the all-night road-house in the story of that name:

A glittering Neon sign like wolves' eyes read: OPEN ALL NIGHT, at which thought a dry weariness pervaded the brain . . .
    The road-house stood at the cross-roads, its row of Christmas card windows shedding a fictitious glow . . . But

> inside there was no-one. A long row of swinging lanterns
> bobbed in their own horrid light as they pushed open the
> door. The lounge was empty and bald as the inside of a band-
> box, glazed with synthetic panelling. The chairs were askew,
> empty, with flattened cushions; ashtrays sent up a cold fume;
> the place wore an air of sullen, sheepish vacuity, as though a
> large party had just got up and gone out. The barman leaned,
> yawning, just inside the bar shutter. When they came in, he
> took no notice. Davina's friends had not come.[7]

The place stands for a spiritual malaise, not just the feckless
Davina's, but a whole generation's with lost traditions and no
homes of their own. There are similar venues in *To the
North*, from the station at Milan to the 'jaded glare of an all
night café' glimpsed by Markie on the final journey. Travel,
which provides the *raison d'être* for such settings, has a moral
as well as symbolic significance, caricatured in a platitude of
Lady Waters's: '*This* age . . . is far more than restless; it is
decentralized.' Markie's sinister flat, cut off at the top of his
sister's 'very high, dark-red house in Lower Sloane Street',
with its shadowy corners and its invisible cook whose 'reedy,
ghostly whistle' makes Emmeline jump, is the main example
in the novel of such impermanent 'nowhere' places, symptoms of deracination. Set against them are places offering
peace and stability. But they are all potentially lost paradises,
like Danielstown. Emmeline's office, 'a studio to her, even a
shrine', dwindles to a scene of horror. Oudenarde Road,
leafy, secluded, and charming, is lost to Emmeline in her
imagination.

> Emmeline said: 'She's going to marry Julian' . . . Timber by
> timber, Oudenarde Road fell to bits, as small houses are
> broken up daily to widen the roar of London. She saw the
> door open on emptiness: blanched walls as though after a fire.
> Houses shared with women are built on sand. She thought:
> 'My home, my home.'

The burning of the house, Bowen's most potent image of
dispossession, reappears here, out of the Anglo-Irish context.
And it enforces the sense that Emmeline lives in a disinherited
world.

There is a Big House of sorts in *To the North*, Lady Waters's old-fashioned country residence 'Farraways' (an unapologetically significant name) which the urban Cecilia finds depressing, but which is a garden of Eden for Emmeline:

> Here Emmeline, step-child of her uneasy century, thought she would like to live ... But already a vague expectation of Monday and Tuesday filled her; looking out from the shadow of the limes already she saw the house with its white window-frames like some image of childhood, unaccountably dear but remote.

Farraways is decorous and pastoral; but, weaker even than Danielstown, it provides no defence for Emmeline against the modern world – Markie's domain – a world inhabited, in hand-to-mouth fashion, by spiritual exiles. Country retreats provide no protection in this world, as we can see from Emmeline and Markie's last weekend together, in a friend's cottage near Devizes. Markie's impatience and discomfort at the idea of a rural idyll is painfully set against Emmeline's romantic enthusiasm. She packs enough food for a week, but Markie insists on going back to the town, to eat in Devizes. The small business of the meal is telling:

> The cottage, the late lovely sense of arrival, tugged at her heart. 'Here we are', she had thought, coming in: but she had been wrong, they were not. For ever coming and going; no peace, no peace. What did Markie always want to avoid?

Emmeline's betrayal is meant to be a symptom of a more general, historical state of loss and dispossession. The emphasis on material things, as well as being necessary for the novel's social, comic vein, is also emblematic. Middle-class, cosmopolitan or suburban life is presented as purgatorial. By contrast, sheltered, gracious living in a place with its own past is seen not only as a good thing in itself but also as a symbol of innocence. This implies an opposition between rural and urban values. Oudenarde Road (rather like the Schlegels' home in Wickham Place, in Forster's *Howards End*) is as much of a safe retreat as one can find in London, but its peace is destroyed by Markie, an essentially cosmopolitan villain.

To underline this theme, landscapes of dereliction are made to illustrate states of mind. These passages are like miniature short stories – especially as they anticipate so many of the settings in the short-story collections, *The Cat Jumps* or *Look at All Those Roses*:

Markie, for the good of his liver, went for a walk by himself after Sunday lunch, uphill into the woods. No birds sang: it had been worse than that day in Keats. Leaves, rotting and rusty, deadened his steps; the afternoon had been sodden and quite toneless; it began to be dark early. Down there, between the dreary trunks of the beeches, houses lay like a sediment in the cup of the misty valley: great gabled carcasses, villas aping the manor, belfried garages where you could feel the cars get cold. There were no lights, not a thread of smoke from a chimney. Afternoon stupor reigned; there was nothing more that they wanted; down there they all sat in the dark . . . Then someone's wife opened a cold piano: she tinkled, she tippetted, she struck false chords and tried them again. God knew what she thought she was doing. The notes fell on his nerves like the drops of condensed mist all round on the clammy beech branches. Markie's left shoulder-blade had begun to itch violently: he ground it against a tree. Penetrated by all these kinds of discomfort he had raged in the bare meek woods . . . the piano stopped, he went downhill again to tea.

. . . He had said: 'How nicely you play!' She said, 'But I wasn't playing. I don't know what I was doing: what was I doing?' Her husband did not know either: he knocked the ashes about in the fire and said it was out. 'Did you have a nice walk?' they had asked him.

'Where did you go?' Markie could not remember. 'Oh well, they said, 'all the walks are the same round here. But it's pretty country, isn't it?' No one else came in: they said they lived very quietly. 'Still,' Markie's friend had said, 'it does grow on one.'

Emmeline, considering this when he angrily came to an end, had enquired: 'Is it a ghost story?'

The point of this landscape (which is superfluous to the plot of the novel) is not just to show up Markie as a lost soul, equally alienated from human beings and from the 'meek' countryside which they have colonised, but to put him in a place which isn't a home for anyone, a place entirely populated with lost souls. The grotesquely fraudulent architecture, the cars getting cold like corpses, the horrid, inexplicable piano playing, the people sitting 'down there in the dark', the dead fire: these purgatorial touches suggest much more than a chillingly exact picture of a familiar scene. Something has gone wrong with the civilisation: it has become a kind of morgue.

The emotional deprivations from which Bowen's characters suffer (either as a temperamental disability or in response to blows of fate) are so often turned into images of place that an eerie overlap results between interior and exterior landscapes. A set-piece of description, looked at again, becomes a metaphor for the state of a soul:

One has to live how one can – it is meaner living, gaudy, necessitous, full of immediate pleasures like the lives of the poor.

When a great house has been destroyed by fire ... the master has not, perhaps, the heart or the money to rebuild. Trees that were its companions are cut down and the estate sold up to the speculator. Villas spring up in red rows, each a home for someone, enticing brave little shops, radiant picture palaces: perhaps a park is left round the lake, where couples go boating. Lovers' lanes in asphalt replace the lonely green rides; the obelisk having no approaches is taken away. After dark – where once there was silence, a tree's shadow drawn slowly across the grass by the moon, or no moon, an exhalation of darkness – rows of windows come out like lanterns in pink and orange; boxed in bright light hundreds of lives repeat their pattern; wireless picks up a tune from street to street ... Life here is liveable, kindly and sometimes gay; there is not a ghost of space or silence; the great house with its dominance and its radiation of avenues is forgotten. When spring is sweet in the air, snowdrops under the paling, when blue autumn blurs the trim streets' perspective or the low sun in winter dazzles the windows' gold – something touches the heart, someone, disturbed, pauses, hand on a villa gate. But not to ask: What was here?

With the quick fancy, the nerves and senses Cecilia could almost love ... With her, the gay little streets flourished, but, brave where her house fell, she could not regain some entirety of the spirit. Disability seems a hard reward for courage.

That Bowen should use the destruction of the Anglo-Irish Big House to stand for the personal impoverishment of her English characters shows how the Burkean idea, of the moral necessity for property and tradition, persists throughout her work. Emmeline's tragedy, Cecilia's inadequacy, are examples of what a disinherited society must expect. Their ruined lives are symptoms of an 'uneasy century'. So there is a tension between their violent, passionate experiences, and the clinical use to which they are put by the author. The effect is not cosy or endearing (particularly given the social assumptions: there can be no doubt, for all their gaiety and courage, that the little villas are inferior to the Big House). But it shows that the losses Bowen chronicles are more than merely personal.

4

THE FATAL HOUSE

The fatal house in Paris still so possessed her that nothing was real that happened outside that.

IN 1933, TEN years into her marriage, Elizabeth Bowen embarked on a painful love affair with the Oxford academic Humphry House, who was engaged to be married, and was several years younger than her. It lasted for three years, and though it didn't break up either of their marriages, it was a disturbing and intense experience which made its way into the emotions of the next novel, *The House in Paris* (1935). (Max, the lover in the novel, seems to have been nothing like Humphry House, but Naomi, his fiancée, was, according to Victoria Glendinning, closely based on Madeleine House: 'Naomi Fisher I see the whole time, even her clothes.')[1]

Meanwhile, Bowen's social and professional life was thriving. She had lively house parties at Bowen's Court, where Virginia Woolf – who was becoming a closer friend – was a guest in 1934. And in 1934 she published a dazzling collection of stories, *The Cat Jumps*.

The title of *The House in Paris*, the novel after *To the North*, is at once factual and ominous. It has an air of documentary realism – this is where it all happened – and it also suggests that, like Danielstown, the house will be a participant in the novel. Like other titles which name a building – *Mansfield Park*, *Castle Rackrent*, *Bleak House*, *Howards End*, *Bowen's Court* – it gives the place a kind of symbolic importance. 'The house in Paris' has no name; it is 'the' house – significant, central – and takes its character from the city it belongs to. That it is both anonymous and foreign is sinister; there is a faint evocation of the Gothic (*The Castle of Otranto, Headlong Hall, Northanger Abbey, Wuthering Heights, The House of the Seven Gables*), implying that *The House in Paris* might belong in that tradition.

And it *is* a kind of haunted house, 'possessed' by the presence of its dying mistress, Mme Fisher, and by the past horrors she has brought into being. Its dark hall with the red wallpaper 'with stripes so artfully shadowed as to appear bars', its stiff, prim salon with the crimson sofa, bare, waxed parquet floors and curtains that don't draw, its airless, obscure sick room upstairs are to seem increasingly macabre. By the end of the novel, phrases such as 'I saw then, that evil dominated our house' or 'the charnel convent room' or 'the fatal house in Paris' seem apt. The novel resembles Le Fanu's *Uncle Silas* in that it never quite becomes a ghost story, but allows itself hints of the supernatural. Mme Fisher is described as a 'witch'; she seems ubiquitous, disembodied: 'You know our hall is dark and she wears black; I only saw her face, which seemed to be hanging there.' The house haunts those who leave it. This is a sensation novel, a horror story, a melodramatic tale of doomed love and violent death.

But *The House in Paris* is also a comedy. It begins with the arrival of the pragmatic Henrietta, perfectly ignorant of the tragedy which took place in the house ten years before. She is eleven years old, her mother is dead, and her father has sent her to stay with her grandmother in the South of France. She arrives at a strange house, where she is to be looked after by someone she does not know, Naomi Fisher, a friend of her grandmother's and daughter of the mysterious invalid Mme Fisher. Miss Fisher has warned Henrietta that the house also contains for the day, by an unfortunate coincidence, a small boy called Leopold, who is waiting to meet his mother. He has never seen her; Miss Fisher tells Henrietta that 'the circumstances are very strange and sad'.

So the ingredients of Gothic suspense are established. Like Catherine Morland arriving at Northanger, or Maud Ruthyn going to Bartram-Haugh in *Uncle Silas*, Henrietta is the unprotected maiden in a strange, possibly threatening environment. But her matter-of-factness, her social prejudice, and her immense disdain for anything melodramatic or soppy, make her, as Leopold sees at first sight, into a twentieth-century Alice in Wonderland. She is the archetypal English heroine, protected from strange experiences by her 'clear-sighted, overriding good sense'. Henrietta's situation may be appropriate to a Gothic novel, but her character undercuts that convention. She dislikes the house, finding it 'antagonistic' and 'unnatural' ('Henrietta thought, if *this* is being abroad . . .'), but she is not frightened by it.

Henrietta's self-protective and limited view of the house (it *is* frightening) is set against the earlier experience of another English girl. Until ten years before Henrietta's visit, Mme Fisher's 'small house in the Rue Sylvèstre Bonnard' had been an exclusive guest-house for 'well-bred, well-fed, well-read English-speaking girls', in Paris to be 'finished' by studying art or music. The novel's adult heroine, Karen Michaelis, daughter of one of Bowen's usual upper-class English families, who stayed in the house when she was eighteen, formed an attachment to Mme Fisher's daughter Naomi, made an impression on Mme Fisher, and fell in love with Mme Fisher's friend, Max Ebhart. Karen, like Henrietta, found the house strange; Mme Fisher's authority seemed almost uncanny.

> She asked questions, but knew: she knew where you went, why, with whom, and whether it happened twice. Though Paris was large, you were never out of her ken. The girls, discussing this, hovered between an idea of the supernatural and Naomi's having been told off to shadow them. Nobody knew how Naomi spent her days – but how could Naomi shadow two girls at once? There must be more to Mme Fisher than that: her marked unobservingness and withheld comment gave her terrific power over the girls' ideas.

There are reminders here of *Villette*: 'Charnel convent room' might have been used for Mme Beck's salon too, and Mme Beck's system of 'surveillance' and 'espionage', her 'ghostlike' glides through the house, 'watching and spying everywhere, peering through every key-hole, listening behind every door'[2] resemble Mme Fisher's almost spectral powers.

Like *Friends and Relations* and *The Death of the Heart*, *The House in Paris* is divided into three parts, the central one taking the reader back to a period five years after Karen's stay in the house. Mme Fisher's emotional stranglehold over Max has led him, in search of peace and escape, to propose to Naomi, who has always loved him. Naomi and Max visit Karen in England, who is also engaged, to Ray Forrestier, a friend of her family's. The latent relationship between Karen and Max surfaces; they have a short intense affair. Mme Fisher revenges herself on Max by 'poisoning' his love for Karen; he kills himself by slitting his wrists in the 'charnel' salon of the house. Karen later marries Ray and allows Naomi to organise the adoption of her son Leopold, born of the affair with Max, by a childless expatriate couple living in Italy.

Henrietta, dropped down like Alice into the house on the very day when Karen has at last, under pressure from her husband, agreed to meet her nine-year-old son, finds that 'she had dropped down a well into something worse than the past in being not yet over.' The very long day which she and Leopold spend in the house seems, by means of some cunning narrative delaying tactics, to be going on endlessly. When we return from the past – the middle section of the novel – to the children in the house, it feels as if they have been waiting for Leopold's mother for years.

The three-part structure of the novel makes us see that its main subject is the relationship of identity to time. In the three parts, different speeds of time are contrasted. The long day of the children is set against the ten years which, to the adults, can seem as nothing; the sense of pause during Karen's visit to Ireland, with which the middle section begins, works against the urgency of her clandestine affair. And in all three sections, very strong wills are pitted against the force of time and fate. Henrietta's self-assertion in the face of Leopold's fanatic egotism is matched with the monstrous power of

Mme Fisher's will, Naomi's obsessiveness, the lovers' need to break through barriers of conscience and circumstances and, finally, Ray Forrestier's decision to do what is right for himself, Karen, and Leopold. And all the minor characters – Henrietta's cunning grandmother, Karen's placating mother – have to assert their wills. Though individuals live in a highly socialised world, their impulses are anarchic. They must press on to their own ends, though these may be disguised by pity, altruism, or hypocrisy.

Children, who have to be protected, and prevented, provide extreme examples of the pointlessness of trying to restrict the will. (This is comically illustrated by the attempts of Leopold's awful foster-parents to censor experience on his behalf: 'We do not consider him ripe for direct sex-instruction yet, though my husband is working towards this through botany and mythology.') No amount of warning will prevent children from pursuing their ends as well as they can. The novel's structure works so well because of the parallels it draws between the childrens' expressions of self and the adults' clashes of will.

What subdues the force of will is not, in this novel, (as in *Friends and Relations*), practical circumstances or the pressure of other wills, but the uncontrollable force of time. Karen is at one point described as being 'in that flagging mood when to go on living seems only to be to load more unmeaning moments on your memory.' If life is to be anything more than this mechanical accumulation, it must involve moments of expectation and desire. But to invite such moments is to put oneself at risk. Bowen follows Proust and Woolf in the contrast between full, significant moments (which have the status of works of art) and mechanical time, described like this in *The Waves*: 'Something always has to be done next. Tuesday follows Monday: Wednesday, Tuesday. Each spreads the same ripple.'[3]

Bowen's characters, particularly in this novel, are heroic, not in their defiance of morality or religion, but in their eagerness to take on the challenge of time for the sake of intense moments. To want something badly without allowing for 'Afterwards' is to risk the revenges of time: bathos, humiliation. There is a minor, unheroic, Larkinesque illustration of this on Karen's journey back from her weekend in Kent with Max. It has been raining:

> Rain *had* been disaster to many people; in the train you saw how hard it had come on them by the way they all sat, knees apart dejectedly, reading the notices or staring up unblinkingly at the carriage lights. You hope so much of a summer Folkestone week-end: they had been made fools of through no fault of their own. 'It costs money, too,' someone said, as the train quickened on the embankment over the churchyard: now there was nothing ahead but the week's work. To foresee pleasure makes anybody a poet – all sorts of intense fancies must have quickened during the journey down – to seek pleasure makes a hero of anyone: you open yourself so entirely to fate. Spoilt pleasure is a sad, unseemly thing; you can only bury it.

The risks attendant on hope are most intensely felt in Leopold's expectation of his mother, and in Karen's affair with Max. Leopold, like his mother, is a sensationalist, exciting himself by his mental experiments with time:

> That very door will open before it's dark, before it's three o'clock, before Henrietta has got to the Trocadéro. From that door opening, I shall remember on. If I opened that door *now* there would be the hall-wallpaper. *Then* when it opens there will be her face. I shall see what I cannot imagine now.

Karen played with the same idea: 'Whatever may happen this morning, it will be part of afterwards.' Mother and son are both heroic, willing to risk the danger of 'Afterwards'. Leopold is as yet unaware of the danger – it is one of the day's lessons – while Karen is consciously reacting against her parents' refusal to take risks:

> She found she had come to hope everything of change . . . In her parents' world, change looked like catastrophe, a thing to put a good face on: change meant nothing but loss. To alter was to decline. 'Poor So-and-so is so changed.' You lived to

govern the future, bending events your way. If change did break in, you bowed and accepted it.

As usual in Bowen's opposition between inexperience and disenchantment, the narrative gives a lot of weight to disillusionment:

> It is a wary business, walking about a strange house you know you are to know well ... you will never be quite the same again ... By having come, you already begin to store up the pains of going away. From what you see, there is to be no escape.

Karen's defiance of time and circumstance is belittled by its position in the book – it has long become 'afterwards' by the time the books opens. Leopold's extreme demands on time and his extreme disappointment, are diminished by the reasonable witness of Henrietta. She too is disappointed when Karen does not come: 'She would grow up to date her belief that nothing real ever happens from Leopold's mother not coming this afternoon.' But she assimilates it into the continuing pattern of her existence. And long before the terrible scene of Leopold's grief, the disenchanted narrator has suggested that his disappointment may be a lucky thing:

> By her not coming the slate was wiped clear of every impossibility; he was not (at least that day) to have to find her unable to speak in his own, which were the true, terms ... The meeting he had projected could take place only in Heaven – call it Heaven; on the plane of potential not merely likely behaviour. Or call it art, with truth and imagination informing every word. Only there – in heaven or art, in that nowhere, on that plane – could Karen have told Leopold what had really been ... The moment, with its apparent reality, dwarfs and confuses us. But as she did not come he was never to know this.

Leopold's disappointment has redeemed the moment from the 'dwarfing' reality of actual time – where, as Karen knows, there has always to be an 'afterwards'. The moment thus remains in his imagination like a work of art, perfected beyond any actual possibility. It is a Pyrrhic victory, the only kind of victory over time there can be. Better this kind of disappointment than a wet weekend in Folkestone.

Max and Karen's affair can be viewed as a heroic act of bravado against the demeaning power of time. This gives stature to the cliché of clandestine lovers who must snatch their minutes together in anonymous meeting places:

> When the waiter had gone, they both looked at the clock. Already, there was one hour less. She saw her boat going one way, his train the other . . .

These are rather ordinary romantic touches, but they build up the urgent feelings about travel and distance in the novel. Bowen has commented on this:

> Bowen characters are in transit *consciously*. Sensationalists . . . when they extend their environment . . . what goes on in them is magnified and enhanced: impacts are sharper, there is more objectivity . . . Speed is exciting to have grown up with. It alerts vision . . . By contrast, it accentuates the absoluteness of stillness. Permanence . . . stands out the more strongly in an otherwise ephemeral world. Permanence is an attribute of recalled places.[4]

As in *To the North*, travel is an activity for the dispossessed. There are many sombre comments on this:

> Someone soon to start on a journey is always a little holy.

> Goodbyes breed a sort of distaste for whoever you say goodbye to; this hurts, you feel, this must not happen again. Any other meeting will only lead back to this.

> Going to meet a stranger or semi-stranger, can you help asking yourself what *they* are coming to meet?

The novel's journeys make for betrayals and disappointments. These can be funny as well as tragic. Henrietta's journey through Paris is amusingly well organised. Clever, managing Mrs Arbuthnot, her grandmother, has invented 'a dear little system of cherry-pink cockades' by which Henrietta's two escorts to and from Paris can recognise her and

Miss Fisher. Henrietta is further protected by her toy monkey, Charles, and by her dispatch case, bought for the journey and containing all she needs ('two apples, a cake of soap and an ebony-backed hairbrush ... sponge-bag, *The Strand Magazine* and the pink *Malheurs de Sophie*'). But though her journey is made from and to a secure well-organised world, even Mrs Arbuthnot has not reckoned with the coincidence of Leopold. Henrietta's journey exposes her to the unmanageable. The beginning of the novel, in which she and Miss Fisher ride in a taxi from the Gare du Nord to the house, suggests (like the first paragraph of *To the North*) that Henrietta is at risk. The taxi is 'skidding' away from the station, the same streets seem to 'unreel past again and again', 'the frightening cardboard city was waking up', 'violent skidding traffic foreignly hooted'. As they get nearer the house, the taxi 'darts' and 'swerves' into yet more sinister realms (like the taxi in 'The Demon Lover' story), 'a complex of deep streets, fissures in the crazy gloomy height'. Henrietta thinks of 'how much blood has been shed in Paris'. This historical observation is to be justified. After the shedding of blood, literal and figurative, has been re-enacted, and after the childrens' lives have both been radically affected, they leave the house, again by taxi. This time the journey is made with Ray, Karen's husband, who has come to fetch Leopold away, and who is also charged with delivering Henrietta to the next stage of her journey. The taxi, 'impatient as a new world outside their door', leaving behind Miss Fisher with the past, 'swerves' and 'pumps' itself through the wet streets of Paris (which, after all, Henrietta hasn't seen) lit up for the evening. At the station, Henrietta is packed off back to her Arbuthnot life. The firm Miss Watson ('And come along now; now we must come along') detaches her, leaving Ray to cope with Leopold alone. The sense of his daunting responsibility is summed up in his feeling about the big station. Travelling is the book's last, dominant image:

> Where are we going now? The station is sounding, resounding, full of steam caught on light and arches of dark air: a temple of the intention to go somewhere. Sustained sound in

the shell of stone and steel, racket and running, impatience and purpose, make the soul stand still like a refugee, clutching all it has got, asking: 'I am where?' You could live at a station, eating at the buffet, sleeping on the benches, buying your cigarettes, going nowhere next. The tramp inside Ray's clothes wanted to lie down here, put his cheek on his rolled coat, let trains keep on crashing out to Spain, Switzerland, Italy, let Paris wash like the sea at the foot of the ramp.

So the book ends, with Ray and Leopold waiting for another taxi, in anticipation of a further journey towards their life together. This is Bowen's favourite kind of ending – Matchett going for Portia in a taxi, Cecilia and Julian waiting for Emmeline's return, Maud meeting Richard Priam off the plane – and it implies that these characters are not yet done with.

Set inside the frame of the childrens' journeys are Karen's journeys, beginning with the visit to Ireland made to escape the constricting cosiness which a just-engaged girl in London (as in *Friends and Relations*) is subjected to. Karen's mild, determined Aunt Violet has moved out of that world through her second marriage to Colonel Bill Bent, whose Big House, Montebello, was burnt in the Troubles, and who has moved, in the aftermath of disaster, to an enclave of 'Protestant gentry, living down misfortunes they once had', in Rushbrook, County Cork, overlooking Cobh Harbour. The Irish visit is the best part of the novel's middle section: for the first time since *The Last September* Bowen is returning to her primary sources. It's delicately evocative, palely coloured by contrast with Gothic Paris, and it quietly undermines any hopes of a refuge from time. The visit seems in retrospect like 'a long afternoon with three telegrams'. It is broken into by the news that Max is to marry Naomi, and that Aunt Violet is ill and must be operated on. Danger makes itself felt in this peaceful backwater, where it's least expected. Aunt Violet's imminent death intensifies Karen's dissatisfaction with her 'safe' engagement and her comfortable world. Like Lois in *The Last September*, she wants change: 'I wish the Revolution would come soon; I should like to start fresh while I am still young, with everything that I had to depend on gone.' Aunt Violet puts this rhetoric in its place by guessing what Karen is really thinking about: she asks if she has ever been in love with anyone other than Ray.

The visit is a calm before the storm. As usual, Ireland stands for a lost innocence. But the country's deceptively peaceful look, brilliantly described as the ship draws in to Cobh Harbour, is an image for all quietness at risk:

Houses asleep with the eyes open watched the vibrating ship pass: against the woody background those red and white funnels must look like a dream. Seagulls, circling, settled on mown lawns. The wake made a dark streak in the glassy river; its ripples broke against garden walls. Every hill running down, each turn of the river, seemed to trap the ship more and cut off the open sea.

On the left shore, a steeple pricked up out of a knoll of trees, above a snuggle of Gothic villas; then there was the sad stare of what looked like an orphanage. A holy bell rang and a girl at a corner mounted her bicycle and rode out of sight. The river kept washing salt off the ship's prow. Then, to the right, the tree-dark hill of Tivoli began to go up, steep, with pallid stucco houses appearing to balance on the tops of trees. Palladian columns, gazeboes, glass-houses, terraces showed on the background misted with spring green, at the tops of shafts or on toppling brackets of rock, all stuck to the hill, all slipping past the ship. Yes, this looked like a hill in Italy faded; it stood in that flat clear light in which you think of the past and did not look like a country subject to racking change.

Uncle Bill, wanting to keep everything as it has always been in this dreamlike treacherous countryside, tries to batten down the hatches against the onslaught of time. His neurotic fear of lateness – he wakes sweating in the night from 'dreams of unpunctuality' – comically tells us that he is over-protecting himself. The narrator passes an oracular comment: 'Here they hung on their hill over the inland sea, and seemed as safe as young swallows under an eave. But fate is not an eagle, it creeps like a rat.'

On her way back to England, Karen talks to a vulgar Irish

girl who admires her engagement ring ('you know what's coming, all right') and increases Karen's sense of dissatisfaction. This sharp, funny encounter (as good as the 'Waikiki' section in *The Death of the Heart*), also develops the novel's themes of travel and foreignness:

> Her eyes, running over Karen, made it plain that she thought well, if not very much, of her. She did not wonder about her, they were much too unlike. Karen saw she must look to Yellow Hat like something on a Zoo terrace, cantering round its run not knowing it is not free and spotted not in a way you would care to be yourself. She thought: She and I belong to the same sex, even, because there are only two: there should certainly be more. Meeting people unlike oneself does not enlarge one's outlook; it only confirms one's idea that one is unique . . .
> 'D'you dance much?' said Yellow Hat.
> 'Yes, quite often. Do you?'
> 'I'm crazy about it,' said the great strapping girl. 'D'you know the Empress Rooms? Aren't they grand?'
> 'Grand.'
> 'Well, who knows we may run into each other there! I wear emerald green and I've got a mole on me back. If you see me passing, give me a good slap.'

Back in London, Karen meets the newly engaged Max and Naomi and begins the impossible affair with Max. Again the key image is of voyaging: Max and Karen fall in love, awkwardly, as travellers saying goodbye:

> Stout men agitating from carriage to carriage bore down on Karen and Max, who, standing with their shoulders against the window, found themselves jammed face to face. There was no escape. She stared at his right shoulder. This undid their touch on the lawn yesterday; they faced each other unwillingly, defiant, dead. Then their eyes met; they looked steadily into each other's pupils . . .
> A porter passed, with baggage pitching on his shoulder; Max put up his hand to shield Karen's head. The people had found places; the corridor was now empty. The train stood as though built on to the platform, but Karen walking away

down it, steadied herself against the frames of the windows as though the train was rocking at top speed.

The stout men 'agitating' and bearing down, the baggage 'pitching' on the porter's shoulder, the imaginary 'rocking' of the train already give Max and Karen the air of reckless travellers, though this train is standing still at Victoria Station. When Karen's mother learns of their affair, she comments acutely: 'So you went more than half-way to meet him'; and Karen herself recognises that by loving Max she is dispossessing herself of her own country:

> Karen, walking by Max, felt more isolated with him, more cut off from her own country than if they had been in Peru. You feel most foreign when you no longer belong where you did . . .

Their love affair consists of two journeys which gather up all the travel images of the novel, the first made by Karen to Boulogne, the second by Max to Folkestone. In both, the weather counts for a lot. In sunny Boulogne, 'a painted scene', they behave like sightseers, though that isn't what they have come for. They are trapped in an artifice of enjoyment: what they are doing (making a journey, being in love, spending a sunny day together) is what people do to be happy: 'After all, after all, were they not meeting for pleasure?' But their feelings and their circumstances are ironically at odds with the conventions of a pleasurable day trip. At Folkestone, and then at the hotel in Hythe where Leopold is conceived, the dank, sombre Kentish scene (described with the passionate exactness of childhood recollection) puts their emotions at risk in a different way: they feel abandoned by the sun. Though Max writes to Naomi breaking off their engagement, and though Max and Karen envisage some sort of life together beyond their immediate 'compulsion', the images of travel (and sexuality) on their separate journeys home are ominous. 'Everyone waited for the train to impale them on London . . . Past midnight, that other train would crash into the Gare du Nord.' Both, as it turns out, are parting to their destruction.

The lovers' transitory weekends act out the predicament of those who, like Max and his son Leopold (and like Elizabeth Bowen), don't have a secure sense of belonging to a country. Max's mother was French, his father an English Jew; he has been brought up by an uncle and aunt, whom he disliked, in the South of France. As an ambitious young Jewish banker in France, he suffers from his 'lack of a home, of any place to return to ... In France to have no family can be more humbling than poverty.' Mme Fisher, knowing intimately about Max's insecurity, has always accused him of wanting an advantageous marriage, and it is on these lines that she 'poisons' his feeling for Karen. Her matriarchal counterpart, Mrs Michaelis, thinks of him as a 'womanish' 'astute' Jew, pursuing Karen as a better option than Naomi. Her middle-class English anti-semitism, typical of its time, is only partly satirised: Max's Jewishness *is* meant to make him seem suspect. Socially and racially, Max is an undesirable lover. His dubious, foreign, rootless qualities make him a shadowy figure; but it's right that the reader should also feel doubtful about him. By falling in love with Max, Karen too becomes a 'refugee'. Their relationship is alien to her, and alienates her from her own world. They communicate stiffly: 'Talk between people of different races is serious; that tender silliness lovers employ falls flat.'

Karen is disconcerted by the foreignness of Max's rival emotional ties, his fatal intimacy with Mme Fisher and his pitying dependence on Naomi ('You two have another language'). Unlike 'provincial' lovers, they have no common ground to fall back on: 'Their worlds were so much unlike that no experience had the same value for both of them.' Their only resort, in lieu of small talk and endearments, is to talk about history: this allows them to go 'into company together', to find some impersonal mutual ground.

Their dangerous lack of common assumptions (very perceptively treated) is one of the risks of Karen's 'revolution' against her race and class, so solidly entrenched in history. In *The House in Paris*, unlike *Friends and Relations*, the life-denying, well-behaved philistinism of the English middle classes is not the central theme, but it is presented vividly enough to show that you might want to escape from it.

> The Michaelis lived like a family in a pre-war novel in one of the tall, cream houses in Chester Terrace, Regent's Park. Their relatives and old friends, as nice as they were themselves, were rooted in the same soil. Her parents saw little reason to renew their ideas, which had lately been ahead of their time and were still not out of date. Karen had grown up in a world of grace and intelligence, in which the Boer War, the War and other fatigues and disasters had been so many opportunities to behave well . . .
>
> Her marriage to Ray would have that touch of inbreeding that makes a marriage so promising; he was a cousin's cousin; they had met first at her home. Her only brother, Robin, had come safely through the war to marry a very nice woman with property in the North; he managed his wife's property, hunted two days a week, sometimes published clever satirical verses and experimented in artificial manures. This was the world she sometimes wished to escape from but, through her marriage, meant to inhabit still.

This lethal quiet satire explains Karen's fascination with the Fisher household, which is not 'nice', and her compulsion towards Max. He sharpens her perception of what is wrong with her home. She describes its restrictiveness to him:

> 'I found I was in prison – no, locked into a museum full of things I once liked, with nothing to do now but look at them and wonder why I had. *They* kept me away from everything that has power; they would be frightened of art if I painted really well.'

After the affair, her mother's relentless pretence that she doesn't know about it, her 'savage battle for peace', out of a 'worldliness so deep down that it seems to be the heart', confirms Karen's war against protective 'niceness'. Bowen feels this conflict between the girl's anarchic will and the mother's repressiveness so strongly that she uses it as an example of a general truth:

> Young girls like the excess of any quality. Without knowing,

they want to suffer, to 'suffer' they must exaggerate; they like to have loud chords struck on them . . . they love to enjoy love as a system of doubts and shocks . . . This natural fleshly protest against good taste is broken down soon enough; their natural love of the cad is outwitted by their mothers.

The ironic result of Karen's revolution against her class is that it condemns Leopold to re-enact the dispossession of his father. Karen has refused to bring him up abroad: 'If he is like Max and me he would hate that – hate exile, hate being nowhere, hate being unexplained, hate having no place of his own.' But her retreat from the consequences of her action – marrying Ray, letting Naomi arrange for Leopold's adoption – means that Leopold is punished for what she has done. The novel keeps up a classical aloofness about the results of compulsive passion; it doesn't attribute blame. But Karen's weakness is apparent through Leopold: she hasn't followed her actions through, and he has suffered for it.

Leopold's encounter with Henrietta is a comic parallel to Max's tragic relationship with Karen. Like Karen, but with no desire to revolt, Henrietta is a member of a solid, well-defined tribe.

Having spent hours unwillingly silent with Mrs Arbuthnot and Caroline and their friends, Henrietta had noted their charm, their astuteness, their command of emotion in others, and could no longer doubt that she lived in a world where it was fatal never to make one's mark.

To Leopold, Henrietta represents England and his mother's 'English life'. She is an object of curiosity like *The Strand Magazine*, which he shakes out of her case and reads without understanding. And Henrietta's first impression of Leopold, is of a foreigner: 'She saw a dark-eyed, very slight little boy who looked either French or Jewish.' All this emphasis on foreignness prepares for the last confrontation in the novel between Ray Forrestier and Leopold:

Ray saw Leopold thinking: Oh yes, an Englishman! (It should be clear that Ray looked like any of these tall Englishmen who stand back in train corridors unobtrusively to let foreigners pass to meals or the lavatory . . . He was the Englishman's age: about thirty-six.)

That Ray should be described as though on a train suggests that his relationship with Leopold can only be a temporary compromise between strangers; Ray sees that he is 'up against the force of a foreign cold personality'. The novel's pattern of baffled relationships between foreigners is projected into the future.

The concern with foreignness also gets into the encounter between children. Awkward relationships between adolescents and adults is one of Elizabeth Bowen's best subjects, especially in *The Death of the Heart*. And she has a wonderfully sharp eye for schoolgirls. 'The Mulberry Tree', her account of her own schooldays, gives the source material for these comic – and touching – characterisations, from Theodora Hirdman to Dicey in *The Little Girls*. It's in *The House in Paris*, though, that she most subtly explores the behaviour of children on their own, and most exactly registers the difference between children with a social 'place' and children without one. Henrietta and Leopold speak a formal, mannered, language but it expresses what they would feel in these circumstances. A. S. Byatt puts this well: 'Leopold, and still more Henrietta, are children equipped with the language of the secret thoughts of intelligent children.'[5]

Intelligent children are not kind.

> With no banal reassuring grown-ups present, with grown-up intervention taken away, there is no limit to the terror strange children feel of each other, a terror life obscures but never ceases to justify. There is no end to the violations committed by children on children, quietly talking alone.

Their cruelty to each other is matched by their cruelty to 'Miss Fisher'. Henrietta's and Leopold's oblivion to her suffering is finely presented as the last 'turn of the screw' for Naomi. At the moments when they ruthlessly play on her exposed emotions, they are as sinister as Miles and Flora with their governess in Henry James's story:

> 'I shan't be here long,' said Leopold.
> 'Naturally, naturally not,' said Miss Fisher sending Henrietta a speaking glance. 'Leopold is expecting his mother this afternoon,' she said in a stage voice.
> 'I know,' said Henrietta basely, 'you told me.'
>
> 'Some other day, I *know* you will see your mother!'
> 'I don't see why,' said Leopold.
> 'Something unforeseen must have happened. You know, even grown-up people cannot always do what they want most.'
> 'Oh! Then why grow up?'
> Miss Fisher replied simply, '*I* never could answer any questions, Leopold.'

Henrietta and Leopold are primitive. They can hold on to each other and weep passionately without having to comment on it; when they stand apart it is 'like a grown-up hand coming between their bodies'. Shaking hands at the station to say goodbye, watched by adults, they are like 'people attempting some savage rite'. Though a knowing adult narrator comments on their scenes together, the children are themselves innocent. They have an instinctual relation to their bodies, they can still speak from the heart. But these children are placed in an adult story about knowledge, compulsion, and power so as to show them at the point of losing innocence. They are victims of the action of time like everyone else; they are bound to move into the world of knowledge.

Henrietta (like Alice and also like James's Maisie) is already worldly and self-conscious. She is full of self-imposed conventions, carefully acquired. She has prejudices, like wanting to see the Tocadéro rather than the Arc de Triomphe, or being unwilling to take a bath in a strange house. She has habits, like her awkward relationship with her toy monkey ('Well, I like to think he notices. Otherwise there'd be no point in taking him everywhere'). And she has rules (one does not interrupt people who are thinking, or dip one's bread in one's coffee). These aren't just comic illustrations of the class which Leopold finds so foreign. They enable Henrietta, poignantly, to define her emerging personality:

> Today was to do much to disintegrate Henrietta's character, which, built up by herself, for herself, out of admonitions and axioms (under the growing stress of: If I am Henrietta, then what is *Henrietta*?) was a mosaic of all possible kinds of prejudices. She was anxious to be someone, and, no one having ever voiced a prejudice in her hearing without impressing her, had come to associate prejudice with identity. You could not be a someone without disliking things.

Compared with Henrietta, Leopold is a barbarian. The danger she runs on this long day is of having her carefully developed sense of personality blown to bits by the impact of Leopold and his history. So, when Miss Fisher bids Henrietta goodbye, she hugs her closely: 'You would think she was sorry for me.' Though not entitled to Leopold's level of tragic intensity, Henrietta, as Naomi knows, has been put at risk by her experience in the house. In a way, she *has* been violated, just as if she were in a Gothic novel after all.

What Henrietta finds fearsome in Leopold is not only his fanatical egotism, the 'bastard's pride' ('You go on like God'), but, even more, his use of her as a mirror in which to test out his own experiences. He maddens her much as Alice is infuriated by the imperviousness of the beings she meets to any sense of her own reality. 'Why, you're only a sort of thing in his dream' would apply to Leopold's treatment of her, as much as to the Red King's of Alice.

> 'Look – now your mother's dead so you can't possibly see her, do you still mean to love her, or is that no good now? When you want to love her, what do you do, remember her? But if you couldn't remember her, but heard you could see her, would you enjoy loving her more, or less?'
> 'I don't see what you mean,' said Henrietta, distracted – in fact in quite a new kind of pain. She saw only too well that this inquisition had no bearing on Henrietta at all, that

Leopold was not even interested in hurting, and was only tweaking her petals off or her wings off with the intention of exploring himself. His dispassionateness was more dire, to Henrietta, than cruelty.

Henrietta protects herself from this assault on her identity by mannerisms drawn from the well-observed feminine armory of her sister and grandmother:

> Glancing aloofly to see if her nails were clean, she seemed to become unconscious of Leopold . . . She glanced across at the clock, smothered a yawn politely and said aloud to herself: 'Only twenty-five past ten.'

Leopold, used to the stifling attention of his foster-parents, warms to these affectations of indifference, and so grants Henrietta a kind of victory. All the same there is no doubt that, though the younger and less secure of the two, he has the stronger will, and that though the reader gets fond of Henrietta as a rational witness to the extreme passions in the house, it is Leopold's discoveries which matter more.

Leopold learns about sex in the house in Paris. In the first part of the novel he opens Naomi's handbag and reads his foster-parents' prurient letter ('We dread having Leopold prematurely upset'). In the last part he encounters, not his mother, but Mme Fisher, cynical, implacable, eaten up with the power of knowledge. But it is striking (and typical) that in a novel which deals with the effect of the sexual passion, sexuality is itself muted. The sexual facts about his conception and its aftermath are not the day's most important lesson for Leopold. He learns the power of knowledge; he learns how strength and weakness of will express themselves; he learns about the action of time; and, most importantly (the whole organisation of the novel moves towards this discovery) he learns that people operate independently, outside his will. This knowledge (to which Mme Fisher has never been able to resign herself) suggests that there is hope for him:

> Yes, his mother refused to come; she would not lend herself to him. He had cast her, but she refused her part. She was not, then, the creature of thought. Her will, her act, her thought,

spoke in the telegram. Her refusal became *her*, became her coming in suddenly, breaking down, by this one act of being herself only, his imagination in which he had bound her up. So she lived outside himself; she was alive truly. She set up that opposition that is love.

He was made conscious of someone's being consciously other than Leopold. (He had felt other people *as* other only in opposition.) He had never seen a decision come at before, or been there when a mind went round like machinery in the dark. He had recognised impulse in grown-up people, never yet its adoption by the entire will. Vacillating outside his own iron scheme of things, grown-up dictatorship, therefore, had seemed to Leopold arbitrary and purposeless; his idea was: They dispose of but do not affect me. But *this* present decision being come at was vital. This man affects me; I cannot affect him.

All the characters, not just Leopold, strain their wills against opposing forces. Karen's mother fights to contain her world against ruinous disaster; Karen's will is the stronger, and in forcing her mother out into the open she destroys her. Naomi, apparently humble and pitiful, tries to possess those she loves. She forces Max and Karen together so that she can have them both under her eye at once:

> Under her unassumingness, Naomi had a will that, like a powerful engine started up suddenly, made everything swerve . . .
>
> Karen and Max, two people, were her objects; even with them she did not pursue anything; she was pure in heart. No wonder she frightened you . . .

Awkward, self-punishing, she is the natural victim, the kind of person who will always be baited. She is bullied by the children, dominated by her mother, patronised by Mrs Michaelis ('She did wish Naomi had a less emotional manner') and impatiently, guiltily loved by Karen. Yet she has a greater dignity than all these characters. Like Emmeline in *To the North* and Portia in *The Death of the Heart*, she is one of Bowen's lethal, exalted innocents. It is a painfully intense characterisation. Naomi's lonely abandonment in the house at the end of the day is the novel's most poignant moment.

But the dominant will of the novel is that of the monstrous Mme Fisher. Bowen has already been doing powerful, Machiavellian older women – Mrs Kerr, Lady Naylor – and these harmful mothers or guardians will recur. But Mme Fisher is more outrageous than any of them. She is a Jacobean, *grand guignol* figure. She is capable of driving someone to suicide; she is locked in a horrible, final battle with old age. Mme Fisher is a death's head, the most shocking evidence of the action of time.

Mme Fisher's relationship with Max takes place entirely offstage. (This novel loves dramatic devices – messenger speeches, delayed entrances, characters 'acting' their roles, the house as a stage.) Mme Fisher is only directly described through the eyes of the two children, so that we see her always as sick and old, not as the powerful, attractive woman who, twenty-two years before, first took over the life of the young Max Ebhart. We are meant to feel that Mme Fisher has been sexually potent, but that her sexuality has always been more about power than sensuality. Max describes her influence over him in sexual terms, but it is clear that their relationship is the more terrible for being sterile:

> 'From the first, she acted on me like acid on a plate . . . as she saw me, I became. Her sex is all in her head, but she is not a woman for nothing. In my youth, she made me shoot up like a plant in enclosed air . . . women I knew were as she made me see them: they were not much. Any loves I enjoyed stayed inside her scope; she knew of them all. She mocked and played upon my sensuality.'

This story is partly a conventional plot of sophisticated French women with young lover. Mme Fisher's wrecking of Max's engagement to her daughter and of his love for Karen can be seen, up to a point, as expressions of revengeful sexual jealousy. But the offstage melodrama of Max's suicide only works because Mme Fisher's power over him is evidently much more than sexual.

100

'He could do nothing that she had not expected; my mother was at the root of him. I saw that what she had learnt about you and him pleased her, that she had pleasure in it in some terrible way . . . His love for you had fallen into her hands.'

After the suicide Mme Fisher says, 'He struck myself, himself, my knowledge of him.' Karen, hearing Naomi's account, comments: 'It was her power she loved. That time it overreached itself; that was all.' The words knowledge and power are interchangeable here.

What we see, however, is not the moment of power, but the revenge of time, as Mme Fisher struggles in the presence of Henrietta (and even more with Leopold) to discount her enfeebled body. Leopold diagnoses her as 'prey to one creeping growth, the Past, septic with what had happened'. Henrietta sees her as a fixed, ghastly image of a struggle against fate.

Mme Fisher was not in herself a pretty old lady. Waxy skin strained over her temples, jaws and cheek-bones; grey hair fell in wisps round an unwomanly forehead; her nostrils were wide and looked in the dusk skullish; her mouth was graven round with ironic lines. Neither patience nor discontent but a passionate un-resignation was written across her features, tense with the expectation of more pain. She seemed to lie as she lay less in weakness than in unwilling credulity, as though the successive disasters that make an illness had convinced her slowly, by repetition. She lay, still only a little beyond surprise at this end to her, webbed down, frustrated, or, still more, like someone cast, still alive, as an effigy for their own tomb. Her illness seemed to be one prolonged mistake. Her self looked, wildly smiling, out of her body: what was happening in here was too terrible to acknowledge; she had to travesty it and laugh it off. Unserene, she desperately kept her head.

Mme Fisher's grotesque struggle puts one fleetingly in mind of Aunt Violet's mild protest against fate; that reminder is one of the incidental triumphs of the book's organisation. There is no mildness in the house in Paris. Bowen has worked 'all out' at the sinister, pent-up 'staticness' of this sick-room scene (and will give it as her favourite example of her techniques for suggesting 'withheld energy').[6]

Out of this living death, knowledge and power are still to be gleaned. Mme Fisher is the only character in the novel who chooses to tell children the truth, to break through the 'secret society' which adults set up around the facts of sex and love. This is shocking to Henrietta, who believes in censorship: when Mme Fisher tells her that Leopold's father 'broke Naomi's heart', she feels as though she has seen Miss Fisher undressed. 'She knew one should not hear these things when one was only eleven.' All the same, she is impressed by Mme Fisher's torturing of Naomi (the mutual dependence and tyranny between mother and daughter is brilliantly understated), by her avid curiosity, by 'how frantically and coldly she loved the present'. Leopold, who meets the woman who 'killed' his father instead of meeting his mother, is not appalled by Mme Fisher's revelations. The two scenes between the old woman and each of the children perfectly contrast Henrietta's middle-class sense that information ought to be restricted, with Leopold's barbaric zeal for as much knowledge and power as possible.

Mme Fisher explains Leopold's past to him clearly and relentlessly, and confirms his sense of himself as special. She is like the witch in the fairy story who sends the young man with a sword on his way out of the wood. (And the novel *is* a fairy story, as well as a Greek tragedy and a Gothic novel.) By putting the past in perspective, by cynically belittling the emotions of the previous generation, she points Leopold towards his future. It is a strong climax to the book's conflict between the force of human will and the force of time.

5

THE DEATH OF THE HEART

'Happy that few of us are aware of the world until we are already in league with it.'

ELIZABETH AND ALAN moved from Oxford to London in 1935, when Alan became Secretary to the Central Council of Schools' Broadcasting at the BBC. She found them a house in Regent's Park, 2 Clarence Terrace, at the corner of one of the most beautiful Regency terraces that encircle the park, facing towards the lake. It would be the house of her next novel and several of her stories. It also became a centre (as Bowen's Court, though getting more run-down, continued to be) for intensive entertaining.

In all this, Alan Cameron seems to have played a supportive but increasingly marginal role. The marriage continued steady – and to many onlookers, inexplicable – while admirers of both sexes played their part in Bowen's life in the mid-1930s: May Sarton, who developed a passionate but unrequited love for her; Goronwy Rees, fetching and unreliable; Sean O'Faolain, her Irish contemporary, whose work she admired. Other friendships – with L. P. Hartley, Raymond Mortimer, Desmond McCarthy – were consolidated. She was extremely productive, reviewing widely, editing an anthology of stories for Faber, and writing theatre criticism for Graham Greene's short-lived magazine *Night and Day*. But behind all this, the pressure of political events worldwide was felt, making her diagnosis of the weaknesses and failings of her own civilisation all the more ominous.

The Death of the Heart (1938) ironically exposes the inauthenticity of the English middle classes, among whom Bowen spent most of her time. And it is more painfully about the confrontation between innocence and experience than any other of the novels. It combines ingredients from *The House in Paris* and *To the North*: Portia, the heroine, is partly a child, like Leopold, becoming aware of compromise and betrayal, and partly a woman, like Emmeline, discovering the danger of love. But her effects on others are as powerful and dangerous as their effects on her. *The Death of the Heart* is a severe novel, for which Bowen's judicious authorial commentary seems exactly right. Her general statements here aren't flamboyantly piled on, like the passage on tragedy in *To the North*. They sound more dry and austere. A moral judgement which matters is being passed.

The novel also gives her fullest picture of pre-war England. It distinguishes very precisely between different strata of the English middle class, and one of its main subjects is the behaviour of that class. Portia, like Leopold, is a problem to herself and others because she has no real idea of what social behaviour ought to be, no standard assumptions. Her innocence isn't only to do with age and sex. It's also a social innocence.

Portia Quayne moves between different class levels like Fanny Price in *Mansfield Park* or Maisie in *What Maisie Knew*. Like Fanny, she is divided from her closest relations and is living with an alien, and superior, branch of the family. Like Maisie, she has the air of a transient: it's never certain whether or not she will have to move on. The novel covers half a year (from an icebound January to a promising June) of Portia's stay with her half-brother, Thomas Quayne, and his wife Anna, in their well-appointed house at 2 Windsor Terrace, Regent's Park. The Quaynes are a wealthy, stylish couple in their mid-thirties. Thomas has inherited his mother's money, her excellent furniture, and with it her housemaid, Matchett. He makes £2,500 a year and is co-partner of an advertising agency. Anna, when he married her eight years before, had been 'an accomplished, on the whole idle girl, with various gifts, who tried a little of everything and had even made money.' When her father died she inherited £500 a year.

In the Quaynes, Elizabeth Bowen indicts the wealthy English middle classes more severely than ever before. The whole novel is an attack on the cold inadequacy of their 'life-style'. Portia's family history, the first thing we hear about, sets up a critique of the bourgeois desire to protect itself against vulgarity and emotional mess, and to cast out the misfits from its clan. (It's like Forster's *Where Angels Fear to Tread*, with the manipulative Mrs Herriton trying to control the errant branch of the family.)

Thomas's mother, Mrs Quayne, is, like Mrs Herriton, 'implacable,' ruthlessly bent on doing right – right, rather than good – and on coming out of things well. When her weak-headed, susceptible, and conscience-struck husband breaks out of his cosy Dorset retirement at the age of fifty-seven to have an affair with a 'little widow' much younger than himself, Mrs Quayne drives him out of her home (to which he is really devoted) with self-regarding zeal. 'Sacrificers', as Matchett says, telling the story to Portia, 'are not the ones to pity. The ones to pity are those that they sacrifice. Oh, the sacrificers, they get it both ways. A person knows themselves what they're able to do without. Yes. Mrs Quayne would give the clothes off her back, but in the long run she would never lose a thing.' Mrs Quayne expels Thomas's father in order to control his marriage to Irene and the fate of their daughter, Portia.

To Thomas, child of a cold mind and a weak heart, his father's adultery and subsequent remarriage seem grotesque. His visits to his father's new family fill him 'with obscure shame – on behalf of his father, himself and society'. Mr Quayne, dying of chills in European hotels, writes to Thomas imploring him to give Portia a taste of 'normal family life' after his death. But Irene is well aware of the Quaynes's attitude to her. She keeps back the letter and goes on bringing Portia up alone, abroad. They lead a vagrant sisterly life in out-of-season cheap pensions and villas, the kind of life

Karen and Leopold might have had together, suggestive of Elizabeth Bowen's childhood with her mother in Kent. It is only after Irene's death that Mrs Quayne's letter is sent on, and Thomas, overriding Anna's objections, opens his doors (at least for a year) to the sixteen-year-old orphaned Portia. Anna and Matchett prepare her room, Anna buys clothes for her, takes her out of mourning, and arranges for her to have classes at a select, expensive school in Cavendish Square. The orphaned waif is brought back into the mainstream of middle-class life.

Bowen could have told the story of Portia's background in a flashback, like the middle section of *The House in Paris*. But Mr Quayne and Irene are not meant to be as important as Portia; their unassertiveness extends to their non-appearance in the novel. The Quayne story is filtered through different points of view: Anna's opening account to her friend the novelist St Quentin, Portia's memories of her life abroad, Matchett's long speeches to Portia. This emphasises one of the novel's main concerns: responsibility to the past.

Anna's uncharitable account of Thomas's family ('Irene, you know, was not what anybody would want at all') contrasts with Portia's tender recollections of her mother, who knew 'that nine out of ten things you do direct from the heart are the wrong thing, and that she was not capable of doing anything better.' Both these versions, though, are dwarfed by Matchett's judicious account of Portia's history. Matchett has registered Mrs Quayne as the original source of cruelty, and she makes Portia aware of the way that she and her parents have been abused by a powerful, entrenched class. Matchett's account dwells on the likeness between Thomas and Portia, which, as Portia comes to realise, unites them against Anna:

> After all he and I have our father. Though he and Anna have got that thing together, there is not the same thing inside him and Anna, like that same thing inside him and me.

Past history is a challenge to the present. Anna rejects the past by refusing to have feelings about it; Matchett insists on its significance; Thomas grudgingly admits to it (to the extent of warning Portia not to repeat the family's mistakes) and Portia learns the meaning of the past in the course of the novel. When she finally runs away from Windsor Terrace, she refers her own position to the treatment of her parents:

> 'They were cruel to my father and mother, but the thing must have started even before that ... My father often used to explain to me that people did not live the way we did ... he was quite certain ordinary life went on – yes, that was why I was sent to Thomas and Anna. But I see now that it does not: if he and I met again I should have to tell him that there is no ordinary life.'

2, Windsor Terrace, where Portia discovers that there is no ordinary life, is like the house Elizabeth Bowen lived in. It will recur in several of the wartime stories, and it's next door to the Michaelis house in *The House in Paris* or the Weymouth Street flat in *The Heat of the Day*. But in *The Death of the Heart* the bombs have not yet started to fall. To compare the Regent's Park scenes in this novel and in *The Heat of the Day* is to have an extraordinarily vivid sense of what the war did to this part of London.

The grand, elegant Regency terraces in the park's Outer Circle, first seen in the novel's brilliant opening scene of a winter walk in the frozen park, as 'pallid' and 'withdrawn' in January ice, give off exactly the sort of chilly hollowness which Bowen needed for the Quaynes. They look 'empty, stagy, E-shaped, with frigid pillars cut out on black shadow; a façade with no back'. Inside the house, the air is 'neutral'. The living areas – Anna's luxurious sitting-room, Thomas's fume-choked study, Matchett's secret basement and Portia's upstairs room – are segregated. Thomas's and Anna's separate areas are connected by room-to-room telephone – a sure sign, like Markie's arrangement with his cook, that human relations are inadequate here.[1]

The atmosphere of the house evokes the Quaynes' spiritual limitations, and the opposition between Anna and Portia. Anna has prepared a pretty room for Portia; Portia fills it with a sort of savage clutter which Matchett respectfully indulges, but which enrages Anna:

> 'She has all sorts of arrangements Matchett will never touch . . . I made that room so pretty before she came. I had no idea how blindly she was going to live. Now I hardly ever go in there, it's simply discouraging . . . She is so unnaturally callous about *objects* – she treats any hat, for instance, like an old envelope. Nothing that's hers ever seems, if you know what I mean, to belong to her . . .'

Portia, who hoards objects which have personal associations with primitive fervour, carelessly loses the stylish accessories Anna has bought for her: gloves, coat, dispatch case. Anna, by contrast, expresses herself through her things – Thomas is originally attracted to her partly through 'her clothes, as part of her style'. This opposition marks irreconcilable attitudes to life. Bowen has used the idea before in an early short story:

> 'Oh, come, Gilda, if one's own skin isn't personal, what is!'
> 'I don't know,' said Mrs Roche slowly. 'I don't think it's very personal. After all, it's only the husk of one – unavoidably there. But one's clothes are part of what one has got to say. Eve was much more herself when she began putting flowers in her hair than when she sat about in just – no fig-leaves. And she was much more herself than ever when she had got the fig-leaves on, and you and I are much more ourselves than she was.'
> 'Then do you think covering oneself up is being real?' asked Laura. She entered the conversation with heavy, serious grace, as she would have entered a room.
> 'I don't know,' said Gilda Roche. 'The less of me that's visible, the more I'm there.'[2]

This is like Isabel and Mme Merle in James's *The Portrait of a Lady*, discussing whether 'one's self . . . is one's expression of one's self' ('I've a great respect for things!') or whether, as Isabel says, 'nothing else expresses me. Nothing that belongs to me is any measure of me; everything's on the contrary a limit, a barrier, and a perfectly arbitrary one.' Mme Merle closes the discussion by asking lightly whether Isabel would prefer to go naked.[3] The conflict about 'things' between Anna and Portia similarly contrasts innocence with corruption.

But Portia does have a strong feeling for inanimate objects. She is highly susceptible to things and their effects, and writes about this a lot in her diary, where she keeps an unforgiving record of life at Windsor Terrace. Matchett, too, who has stayed on as housemaid 'with the furniture', has a mystical sense of the historical consciousness embodied in things: 'Unnatural living runs in a family, and the furniture knows it, you be sure.' Like Portia and Matchett, the novel's narrator believes in the emotional significance of objects:

> After inside upheavals, it is important to fix on imperturbable *things*. Their imperturbableness, their air that nothing has happened renews our guarantee . . . these things are what we mean when we speak of civilization . . . In this sense, the destruction of buildings and furniture is more palpably dreadful to the spirit than the destruction of human life.

Portia and Matchett both feel that objects at Windsor Terrace point to a gap: the 'normal family life' that ought to be there and isn't. But Windsor Terrace raises the question of whether there *is* such a thing as 'normal' life. This makes a kind of bleak running joke between Anna and Thomas:

> 'Yes, it often does seem to me that you and I are not natural. But I also say to myself, well, who is natural, then?'

> 'What proof have you,' said Thomas, '. . . that much nicer people do really exist?'

Anna satirises the idea of normality when, at a moment of crisis, she calls on St Quentin as 'an old family friend'. The clichéd phrase rebounds from the texture of life at Windsor Terrace. It is not a place for old loyalties or family traditions. Portia has invaded a house which is profoundly unconvivial; the comforts of Anna's sitting-room have no warm domestic foundation. The Quaynes sit round 'a painted, not a burning, fire, at which you tried in vain to warm your hands'. Their friends are few and not much liked, and no one is ever expected to drop in:

Callers were unheard of at Windsor Terrace. They had been eliminated; they simply did not occur. The Quaynes' home life was as much their private life as though their marriage had been illicit.

The reluctance to be surprised or exposed works from inside. Feelings are concealed, looks and glances are always failing to meet. Portia's looks are too naked, Eddie's too stagey, Anna's too evasive. Anna finds and reads Portia's diary, but the last thing she will do is tell her this. Anna and Thomas come back from holiday, and find nothing to say about having been away, or about coming back – though Anna makes a half-hearted try, since a response would be the 'natural' thing to have: 'Our life goes by without any comment ... We're *home*, Thomas: have some ideas about home – ' They have organised themselves into a vacuum, and their isolation produces not intimacy but separateness:

> 'I'm never with you,' he said.
> 'Well, look how we live.'
> 'The way we live is hopeless.'

The narrator is severe about the political basis of the Quaynes' over-selective approach to life:

> Not only is there no question of solitude, but in the long run we may not choose our company. The attempt at Windsor Terrace to combat this may have been what made that house so queasy and cold. That mistaken approach to life – of which at intervals they were all conscious, from Thomas Quayne down to the cook – produced the tensions and hitches of an unpromising love affair. Each person at Windsor Terrace lived impaled upon a private obsession, however slight ... Something edited life in the Quaynes' house ... At the same time, no one seemed clear quite *what* was being discarded, or whether anything vital was being let slip away. If Matchett were feared, if she seemed to threaten the house, it was because she seemed most likely to put her thumb on the thing.

Matchett, the unforgiving judge of the Quayne family, finds that the 'thing' is lack of continuity. Anna has no children, for which Matchett holds her morally to blame; and she refuses to preserve memories and traditions. So the couple is immolated inside a pointless present. Matchett explains this to Portia:

> 'No, there's no past in this house.'
> 'Then what makes them so jumpy?'
> 'They'd rather no past – not have the past, that is to say. No wonder they don't rightly know what they're doing. Those without memories don't know what is what.'

The Quaynes may be morally disapproved of, but their relationship is very subtly and feelingly done. It's one of the great studies of an inhibited English marriage, to be set beside the Goulds in *Nostromo*, the Brookenhams in *The Awkward Age*, or the Ashburnhams in *The Good Soldier*. *The Death of the Heart* is a painful book because of what happens to Portia, but also because of unacknowledged pain in the Quaynes' marriage.

Anna's temperament is marvellously done: her liking for admiration, entertainment, gossip; her reluctance to deal with her own memories; her tolerant, malevolent attitude to Thomas; her nervous control, which makes a fidgeting gesture, with her, into 'an act of passion'; her resistance to nature (on a trip to Epping Forest, she stays in the car and reads a detective novel,[4] on board ship to Capri she keeps her back to the sea); her permanent dissatisfaction:

> 'You don't much like anything, do you?'
> 'No, nothing,' said Anna, smiling her nice fat malign smile.

She is interesting because her defences are incomplete – Portia gets under her skin – and because her scepticism rings true. Anna is felt to be accurate: 'Let's face it – whoever is adequate? We all create situations each other can't live up to, then break our hearts at them because they don't.'

Anna and Thomas seem to show that love is not a good idea. Both their hearts are defunct. Anna was betrayed in the one love affair that mattered to her before she met Thomas. Thomas has fallen in love with Anna since their marriage, but is 'prey to a passion . . . that nothing in their language could be allowed to express, that nothing could satisfy.' In all his other relations Thomas is bored, self-disgusted and suspicious. He assumes that everyone he meets is on the make, is easily embarrassed, and has little idea of how other people feel. He is a malcontent of the 1930s, and his bad faith is meant to represent a whole class. He knows he is typical:

'I know there must be something all you people get together about.'

'There may be,' said Thomas, 'but I don't think there is. As a matter of fact, I don't think we get together. We none of us seem to feel very well, and I don't think we want each other to know it. I suppose there is nothing so distintegrating as competitiveness and funk, and that's what we all feel. The ironical thing is that everyone else gets their knives into us bourgeoisie on the assumption we're having a good time . . . They seem to have no idea that we don't much care for ourselves . . . We're just a lousy pack of little Christopher Robins. Oh, we've got to live, but I doubt if we see the necessity. The most we can hope is to go on getting away with it till the others get it away from us.'

Thomas's speech is made to Major Brutt, 'the man from back somewhere', who's failed to make a go of it 'out in Malay', and who is waiting in a grim London hotel for something to turn up before the money runs out. 'Makes of men date, like makes of cars; Major Brutt was a 1914–18 model: there was now no market for that make.' There is a job for a flashy young man like Eddie in Thomas' firm, but not for the decent, pathetic Major, too loyal to his class and country to realise that they have dished him.

Major Brutt's connection with Windsor Terrace is coincidental. He was a friend of Robert Pidgeon, Anna's past lover, and once met them together. Pidgeon is his hero, and, being a romantic, he has invested that evening with an illusory glamour. Meeting Anna again, finding her married to someone else, is a blow. But illusions, as the narrator drily comments, can be re-invested:

It is the emotion to which we remain faithful, after all: we are

112

taught to recover it in some other place. Major Brutt, brought that first night to Windsor Terrace . . . already began to attach himself to that warm room. For hospitality, and that little girl on the rug, he began to abandon Pidgeon already. Even he had a ruthlessness in his sentiments – and he had been living alone in a Cromwell Road hotel.

Major Brutt attaches himself to Windsor Terrace; he drops in, sends Anna pink carnations and Portia jigsaw puzzles. He is an embarrassment to the Quaynes because they assume he wants something from them, and because he reminds Anna of the past. With his illusions about their happy home, and his tender memories, he constitutes the same 'undermining reproach' as Portia. Both innocents, both transients, Portia and the Major forge a pathetic bond. At the end of the novel, she goes to the Major as her last refuge from Windsor Terrace, and proposes that they should live together. This strange moment in the novel is at once funny, disturbing, touching and desperate. In order to enlist Major Brutt, Portia, 'in a very small voice that was implacable', disabuses him of his fantasies about Windsor Terrace:

> 'You are the other person that Anna laughs at . . . She says you are quite pathetic. She laughed at your carnations being the wrong colour, then gave them to me. And Thomas always thinks you must be after something. Whatever you do, even send me a puzzle, he thinks that more, and she laughs more. They groan at each other when you have gone away. You and I are the same.'

Major Brutt, like other characters in the novel, teaches Portia a lesson in experience. Like *The House in Paris*, this is the story of an education. School itself, a silly, dilettantish place chosen by the Quaynes, is not much use. Bowen has some pointed fun with it: 'We were to have a lecture on the Appreciation of Mozart, but because of the fog we had a Debate on Consistency being the Hobgoblin of Small Minds. We also wrote essays on Metternich's policy.' But what

Portia actually learns there is that she doesn't fit in. Also that the person you choose as confidante (vulgar Lilian, an excellent schoolgirl caricature along the lines of Theodora and Pauline) is bound to prey on your emotions.

Outside school, everyone Portia encounters teaches her something about social, moral, or emotional experience. This process is very clearly patterned, like the opposition between good and evil in *To the North*. *The Death of the Heart* has three sections, weightily entitled 'The World', 'The Flesh', and 'The Devil'. In the first section (winter) Portia gets used to life at Windsor Terrace. Anna finds her diary, Major Brutt encounters the Quaynes and Portia falls in love with Eddie. In the second section (spring), Portia is sent to stay with Mrs Heccomb and her stepchildren in Seale while Thomas and Anna escape from her on holiday; Eddie comes to visit her. In the third section (summer), all return to London. St Quentin tells Portia that Anna has read her diary, and Portia discovers that Eddie is in league with Anna. She runs away from Windsor Terrace to Major Brutt, and the Quaynes send Matchett to fetch her home. In these three sections, the triangular relationship between Portia and the Quaynes is posted round with four guardians, or teachers: two benign (Matchett and Major Brutt) and two malign (Eddie and St Quentin), with a comic interlude of instruction from the inhabitants of 'Waikiki'.

Of the four instructors, Matchett is the most daringly unnaturalistic. She equips Portia for her journey by telling her the secrets of the past. Like a Greek chorus, she knows what is wrong with Windsor Terrace, with Eddie ('he's a little actor, he is') and with Portia herself, but she is not empowered to act on this knowledge until the very end of the novel. Only after Portia's flight and the lapse of Eddie's influence, do the authorities give up their jurisdiction to her. Those who live without the past finally entrust Portia to the spokesman of the past, thereby admitting to and ensuring a kind of continuity. This may seem a grandiloquent description of a housemaid's taxi ride to fetch back a runaway girl to

her comfortable home. But the narrative makes that significance felt, because it attaches such momentousness throughout to the impassive, unconciliating, obscure presence of
Matchett:

> She sat sideways on to the bed, her knees towards Portia's
> pillow, her dark skirts flowing into the dark round, only her
> apron showing. Her top part loomed against the tawny square
> of sky in uncertain silhouette; her face, eroded by darkness
> like a statue's face by the weather, shone out now and then
> when a car fanned light on it. Up to now, she had sat erect,
> partly judicial, partly as though her body were a vaseful of
> memory that must not be spilt – but now, as though to shift
> the weight of the past, she put a hand on the bed, the far side
> of Portia's body, and leant heavily on it so that she made an
> arch.

That sort of significant language is not given to St Quentin.
His shark-like features, his liking for physical comforts, his
dread of personal exposure are comical, not villainous; he is
not powerful enough to be 'the Devil'. He is a Jamesian
observer, unexplicitly homosexual, who attaches himself to
other people's dramas, and who prefers to avoid commitment. But in the end St Quentin finds that action is inevitable.
No one can merely observe. He partly gives an amoral,
aesthetic view of the Quaynes' relationship to Portia. He is
interested in the style, rather than content, of Portia's diary.
But he is also involved in the betrayals which make up the
novel. Portia breaks faith with Matchett by 'going off' with
Eddie, Eddie is disloyal to Anna by mocking her with Portia.
At Seale, Eddie betrays Portia socially and physically; back in
London, he betrays her confidence to Anna. St Quentin
betrays Anna's secret about the diary to Portia; and Portia
betrays Windsor Terrace to Major Brutt, wrecking his
illusions. The 'devil' of the last section has been thought to
stand for St Quentin,[5] but it seems more to mean the whole
idea of betrayal. Like Henry James, who has a strong
influence on this novel, Bowen makes a severe moral
judgement of betrayal, through a satirical, worldly narrative.

It's clear from the start of the novel that Portia is bound to trust Eddie and that Eddie is bound to betray her. There is some interesting autobiographical material hidden in here. Victoria Glendinning describes a house party at Bowen's Court in 1936 at which Goronwy Rees, in whom Elizabeth Bowen was interested, began an affair with Rosamond Lehmann.[6] Rees was in his twenties, ten years younger than Elizabeth Bowen, very bright, attractive and irresponsible. When *The Death of the Heart* was published, he was at first amused, but then considered suing for libel. In later life Rees recalled the affair coolly: 'Anyway, these people were always more in love with me . . . I didn't believe in love.'[7]

The information is particularly intriguing because of Goronwy Rees's connections with Russian spies in Britain in the 1930s, – which I'll come back to with *The Heat of the Day*.[8] It suggests that Bowen projected herself equally into Anna and Portia, and it also explains the fictional treatment of Eddie. This does sometimes have the feeling of a revenge being taken on an affected and opportunist ex-lover. We get a lot of Eddie's mannerisms, the horrid faces he pulls ('I do that when I wish I had no face'), the glittering eyes with their inner 'vacuum', the actorly gestures of a body that is 'losing its naivety'. But Eddie's behaviour, which, as St Quentin says, denotes 'a permanent state of hysteria', reflects on the people who have taken him up. As he is aware, he has been 'bought':

> Everyone seemed to get a kick out of their relations with Eddie; he was like a bright little cracker that, pulled hard enough, goes off with a loud bang. He had been the brilliant child of an obscure home, and came up to Oxford ready to have his head turned. There he was taken up, played up, played about with, taken down, let down, finally sent down for one idiotic act. His appearance was charming: he had a proletarian, animal, quick grace. His manner, after a year of trying to get the pitch, had become bold, vivid and intimate. He became a quite frank *arriviste* . . .

Eddie is a social prostitute, at once passive and calculating, who caters to the worst kind of middle-class sensationalism

116

and patronage. This is merciless. But while Bowen shows us Eddie's spoiling quality, she makes clear too that he is being spoiled. His face is at once 'degenerate' and 'innocent'. In a crisis he displays hysterical despair, not policy. He feels guilty about having cast off his provincial working-class family, and bitterly resents having to play up to his patrons. All this is summed up in his discreditable relationship with Anna, who patronises him as a 'troubadour' but fends him off sexually:

'If I have to know people who ruin me, I mean to get something out of it.'
'I don't understand. Ruin you? Who does?'
'You do, and your whole lot. You make a monkey of me, and God knows what else worse. I'm ashamed to go back home.'

Eddie is drawn to Portia because she has acquired no standards by which to judge him, and he finds her, at first, a sweet peaceful contrast to Anna's constant 'What then?' But in the end she appals him because she has no sense of what to expect. Portia's not having anything to go by becomes alarming as well as pitiful to Eddie, as it is to the reader.

Portia thinks Eddie is 'ordinary' because he seems to be like her. She fails to realise that he has been bought by the world which he despises. Their conversations, at once quaint and appalling (the novel depends heavily on dialogue), brilliantly chart Portia's emotional literal-mindedness and Eddie's growing exasperation.

'Have I been unkind?'
'I've got no way of telling.'
'I wish you had ... Because I don't know, do you know. I may be some kind of monster; I've really got no idea ... The things I have to say seem never to have had to be said before. Is my life really so ghastly and so extraordinary? I've got no way to check up. I do wish you were older; I wish you knew more.'
'You're the only person I ever –'
'That's what's the devil; that's just what I mean. You don't know what to expect.'

> Not taking her anxious eyes from his face – eyes as desperately concentrated as though she were trying to understand a lesson – she said: 'But after all, Eddie, anything that happens has never happened before. What I mean is, you and I are the first people who have ever been us.'
>
> 'All the same, most people get to know the ropes – you can see they do ... You expect every bloody thing to be either right or wrong, and be done with the whole of oneself.'

The innocent person behaves as though every action is absolute and original; but, as Eddie says, 'My God, we've got to live in the world.' Actions and emotions – love, betrayal – are not original. They turn out to have happened before to someone else. 'Motives and passions', the narrator comments, with a jaundiced realism equal to Anna's, 'are alarmingly few.' The death of the heart sets in when what seemed unique, absolute and permanent turns out to be usual, relative and transient. But, in the process, the demands of the innocent characters prove to be extremely dangerous to the world they must live in:

> Incurable strangers to the world, they never cease to exact a heroic happiness. Their singleness, their ruthlessness, their one continuous wish makes them bound to be cruel, and to suffer cruelty. The innocent are so few that two of them seldom meet – when they do meet, their victims lie strewn all around.

There are two stages to Eddie's betrayal of Portia. Her final disillusionment takes place in London, but it begins during her visit to the Heccombs at Seale. This setting (recognisably Hythe) takes up a third of the novel, and is the comic high point of Bowen's work. The book's tactics alter here: the vulgar Heccombs are treated with gusto, quite unlike the meticulous coldness of the Windsor Terrace scenes. Portia has moved into a ruder, less dangerous world; the manner of the book lets go, with a sense of relief, making the return to London after it all the more enclosing. Also it's like Fanny Price's long visit to Portsmouth in *Mansfield Park*. Like Fanny, Portia thinks more warmly about her adoptive home when she is away from it: 'She had not been kind to Anna ... She had lived in that house with an opposed heart.' And, like

Fanny, she has to get used to a more robust style of seaside living:

> Mrs Price, Rebecca, and Betsey, all went up to defend themselves . . . the whole of which, as almost every door in the house was open, could be plainly distinguished in the parlour, except when drowned at intervals by the superior noise of Sam, Tom and Charles chasing each other up and downstairs, and tumbling about and hallooing.
> Fanny was almost stunned. The smallness of the house and the thinness of the walls brought everything so close to her . . .⁹

> She heard the bang that meant Daphne was in. Waikiki, she was to learn, was a sounding box: you knew where everyone was, what everyone did – except when the noise they made was drowned by a loud wind . . .
> Through the floor, Mrs Heccomb was to be heard hush-hushing as Dickie crashed open the glass door. Then he rolled an armchair round and kicked the fire: it sounded like a giant loose in the lounge.

Bowen has a wonderful time doing Waikiki as the 'fount of spontaneous living'. It's a very full and highly coloured period piece, which feels snobbish but accurate. Mrs Heccomb (once Anna's governess, now a widow living with her late husband's children), a kindly, vacillating lady, is comically contrasted with her two commanding stepchildren. Daphne's staggering brilliantine, her tangerine lipstick, her 'ruthless manners', Dickie's brutal chauvinism, and the stolid unthinking high spirits of their seaside 'set' are easy targets, and not a chance is missed. We have Mrs Heccomb shopping ('One bottle of Bisurated Magnesia tablets (small size), One bottle of gravy browning', etc.), taking a nap ('Mrs Heccomb woke with a little snatch at her hair, as though she had heard something in it') and meeting Eddie ('Portia could almost hear Mrs Heccomb's ideas, like chairs before a party, being rolled about and rapidly rearranged'). We have the Saturday night 'hop' at Waikiki, the Sunday walk on the cliffs, the outing to the cinema, Sunday dinner ('they ate as though taking part in an eating marathon'), a trip to Southstone's

Pavilion (Folkestone, of course) and a visit to Smoot's library, where Daphne, pinned to her chair like 'a furious Lady of Shallot' 'added *cachet* . . . by her air of barely condoning the traffic that went on there'. We have several noisy altercations between Daphne and Dickie, and we have Dickie's views on girls:

> 'If one is to know a girl, it is much better to tell her what one thinks. Another thing I don't like is messed-up mouths. When I give a girl tea, I always look at her cup. Then, if she leaves any red muck on the rim, I say, "Hullo, I didn't know that cup had a pink pattern." Then the girl seems quite taken aback.'

Passions run high at Waikiki: there's no holding back and no diplomacy. Portia looks for dissimulation and restraints – what keeps people in check here?

> The uneditedness of life here at Waikiki made for behaviour that was pushing and frank. Nothing set itself up here but the naivest propriety – that made Daphne shout but not swear, that kept Dickie so stern and modest.

Under this modest veil, nature is in full force. The contrast to Windsor Terrace means that Portia has to start again: is *this* normal life? The Quaynes look more dubious than ever from Waikiki. But Waikiki's reliance on conventions seems inadequate too, as Portia notes in her diary, after a conversation with Dickie:

> He said he judged people by their characters. I said was that always a quite good way of judging, as people's characters get so different at times, as it depends so much what happens to them. He said no, I was wrong, that what happened to people depended on their characters.

Dickie's moral certitude is not much use to Portia. Events at Seale confirm her suspicion that behaviour and experience are not absolute, but relative and ambiguous. Daphne's drunken friend, the badly behaved Mr Burseley, tells Portia at the Saturday night dance that she is 'a sweet little kid'. Portia is grotesquely reminded of Eddie, and for the first time is made aware of the humiliating lack of uniqueness in love. Could a feeling, she is made to wonder, 'spring straight from the heart, be imperative, without being original'? When Eddie arrives at Waikiki, the havoc he causes intensifies Portia's new uncertainties. There is a messy little betrayal: they all go to the cinema, and Eddie 'gets off' with Daphne. Portia, like everyone else in the row, sees them holding hands.

The Death of the Heart isn't primarily a novel about sex. Sexuality at Seale is rampant, but everyone is coy and conventional about it. The sexual drive of the Waikiki set is rendered as comedy (a very funny show-down with Daphne follows the cinema scene). Sexuality at Windsor Terrace is indirect and muffled. Anna is furious with Eddie when he tries to kiss her; she wants a *protégé*, not a lover. Eddie doesn't seduce Portia physically. Bowen is reticent about lust, which she makes incidental, or clownish. In the painful scenes between Portia and Eddie in the woods and the empty lodging house, it's not Portia's sexual jealousy which Eddie fends off, but her consuming trustfulness:

> 'I cannot feel what you feel: I'm shut up in myself . . . I don't want you; I've got no place for you; I only want what you give . . . What you want is the whole of me – isn't it, *isn't it?* – and the whole of me isn't there for anybody. In that full sense you want me I don't exist.'

Portia's defencelessness is very insistently done. Her 'perfectly open face', the intentness of her eyes, her awkward body, her self-abnegation with Eddie, her 'terrible meek tears', are almost too pathetic. There are a lot of poignant details like the comparisons with a captive bird, or the childish arrangements in her room ('I noticed some toothpowder had come off the top of one of my bears' cakes'). It's hard now to think of a sixteen-year-old as being quite so vulnerable. You might want to put her age back to thirteen or fourteen. At the same time, her diary has all the subtle perceptiveness of the adult narrator:

> Tonight there is quite a fog . . . When I woke . . . it was not like night but like air being ill.

> Today it is not raining but quite dark, black is all through the air though the green looks such bright green.

> This house makes a smell of feeling.

Altogether, Portia's pathos and extremism have an alarming effect. And they make the novel work at a symbolic, as well as a social level.

The section-titles of *The Death of the Heart* refer to the Litany: 'From all the deceits of the world, the flesh, and the devil, Good Lord, deliver us.' Portia's 'heart' is sacrificed to the world, and there is a suggestion that the sacrifice may be redemptive. Images of death, particularly of death in childhood, are everywhere. At the end of the night-time dialogue between Portia and Matchett, Matchett switches the light on to see Portia lying 'in a sort of coffin of silence'. The sudden light creates the feeling of a hospital: 'As though she lay in a sickroom, her spirit retreated to a seclusion of its own.' That same room, empty on the day Portia refuses to return to Windsor Terrace, 'seemed to expect nobody back . . . the day had died alone in here.' Earlier, Eddie, going to Windsor Terrace while everyone is away, finds Matchett in possession and the rooms draped for spring-cleaning. 'Everything really had a charnel echo and I said to myself, "She died young."' The idea of Portia as the child-bride of Death,[10] doomed for early sacrifice, is every so often suggested by her physical demeanour. On her way to her last meeting with Eddie she seems to bob along 'with the gaseous lightness of a little corpse'. Taking possession of Major Brutt's room in the hotel, she seems to 'obliterate' herself 'like a sick person' or someone who has decided not to get up. Sometimes there's even a suggestion that Portia is suffering from a metaphysical sickness, the disease of fallen man. A recurrent theatrical metaphor makes her, like Emmeline, into a fated, tragic victim:

> She was like one of those children in an Elizabethan play who are led on, led off, hardly speak and are known to be bound for some tragic fate which will be told in a line.

At times, Portia seems aware of her symbolic status. With-drawing in horror from 'the shut-in room, the turned-in-heart' of the Quaynes' house, she thinks that 'individual persons were surely damned.' In her last scene with Eddie, she takes him literally as usual:

'Well, leave me alone, damn you!'
'I don't care if I'm damned.'

The double betrayal she has suffered at the hands of Anna and Eddie 'pushes up to full growth' in her mind 'like a double tree'. So the 'death of the heart' may stand for the original fall from grace. But that interpretation is probably too rigid and limited to make complete sense of the novel. Matchett is the only character in the book who has a sense of religious ritual: 'The impassive solemnity of her preparations made a sort of altar of each bed; in big houses in which things are done properly, there is always the religious element.'

Otherwise, *The Death of the Heart* is set in a thoroughly secular universe. (Church-going is just another comic aspect of Seale.) What judgement, what retribution, what forgive-ness there are must take place here and now. There isn't a theological idea of a fall from grace, but a temporal concept of justice. Portia's name invokes the woman in Shakespeare disguised as judge. What gives the novel its toughness is that Portia isn't just a sacrificial victim; she's also an unforgiving witness, as hard on the world as it is on her. As St Quentin says, 'You put constructions on things. You are a most dangerous girl.' And her diary does 'trap' Anna by making her see her own life: 'she makes me feel like a tap that won't turn on'.

The final scene at Windsor Terrace in which Anna, Thomas and St Quentin decide what must be done about Portia, and in the process admit to their own inadequacies, is like a trial. The house has always been, for Portia, the 'court of an incomprehensible law'. Now it seems as though she has been the detective with 'the clue to the crime'. St Quentin, going to the house on this last occasion, is 'drawn to the scene of his crime – or, more properly, to its moral source'. When Portia doesn't come home, Thomas starts to ask questions; St Quentin and Anna look guilty; 'the air immediately tightened, like the air of a court'. Portia issues an ultimatum: she won't come back from the Karachi Hotel until she finds out whether they decide to do 'the right thing'. The Quaynes have to pass a test. The decision to send Matchett is a judicious move which lets them out and answers to Portia's needs. But in the process they have to examine themselves, to tell the whole truth. They are altered by what has happened. Anna, at last, reveals a passionate unease and a sympathy for Portia, which suggests there may be a possibility of resuscitation for her moribund heart:

> 'Well, how would you feel, Anna?'
> 'If I were Portia? Contempt for the pack of us, who muddled our own lives then stopped me from living mine. Boredom, oh such boredom, with a sort of secret society about nothing . . . Frantic, frantic desire to be handled with feeling, and, at the same time, to be let alone. Wish to be asked how I felt, great wish to be taken for granted –'

To the extent that the Quaynes recognise Portia's needs, some sort of justice is done. But a more general form of 'judgement' operates throughout the novel. Portia's innocence makes a judgement on the world, but the world also passes judgement on innocence. In that way the novel typically refuses a simple romantic opposition. The language of the narrator is a disabused language, speaking of compromise, realism and adaptability. This disillusioned, judicious narrative voice is like Anna's, and, even more, like St Quentin's. It makes it clear that Portia *has* got to change; it stacks the cards against her.

The lesson St Quentin has for Portia is about compromise:

> 'What makes you think us wicked is simply our little way of keeping ourselves going. We must live, though you may not see the necessity.'

This policy (usually given in stylish aphorisms) is elaborated on in his account of Portia, made to the Quaynes:

'Her "right thing" is an absolute of some sort, and absolutes only exist in feeling ... This evening the pure in heart have simply got us on toast. And look at the fun she has – she lives in a world of heroes ... I swear that each of us keeps, battened down inside himself, a sort of lunatic giant – impossible socially, but full-scale – and that it's the knockings and batterings we sometimes hear in each other that keep our intercourse from utter banality. Portia hears these the whole time; in fact she hears nothing else ...'

St Quentin says that Portia is the representative of the extreme, anti-social part of everyone, but makes it clear that this part cannot live in the world. He may be treacherous and unfeeling, but his realistic version of existence is endorsed by the narrator:

We have really no absent friends ... We desert those who desert us; we cannot afford to suffer; we must live how we can.

The strongest compulsions we feel throughout life are no more than compulsions to repeat a pattern: the pattern is not of our own device.

Happy that few of us are aware of the world until we are already in league with it.

The narrator's world is more like the Quaynes' world than like Portia's. So there is no romantic escape for her, as there was for Emmeline. She learns to negotiate and make terms. She will have to go back to Windsor Terrace and accommodate.

But the novel does not end with an explicit conclusion. As with Ray and Leopold standing in the Gare de Lyon, *The Death of the Heart* implies, through open-endedness, a future of compromise and delicate adjustments. In a bold and ambiguous coda, Bowen breaks off the narrative and replaces it with Matchett's voice. The book ends with Matchett's arrival at the Karachi Hotel, where Portia and Major Brutt are waiting. The effect of Matchett's monologue is startling, as though a sphinx had broken silence and turns out to be consumed with small worries about the taxi driver and the address. But out of Matchett's pragmatic, distrustful, even disappointing voice emerges a sense of possibilities. She at least embodies a force for endurance; and once faith, hope and love have been discredited, endurance acquires more distinction: 'We must live how we can.'

6

THE LIFE ROOM

Wandering as it were among the apples and amphoras of an
art school, he had blundered into the life room: woman
revolved gravely.

ELIZABETH BOWEN IS a great twentieth-century writer of
short stories, and if she had written no novels she would have
been valued and remembered for the stories. She started them
before she began writing novels, and she went on writing
them all her life. The form suited her, as it did other Irish
writers – Sean O'Faolain, Liam O'Flaherty, William Trevor,
Mary Lavin. It allowed full play to her talent for dialogue,
vivid atmospheric scene-making, careful shaping of materials,
sensational moments and suggestions of the unsaid. Some of
her best stories are set in Ireland. But they have a rich range
and variety. They are especially good at children, schools,
ghosts, hotels and wartime London.

She wrote over eighty stories, not all of which can be
looked at here. But by paying attention only to a selection, to
those which strike me as the most impressive and interesting
of all, it's possible to see what makes her such an extraordinary, distinctive story-teller.

I don't think it's essential to do this chronologically. Bowen
herself, retrospectively, dismisses the importance of chronology. '"Development" may appear in any one writer's successive novels; in successive short stories I hold it to be a myth.'[1]
Of course, chronology does matter to some extent. In the
same Preface she remarks on some changes in her techniques

127

– 'At the beginning I over-wrote' – and adds that she has moved from a liking for impressionism and 'free form' to a preference for narratives with 'a beginning, a crisis, and an end'. And she later points to the extreme shortness of the sketches in the first two books, *Encounters* (1923) and *Ann Lee's* (1926) as evidence of her being essentially 'a visual writer, with no taste for analysis'.[2] Character came later. There is a great difference between the brief impressionistic early sketches and the major stories of the three central collections, *The Cat Jumps* (1934), *Look at All Those Roses* (1941) and *The Demon Lover* (1945). (Some of the best of these central stories – 'The Disinherited', 'Summer Night', 'Ivy Gripped the Steps' – are long and complex enough to feel like novellas rather than short stories.) The wartime stories, written between 1939 and 1945, are very close in content and feeling to *The Heat of the Day* and I'll return to these in Chapter 7.

But it doesn't seem essential to think of her stories always in terms of chronology. What she calls the 'Bowen terrain', which is a spiritual as well as a geographical locality, has a recognisable atmosphere, a consistency of theme, in stories written forty years apart. They often chart an ominous vacancy, a lack in people or in places of a proper sense of themselves. 'Where shall we be when nobody has a view of life?' asks the wartime visitor to Ireland in 'Sunday Afternoon'. Unlike their characters, these stories do have a distinct 'view of life'.

Bowen is clear about the responsibility of the short story. It must be '*necessary*', and it must have a 'valid central emotion', like a lyric poem.

> However plain or lively or unpretentious be the manner of the story, the central emotion – emotion however remotely involved or hinted at – should be austere, major. The subject must have implicit dignity.[3]

Writing about Irish and American short stories in the Introduction to her own 1936 selection, she praises the 'semi-poetic' art of enforcing 'amazement' through understatement.

She calls this the 'extraverted' short story, 'bare of analysis, sparse in emotional statement', which provides 'general significance' through the particular. For the short story to justify itself, it 'must raise some issue'. This is a severe rubric, resting as it does on words like 'necessary' and 'austere', and recommending 'exact and impassive' narration.[4] It leads her to criticise those of her own early stories which exhibit or betray 'sentiments' too unguardedly.[5]

Paradoxically, though, she feels that the short story allows for extremes that the novel cannot admit: hallucination, dreams, fantasy, the unfamiliar. The short story is in some senses 'a free zone':

> More than half of my life is under the steadying influence of the novel, with its calmer, stricter, more orthodox demands: into the novel goes such taste as I have for rational behaviour and social portraiture. The short story, as I see it to be, allows for what is crazy about humanity: obstinacies, inordinate heroisms, 'immortal longings'. At no time, even in the novel, do I consider realism to be my forte.[6]

But that freedom in the short story can only work through control and focus. Very often a story is 'sparked off' by a particular place or scene. Some 'arose out of an intensified, all but spellbound beholding on my part, of the scene in question'.[7] But then that 'spellbound' inspiration has to be carefully turned into a perfectly mastered structure.

There are obvious examples of this, like the story set in a garden blazing with roses, first seen from a car by a bored couple driving back to London; the story set in suburban woods full of families out for the day, providing no shelter for a pair of lovers; or the story set on a bleak new housing estate which drives a middle-aged woman to the point of madness. As their titles suggest ('Look At All Those Roses', 'A Walk in the Woods', 'Attractive Modern Homes') the effect of these places *is* the story. There is always a connection between place and plot in her work.

'Bowen terrain' is not a wild uninhabited countryside. She is not interested in the aesthetic effects of landscape or in a

Wordsworthian contemplative solitude. The characteristic position of her people in relation to the sea is, like Gavin in 'Ivy Gripped the Steps', to stand with their back to its 'heaving mackerel vacancy', longing to be with the crowd on the promenade. What she likes best, in the stories as in the novels, is to put groups of people into the place they deserve. The moral relationship between places and people, for her crucial Anglo-Irish subject-matter, is very important in the short stories.

She uses places to expose a deficiency in the people who inhabit them, either because they provide a diminished quality of life, or because their decline presents a challenge that can't be met by the occupants. Many of them are not fulfilling their intended function. There are family houses which have fallen into disuse, seaside hotels and esplanades which have become scenes of desolation. Certain locales in 'Bowen terrain' are always bad for the soul. They recur in the stories, which often describe an opposition between experience and innocence, or a withdrawal from a pointless surplus of experience, or a social group so anaesthetised that it's not aware it has lost anything.

New estates on the outskirts of towns impose a baleful unreality and sameness on their inhabitants. The girl narrator of 'Songs my Father Sang Me' – a lament for a lost England – grew up in a wilderness of bungalows near Staines. 'The only point about that region is that it has no point and that it goes on and on.' 'The Disinherited', a powerful satire on middle-class life in the 1930s, begins on an 'exclusive estate' outside a university city. There's no refuge here from the violent rootlessness and dislocation that the story describes:

> You undertook not to keep chickens, put up a frame garage or hang out clothes ... Few houses had gone up so far; those there were stood apart, like Englishmen not yet acquainted, washed by clear upland air and each in its acre of wiry grass that had lost its nature, being no longer meadow and not yet lawn. Half-made roads, like the first knowing cuts of a scalpel, mapped the flank of the hill out, up to the concrete water-

tower upon its crest. No buses approached, and there were and would be no shops.

Bowen shows her social prejudices in the opposition between the desirable, absent 'meadow' and 'lawn', and the reality of 'concrete water-tower'. But what she is lamenting is not only rural or aristocratic seclusion. It is also the absence of houses and shops, a tradition of ordinary life.

By contrast, she allows more feeling to provincial suburbs, which can at least be ambiguous, as in 'The Queer Heart':

> This was one of those roads outside growing provincial cities that still keep their rural mystery. They seem to lead into something still not known. Traffic roars past one end, but the other end is in silence: you see a wood, a spire, a haughty manor gate, or your view ends with the turn of an old wall . . . And, each standing back in half an acre of ground, there were two or three stucco houses with dark windows, sombre but at the same time ornate, built years ago in this then retired spot. Dead lime leaves showered over their grass plots and evergreens.

Anything might happen in those retired, provincial, neo-Gothic houses, which fascinated Bowen all her life. The same ingredients – dead lime leaves, stucco gate-posts, sundials, laurels, church-like windows – recur in story after story.[8] A story called 'Reduced', about a woman with a mysterious past (she has been cleared of murdering her last employer) who is hired by a mean, unpleasant man as a cheap governess for his two daughters, makes interesting use of this kind of dubious setting:

> Pendlethwaite was not a lovable house. Built about 1880 of unpleasing maroon brick, it creaked inside with pitch-pine; its church-like windows peered narrowly at the smiling landscape round; its grounds darkened a valley with belts of laurel and stiff, damp-looking clumps of unindigenous firs. The house looked dedicated to a perpetual January: sunnier seasons beat back from its walls.

The perfect setting, it would seem, for untoward events; this could be a ghost story *or* a murder story. Those ominous

131

verbs suggest that something horrid is imminent. But there's an unexpected outcome. The governess creates a secret world shared by herself and the children, alienated (like Portia with Matchett) from the rest of the house. There's no scene of ugliness or violence, but there is a quiet ominousness about the children's incipient mutiny.

Bowen likes to use that sort of large, chilly house for a family that is falling apart. In 'The Needlecase', a too large house in dismal countryside is kept on for the sake of a prodigal absentee elder son. Another errant son necessitates the auctioning of the family house in 'The Last Night in the Old Home'. In 'The Disinherited', the feckless, impoverished Davina takes the innocent Marianne away from her house on the new estate for a night out. They track down a seedy collection of bored bohemians who have taken over 'Lord Thingummy's' stately home. The language for this incongruous scene is at once elegiac and sinister:

> One door stood open, and light peered in at the glacial sheeted outlines of furniture and a chandelier that hung in a bag like a cheese and glittered inside the muslin. A chill came from the hearthstones: the house was masterless. Along a pathway of drugget over the marble, at a quick muffled shuffle as though conducting a funeral secretly, the revellers passed down the hall to a door at the far end. They shot through with a rush, each unwilling to be the last, and shut the door defiantly on the echoing house.

The relationship between the house and its transient inhabitants – they camp out, lie around, make love, leave some litter – bleakly illustrates an impoverished modern world. And then there's the sinister bungalow ('the papers call it a love nest') which features in the journal of Davina's aunt's chauffeur. Davina is borrowing money from him in return for sexual favours, and he reveals in his journal that he has murdered his upper-class mistress. The chauffeur's soliloquies are melodramatic, but they add to the tawdriness of the whole story, where all the settings – the stifling bungalow, the soulless estate, the decaying Big House – brilliantly convey an idea of purgatorial lives. The empty road-house where Davina's friends fail to show up, with its 'horrid light' and 'ashtrays' sending up a 'cold fume', is hell: 'A glittering Neon sign like wolves' eyes read OPEN ALL NIGHT, at which thought a dry weariness pervaded the brain.'

In the Irish stories, the 'Big House' is rarely described in its heyday. Instead there is a struggle to sustain the tradition, involving personal sacrifice, (as in 'The Tommy Crans') or a sad stoicism (as in 'Sunday Afternoon'). The castle in 'Her Table Spread', one of Bowen's best and strangest stories, is an absurd futureless place of desperate hopes and wild sallies into the wet, bat-haunted night. Only in 'The Happy Autumn Fields' is there a vision of the Big House in all its glory, brimming with a ritualised, traditional family life.

> There was a look like velvet in the darker parts of the air; sombre window draperies let out gushes of lace; the music on the pianoforte bore tender titles, and the harp though unplayed gleamed in a corner, ... The towering vases upon the consoles, the albums piled on the tables, the shells and figurines on the flights of brackets, all had, like the alabaster Leaning Tower of Pisa, an equilibrium of their own. Nothing would fall or change.

But this apparently unchanging place is a lost and, as it turns out, a threatened world, painfully glimpsed in the imagination of a wartime Londoner who is searching for relics in a bombed house. The opposition in this very fine story between a place where it seems that 'nothing would fall or change' and the destruction of the war is central to Bowen's use of place.

It is in Bowen's ghost stories, that her gift for what Sean O'Faolain calls 'compression of suggestion'[9] is most atmospherically and evocatively used. We can see here her attraction to the short story as a 'free zone', where fantastical extremes are possible. Her ghost stories are in the tradition of M. R. James or Kipling ('The House Surgeon', 'They'), or Henry James. Writing about James's *The Turn of the Screw*, Bowen takes its main 'terror-ingredient' to be 'moral dread'.

'I need not point out that it is the stench of evil, not the mere fact of the supernatural, which is the genuine horror of *The Turn of the Screw*.'[10]

Bowen too relies in her ghost stories on accumulative suspense and sharp moments of shock; and also on a creepy uncertainty about what is actually happening. She talks about the same qualities in Sheridan Le Fanu's *Uncle Silas* (itself expanded from a short story), a book which in its Gothic setting, its psychological intensity and its very peculiar tone, had a strong influence on her writing. (The setting is not Irish, but it has all the feeling of 'the hermetic solitude and the autocracy of the great county house'.)[11] Bowen makes a fine analysis of Le Fanu's 'oblique, suggestive art' (both here and in her introduction to *The House by the Churchyard*), and singles out characteristics which can all be applied to her own writing. These are Le Fanu's 'voluptuousness' as a terror-writer, his cunning in playing on the reader's childhood 'helplessness and apprehension', the ambiguity of all the characters (which infects the reader with Maud Ruthyn's 'fatalistic mistrust' of everyone she meets), and the important relationship between outdoor weather and 'psychological weather'. She is also impressed by the claustrophobia of the book, the keynote of her own horror stories.

Her interest in *Uncle Silas* centres on Maud Ruthyn's character, whose responses she calls those of a 'highly intelligent, still more highly sensitive, child of twelve'. The novel, she says, is characteristically Irish in its sexlessness and its 'sublimated infantilism'. 'Maud is, by nature, a bride of Death.' This points towards some of her own characters, Portia and Emmeline, and, in the short stories, the 'child-wife' of 'The Apple Tree', locked in the nightmare of a schoolfriend's suicide; Pepita, in 'Mysterious Kôr', not properly grown up and consoling herself with a fantasy life; Marianne in 'The Disinherited', struck in an angelic, dopey innocence. Bowen's account of Maud Ruthyn explains her own preference for girls who have not quite grown up:

She is an uncertain keyboard, on which some notes sound

clearly, deeply and truly, others not at all. There is no question, here, of Victorian censorship, with its suggestive gaps: Maud, on the subject of anything she *does* feel, is uninhibited, sometimes disconcerting. And equally, in the feeling of people round her we are to take it that, child-like, she misses nothing.[12]

Bowen likes the way we don't quite know where we are in *Uncle Silas*. And in her own stories, the supernatural is often a psychological suggestion rather than an actuality, and she is always careful to root it in ordinariness. This 'normality' is often comical. In 'Green Holly' a bored group of experts secluded in wartime secrecy in 'Mopsam Grange' (one of those sinister pseudo-Gothic houses) find their tired relationships livened up by a pair of romantic ghosts. In 'The Cheery Soul', a visitor who's come to sponge on a rich Midlands couple for Christmas (again in a large chilly house) finds the couple mysteriously vanished, and a rude, but definitely spectral cook, in possession. There's a less affable comic note to 'The Inherited Clock', in which the girl who's inherited a 'skeleton' clock has repressed the violent sexual episodes in her childhood which are connected with it.

These stories involve explicit hauntings. Others take us into the realm of uncertainty, on the lines of *Uncle Silas*. 'Pink May', one of her rare first-person narratives, is told by a silly young girl whose marriage and love affair have fallen apart during the war, and who blames it all on to a 'ghost' who is, as it turns out, the girl's suppressed conscience. 'The Cat Jumps', a wonderfully macabre story, bristles with the implied violence for which she so admires Le Fanu:

> In so far as *Uncle Silas* uses physical horror, the use is extremely sophisticated: Maud's quick and almost voluptuous reactions to sound, sight, touch and smell make her the perfect reagent. The actual *sound* of a murder, a messy butchery, has probably never, in any gangster story, been registered as it is here.[13]

In 'The Cat Jumps', Rose Hill, the scene of a Mr Harold Bentley's indescribably horrible murder of his wife, has

ELIZABETH BOWEN

stayed empty for two years, until it's bought by a no-
nonsense family, the Harold Wrights, and their three ration-
ally brought-up children. 'They had light, bright, shadowless,
thoroughly disinfected minds'; they are uninhibited and up-
to-date. They take the *New Statesman*, and read Krafft-Ebing
and Havelock Ellis (this is 1934), and plan to 'lay' the
Bentleys with no trouble at all. In spite of their busy efforts,
though, a peculiar aroma seems to linger round the house, 'a
smell of unsavoury habitation, of rich cigarette-smoke, stale
in the folds of unaired curtains, of scent spilled on unbrushed
carpets, an alcoholic smell'. Their first weekend house party,
with a collection of like-minded guests, isn't as clear-headed
an occasion as they had intended. One of the female guests
turns out to have an unfortunate passion for the subject of
the Rose Hill murder: Muriel knows where in the house
each bit of Mrs Bentley was dismembered, and with just
what relish Mr Bentley took his time. The weather turns
oppressively dank and dark. By the end of the evening, an
unnerving dissolution has taken effect on these bright modern
personalities:

> On the intelligent sharp-featured faces all round the table
> something – perhaps simply a clearness – seemed to be
> lacking, as though these were wax faces for one fatal instant
> exposed to a furnace. Voices came out from some dark
> interiority; in each conversational interchange a mutual vote
> of no confidence was implicit. You would have said that each
> personality had been attacked by some kind of decomposition.

Bedtime is a moment of horror: to all the women in the
house, it seems as though the spirit of Harold Bentley has
taken over their husbands. And as the story ends on a climax
which is part farce, part nightmare, it looks as if that might
well be so. No summary can do justice to the cunning
obliqueness with which the 'terror-ingredients' – the
encroaching history of the house, the dissolution of the
modern personalities – are brought into play here.

The real subject of this farcical horror-story is, typically,
the relative lack of intensity and passion in the inheritors of

136

this horrid place. A number of stories (especially in wartime) deal with this theme of reduced or diminished lives. In 'The Apple Tree', a young wife is 'possessed' by the suicide at school of an ugly unfriended girl whom she abandoned, and who hanged herself from the apple tree. The image of the tree is haunting the young wife and wrecking her marriage. It is exorcised by the efforts of a worldly older woman (a familiar Bowen type). But, once un-bewitched, the marriage loses its interest. The appalling past is more intense and meaningful, than anything in their ordinary future: 'As one would expect, from then on less and less was seen of the couple. They disappeared into happiness: a sublime nonentity.' In a short sketch from the first volume of stories, 'The Shadowy Third', the ghost of a first wife is felt as an insistent, reproachful shadow over a new marriage – the shadow of someone who has been 'done out of their life' by not being wanted. In another early story 'Foothold', the characters anticipate the Quaynes and St Quentin in *The Death of the Heart*. A tasteful, sophisticated woman and her devoted husband, who have recently moved into a beautiful country house, are visited by the clever, adaptable and (probably) homosexual Thomas, who 'specialized in a particular kind of friendship with that eight-limbed, inscrutable, treacherous creature, the happily-married couple; adapting himself closely and lightly to the composite personality.' The house is charming, the visit is pleasant; but there is the ghost of Clara to be dealt with. What begins as a joke for the husband turns into the presence of a terrible emptiness into which the worldly, controlled Janet is beginning to fall. 'There's more and more room every day. I suppose it must be underneath.' Late at night, both men hear Janet in her room, quietly crying to the ghost: 'Oh, Clara ... I can't bear it. How could you bear it? The sickening loneliness ... Listen, Clara ...' Very quietly, the story insinuates that the ghost has revealed to Janet her own insufficiency. In its way this reserved story is as alarming as the later, more flamboyantly ghoulish 'The Demon Lover'.

Horror and fear work through the placing of details, which

give Bowen's stories their particular power. Each story has not only its weather and its season, its objects and its landscapes, but also its essential quality of light and sound. In 'Human Habitation', a fine story from the 1928 collection *Ann Lee's*, two young men lost on a walk come out of the dark into a house where a woman is waiting for someone who may never turn up. They leave, never knowing 'if he came back'. The story ends: 'They stumbled forward in the dark with tingling minds.' 'Her Table Spread' is an outstanding example of a story plotted through the dynamics of light and weather. The English visitor's wary observation of the Irish castle and its keyed-up occupants is charged with an odd, impressionistic intensity throughout. It's a dark wet night. An English destroyer is anchored in the estuary. Valeria Cuffe, the castle's retarded, clumsy, 'statuesque' heiress, is agog for a romantic visitor from the ship. Once before, when they were all away, sailors did come up to the castle. Valeria's relatives partly share her eagerness, in part try to conceal it. Alban, a timid, self-preserving man, feels at first put out ('he had heard they were all mad') but at the end is momentarily drawn in to fulfil Valeria's wild yearnings.

The atmosphere, which *is* the story, is at once established.

Alban had few opinions on the subject of marriage; his attitude to women was negative, but in particular he was not attracted to Miss Cuffe. Coming down early for dinner, red satin dress cut low, she attacked the silence with loud laughter before he had spoken. He recollected having heard that she was abnormal – at twenty-five, of statuesque development, still detained in childhood. The two other ladies, in beaded satins, made entrances of a surprising formality. It occurred to him, his presence must constitute an occasion; they certainly sparkled. Old Mr Rossiter, uncle to Mrs Treye, came last, more sourly. They sat for some time without the addition of lamplight. Dinner was not announced; the ladies by remaining on guard, seemed to deprecate any question of its appearance. No sound came from other parts of the Castle.

In his comments on the story, Sean O'Faolain remarks on the economical effect of the words 'red', 'attacked', and 'detained'. What's also striking is the negativeness of the description. Alban's inhibitions about marriage, his wariness of commitment, his unenthusiastic response to what seems an over-elaborate reception (a reception which, as it turns out, is not in his honour at all) mix with the negative quality of the occasion. No lamps, no dinner, defensive ladies, no sounds in the Castle: very baffling to the English visitor. Alban's dried-up isolation absurdly comes up against the Castle's breath-held expectations.

The formal, negative opening sets up a rhythmic patterning of light and dark. Inside the house, the ladies glitter, the candles are lit, the standard lamps in the drawing-room give out 'a deep, welcoming light'. The curtains aren't drawn, and the fact that the lights can be seen from the water is constantly stressed. And the ship can be seen from the house by its lights, 'blurred by rain and drawn down deep in reflection into the steady water'. Valeria rushes out with a lantern:

> Her fine arm with bangles went up and down, up and down, with the staggering light; the trees one by one, jumped up from the dark, like savages.

The sentence expresses the violence which Alban finds so alarming. It's grotesque, too, because its elements are mechanical and disconnected. Alban goes out into the wet dark with old Mr Rossiter: they sit in the boathouse and Mr Rossiter settles down with a bottle of whisky. Driven out by the old man's talk of marriage and by a bat flying past his ear, Alban staggers back up in 'absolute' darkness to the Castle. Valeria's lantern has gone out, and when Alban encounters her, she takes him to be her longed-for suitor from the ship. She cries out: the others come out on to the terrace above, 'blind with lamplight'. Alban is transfigured by the mistake: 'For a moment, without moving or speaking, he stood, in the dark, in a flame, as though all three said: "My darling . . .".' The strange romantic climax, bringing together the dark and the flame, is prepared for by the careful manipulation of lighting throughout. In the morning, the destroyer steams away, the castle inmates are 'insensible', and the Castle itself is 'extinguished'.

The unseen ship, providing the story's emotional focus is a typical ploy. In 'Tears, Idle Tears', a small boy who is always disgracing his mother by weeping noisily in public, is told to stay behind in Regent's Park and look at a duck on the lake until he can stop. He's consoled by a bluff, eccentric girl sitting on a bench. Later in life, he forgets the girl, but 'could still remember, with . . . a sense of lonely shame being gone, that calm, white duck swimming off round the bank'. In 'The Last Night in the Old Home', the object which stands for the disintegrating family is a rocking horse. In 'Songs My Father Sang Me', the narrator remembers, as a poignant association with her parents' break-up, a manicure set she was given for her birthday. In 'Sunday Afternoon', the young girl's restless aggression threatens the melancholy dignity of a group of Anglo-Irish friends:

> Her gesture upset some tea on the lace cloth, and she idly rubbed it up with her handkerchief. The tug her rubbing gave to the cloth shook a petal from a Chinese peony in the centre bowl on to a plate of cucumber sandwiches. This little bit of destruction was watched by the older people with fascination, with a kind of appeasement, as though it were a guarantee against something worse.

All these techniques – the fixing of an emotion through objects, the interfusing of place, weather, and mood – work through a charged, discreet, versatile language; what Sean O'Faolain calls 'a language of undertones'.[14] Here it's at work in 'The Cat Jumps':

> An early dusk set in; an oppressive, almost visible moisture, up from the darkening river, pressed on the panes like a presence and slid through the house . . . then Mrs Monkhouse, sniffing, exclaimed: 'Who uses "Trèfle Incarnat"?'
> 'Now, *who* ever would –' her hostess began scornfully, then from the hall came a howl, scuffle, a thin shriek. They sat too still; in the dusky library Mr Cartaret laughed out loud.

These tactics – sinister verbs, nervy fragments of speech, disconnected elements – can also be used for comedy. There is a close relationship in all the stories (it's part of the Anglo-Irish literary tradition) between violence and humour. An early story, 'Recent Photograph', gives an exaggerated example of her liking for the grotesque:

> A Mr and Mrs Brindley lived for some years quietly and unknown to history in one of the more rural of London's outlying suburbs. One spring evening Mr Brindley, returning from business, cut his wife's throat with a razor, and afterwards turned in for the night with his head inside the gas oven, having mitigated the inside's iron inclemency with two frilly cushions.

Later, Bowen will master a subdued, crafty placing of detail almost too insidious to be called ironic. The artificial atmosphere of 'The Little Girl's Room', in which the impressionable Geraldine is being preciously brought up by her elegant grandmother, but has a private fantasy life of extreme, revengeful violence, is done with just such deadly touches. Mrs Letherton-Channing, training up Geraldine in her delightful Italianate country house, watches for results 'ambushed in gentleness'. Geraldine's lessons are 'quartered by silvery ejaculations from the clock', while her grandmother chats with a friend in 'the rose-clotted loggia'. 'Her hands wrinkled slightly at the wrists like white kid gloves.' These details accentuate the theme of the forcing house, of artificial transplantation.

At the beginning of a moving story called 'The Tommy Crans', the child's confused apprehension of a lively, ramshackle party scene is brilliantly achieved by the dislocation of objects from their usual dimensions or places. Things seem to loom larger than life. Parts of the body, bits of clothing, separate themselves from their owners. The Dickensian effect is phantasmagorical; the viewpoint is constantly the child's:

> Herbert's feet, from dangling so long in the tram, had died of cold in his boots; he stamped the couple of coffins on blue-and-buff mosaic. In the Tommy Crans' cloak-room the pegs

were too high – Uncle Archer cocked H.M.S. *Terrible* for him over a checked ulster. Tommy Cran – aslant meanwhile, in the doorway – was an enormous presence. 'Come on, now, come!' he exclaimed, and roared with impatience. You would have said he was also arriving at the Tommy Crans' Christmas party, of which one could not bear to miss a moment.

Now into the hall Mrs Tommy Cran came swimming from elsewhere, dividing with curved little strokes the festive air – hyacinths and gunpowder. Her sleeves, in a thousand ruffles, fled from her elbows. She gained Uncle Archer's lapels and, bobbing, floated from this attachment. Uncle Archer, verifying the mistletoe, loudly kissed her face of delicate pink sugar. 'Ha!' yelled Tommy, drawing an unseen dagger. Herbert laughed with embarrassment.

The fantastic quality of the scene renders the child's experience and it also anticipates the topsy-turvy world of this story in which adults behave like children and the children have to bear the responsibilities.

The family groups in Bowen's stories are under pressure: the pressure of loss, of a dominating will, of someone who doesn't fit in, of distrust. Stories of family tension are frequent. There's a young wife who hates her husband but loves the family she's married into ('Joining Charles'), a daughter in love going against the spirit of her family ('Aunt Tatty'), two sisters in competition for the same absent lover ('The Cassowary'), a man unable to marry the girl he's always loved because of their familial responsibilities ('The Tommy Crans'), a woman escaping from family bonds to visit her lover ('Summer Night'). The mesh of middle-class family loyalties and betrayals is one of her main subjects: betrayals excite her.

The stories are full of misfits. There are the difficult innocents, unworldly, violent, even abnormal, like Valeria Cuffe in 'Her Table Spread', or the backward daughter Annabelle in 'The Last Night in the Old Home'. These characters, fixed inside their own pure vision of things, are unmanageable. They must destroy or be destroyed. And, as in the novels, there are characters consumed with the desire for control. Mrs Vesey's will rules over the group in 'Sunday Afternoon': she is one of many such powerful older women. In 'A Queer Heart', a jolly widow does battle with the will of her daughter and her own sister; 'Their two cold natures ran together . . . They censured her the whole time.' In 'The Girl with the Stoop', a crippled boy woos a mild-natured girl through sheer force of mind. 'I'm all will and you've no will,' he says; but she resists him in the end. The woman in 'The Demon Lover' remembers her dead lover's 'will': 'He was never kind to me, not really . . . Mother said he never considered me. He was set on me, that was what it was – not love.' The force of will in Bowen's stories can be terrifying.

The stories' heroines are often passionate, egotistical, difficult girls at odds with the family group. These women may be attractive, like Emma in 'Summer Night'. They may have an admirable kind of reckless flair, like Geraldine's dead mother in 'The Little Girl's Room', or Rachel in 'The Man of the Family'. They may be a thoroughly bad lot, like Davina in 'The Disinherited', or Margery in 'The Dolt's Tale', or Delia in 'The Last Night in the Old Home', 'as light as a little cat'. None of them is fit for family life. Davina, living off her rich aunt in a state of fierce, concentrated boredom, is the angriest of these reckless heroines:

> At twenty-nine, she had no more money of any kind; she had run through her capital; love-affairs and her other expensive habits had ruined her. To earn was out of the question: she had no idea what to do. In an agony of impatience, she waited about indefinitely.

Like nearly all the heroines, Davina does not earn. (Hence, of course, the importance of family pressures, which are economic. 'The Tommy Crans', in particular, is about the burden placed on two children's lives by the older generation's financial fecklessness.) Davina has somehow to fill time, without money, marriage, or interests. Bowen presents that kind of female middle-class parasitic existence ruthlessly, as in the story 'Foothold':

> 'You know how rather odious I've always been about

143

désoeuvrées women; I've never been able to see how one's day could fail to be full up, it fills itself. There's been the house, the garden, friends, books, music, letters, the car, golf when one felt like it, going up to town rather a lot. Well, I still have all these and there isn't a moment between them. Yet there's more and more room every day. I suppose it must be underneath.'

A pleasant, civilised round; but not enough, evidently, to keep off the dark night of the soul. (Janet, the haunted heroine of 'Foothold', noticeably doesn't include her children in her list of activities: they, of course, are away at boarding school.) Bowen doesn't moralise about the gaps in a cultured middle-class unemployed woman's life, but she likes to take the ground from under such characters' feet.

The pressures inside marriage are on the whole quietly done. In one or two of the earlier stories there are caricatures of male chauvinists: Charles in 'Joining Charles', Herbert in 'The Lover' ('Woman . . . is seldom placed in a position where it is necessary for her to think for herself' . . . 'All women wish to marry'). The mean, tyrannical Godwin Carbury of 'Reduced' is a later version of the type, and 'The Cat Jumps' is a baroque joke about the war between the sexes. But usually Bowen is more subtle about the failings in a relationship. She often has a sophisticated couple who can neither feel for nor get away from each other, like the couple in 'The Storm', 'self-sufficient, travelled, wary, and mutually pitiful', or the Perry-Dentons in 'A Love Story', who 'deadened the air round them with their static, depleting intimacy'. There are several stories, too, about the relentless persecution of a husband by his wife – 'Recent Photograph', 'Songs My Father Sang Me' – in which the husband feels, like Harold Wright in 'The Cat Jumps': 'She lay like a great cat, always, over the mouth of his life.'

The husbands tend to be less sensitive than the wives. Bowen often writes about husbands who don't know what their wives are feeling, or lovers who want to possess, but not to know, the woman. Emma in 'Summer Night', drives at top speed through the Irish countryside to get from the former to the latter. When she reaches the cold, experienced, attractive Robinson (another Markie), her excitement is quashed:

> She was becoming frightened of Robinson's stern, experienced delicacy on the subject of love. Her adventure became the quiet practice with him. The adventure (even, the pilgrimage) died at its root, in the childish part of her mind.

Marianne, the vague, childlike wife (another Emmeline) in 'The Disinherited', inhabits an affectionate but dull marriage. She is unfaithful; but the marriage is still there just the same, like a quiet box:

> Matthew Harvey never kissed in a station, so half-way across the hall he put down his dispatch-case, closed the door to the kitchen, and kissed his wife. Colour rushed up her face, but he did not see.
>
> He returned a book to the shelf and looked through a pile of letters. Meanwhile Marianne's look trailed wearily round the living-room, as though it were she who were just back from a journey and could still find no place to rest.
>
> 'I think,' said Matthew, 'I must get my glasses changed.'
>
> 'Changed?' said Marianne, starting.
>
> 'My glasses, yes,' said Matthew leaning back in his chair and looking at her with affection. Then he stooped to pick up an end of white cotton from a hand-woven rug. He rolled this into a cocoon and flicked it into the fire. 'A bit of white cotton,' he said, 'but I picked it up.'

Of all the pressures in the family group, the most extreme is that placed on – or exerted by – the child. Some of the best of Bowen's stories treat childhood desolation, loneliness, exhibitionism, fantasy and terror. She wants to get back inside the eye of the child.

The stories about children fall into two groups: those about children alone, usually on a visit, trying to adapt themselves to the social demands of the adult world, and those about children talking to each other on their own. (*The House in Paris*, of course, deals with both.) The closest thing in the short stories to Henrietta's and Leopold's alarming private conversations is the talk of the two children, the adopted

Nancy and the fatherless Herbert, at the Tommy Crans' party:

He and Nancy looked at each other gravely.

He saw Nancy, crowned and serious because she was a queen. Advanced by some urgent pushing, he made his way round the table and sat down beside her, podgily.

She said, 'How'd you do? Did you see our lake? It is all frozen. Did you ever see our lake before?'

'I never came here.'

'Did you see our two swans?'

She was so beautiful, rolling her ringlets, round with light, on her lacy shoulders, that he said rather shortly: 'I shouldn't have thought your lake was large enough for two swans.'

'It is, indeed,' said Nancy; 'it goes round the island. It's large enough for a boat.'

... 'How old are you, Herbert?'

'Eight.'

'Oh, I'm nine. Do you play brigands?'

'I could,' said Herbert.

'Oh, I don't; I'd hate to. But I know some boys who do. Did you have many presents? Uncle Ponto brought me a train; it's more suitable for a boy, really. I could give it to you, perhaps.'

'How many uncles – ?' began Herbert.

'Ten pretence and none really. I'm adopted, because mummy and daddy have no children. I think that's better fun, don't you?'

'Yes,' replied Herbert, after consideration; 'anybody could be born.'

That private language, alien to the adult world, at which Bowen excels, is often used to express the child's sense of being in exile, as in 'The Easter Egg Party':

'I can't help *what* you are,' said Hermione, quite dispassionate. 'Couldn't you get some other girl to stay with you? There's nothing for me to do here; I mean, I can't do anything. And all those girls were awful to me today; nobody cared if I found an egg or not. That girl Maisie wouldn't let me play with her brother. No one has ever been so awful to me as they all were; they took all the eggs, and I never found even one. And you never let me talk, all the time, you never let me touch anything. You keep on making me take an interest in things, and you never take the slightest interest in me. Mummy said you were interested in me, but now I don't believe her. I feel just as if I was dead, and I do want to go home.'

This partly takes its comic force from being surrounded by the kind of complacent English environment Bowen loves to satirise:

> West Wallows was more than a village: it was a neighbourhood. From the wide street branched roads that led past the white gates of many homes. The rector was tactful and energetic, the squire unusually cultivated; there were a number of moderate-sized dwellings – some antique, some quite recently built. Inexpensive sociability, liberal politics, shapely antique family furniture, 'interests', enlightened charity set the note of the place. No one was very rich; nobody was eccentric, and, though few people hunted, nobody wrote letters against blood sports. The local families harmonised with the pleasant retired people who had settled here. Probably few neighbourhoods in England have such a nice atmosphere as West Wallows. In the holidays all the children had a jolly time . . .[15]

But the inability of the dreadful Hermione to fit into this society, her profound feeling of alienness, is not funny: 'I feel just as if I was dead' (not, I wish I was dead) is the voice of despair.

Childhood despair is often witnessed, though it may not be understood. The eyes of the child Frederick, in 'Tears, Idle Tears', weeping terrible and involuntary tears inherited from the suppressed grief of his widowed mother, are watched by a sympathetic onlooker, to whom they seem like 'wounds, in the world's surface, through which its inner, terrible unassuageable, necessary sorrow constantly bled away and as constantly welled up.'

Not all Bowen's observers are as humane. She has a Jamesian interest in the character (usually male) for whom disengaged observation is a way of life – and a form of tragedy. The short stories are full of such characters. In 'The Secession', an early story set in Rome, Humphrey Carr drives one woman to suicide and another to distraction through a chronic incapacity for action. William, who unsuccessfully attempts to interfere in a family quarrel in 'The Man of the Family', then withdraws to his usual vantage point of aloof scepticism: '"It really doesn't much matter", thought William. "They're all fools."' Henry in 'Sunday Afternoon', is one of the most painful examples of this type, poised between the seclusion of his old Irish friends, and 'the new catastrophic *outward* order of life ... At his age, between two generations, he felt cast out.'

He is like Alban, the English visitor in 'Her Table Spread', one of the Bowen stories that most haunts me. Alban is something of a joke, because he is prissy and self-regarding, and because what he has to engage with is so bizarre. Yet his sense of having missed everything is not funny:

> The piano was damp, but Alban played almost all his heart out. He played out the indignation of years his mild manner concealed. He had failed to love; nobody did anything about this; partners at dinner gave him less than half their attention. He knew some spring had dried up at the root of the world. He was fixed in the dark rain, by an indifferent shore.

As the events of the evening begin to overwhelm him, he becomes alarmed; he's not prepared for this sort of thing: 'Wandering as it were among the apples and amphoras of an art school, he had blundered into the life room: woman revolved gravely.' The image combines sadness and absurdity. And the story sustains both moods. Though it is a ridiculous moment, there is also nothing absurd about Valeria's greeting Alban as her long-awaited lover, and rescuing him, momentarily, from the condition of alienation and disinheritance – personal and national – in which Bowen's characters are usually caught.

> She laughed like a princess, magnificently justified. Their unseen faces were all three lovely, and ... such a strong tenderness reached him that, standing there in full manhood, he was for a moment not exiled.

148

7

AN AWFUL ILLUMINATION

'I say, this war's an awful illumination; it's destroyed our
dark: we have to see where we are.'

BOWEN'S WAR YEARS, some of the most intense and
exciting of her life, were spent in London and Ireland. Like
the heroine of her next novel, she was one of the 'little shoal'
of 'stayers-on in London'. She was in the thick of everything.
She volunteered as an ARP warden for Marylebone, and Alan
Cameron joined the Home Guard. During the Blitz, their area
of London was badly bombed, and they once had to evacuate
Clarence Terrace in the middle of the night. She walked
through ruined London with Virginia Woolf – whose death in
1941 was a severe blow to her. In July 1944 their house was
blown hollow inside by a V1, and they moved out until
October of that year. One of their friends lamented, 'It was
the last house in London which still felt like a pre-war
house.'[1]

That friend was the Canadian diplomat Charles Ritchie, a
stylish, clever, charming, very interesting man whom Bowen
met in 1941. By 1942 they were lovers, and their affair
continued throughout the war. Ritchie returned to Ottawa in
1945, but they saw each other at regular intervals in the years
to come. Though he married his cousin in 1948, his intimate
friendship with Bowen continued to the end of her life.

They spent a great deal of time together in London, alone,
and, socially, with Alan and with friends. But Bowen also
travelled regularly to Ireland. This was possible for her in

wartime because of her offer in 1940 to work for the Ministry of Information. Like Stella Rodney in *The Heat of the Day* (1949), she became involved in 'secret, exacting, not unimportant work'. What she called her 'Activities' allowed her to get to Ireland during the war, and tested her own ambivalent relationship to her two countries. She identified both with Irish neutrality and with the British war effort. She was engaged in 'ascertaining Irish attitudes to the war, specifically in the question of the Treaty Ports in the south and west of Ireland, to which Churchill tried to persuade de Valera to allow British access'.[2] Her reports (praised by Lord Cranborne as 'sensible and well balanced') said that any threat of violation of Ireland's neutrality would produce 'chaos'.

Bowen's wartime experiences and her emotional life were adventurous, rich and active. But in her writing of these years, some of her best work – her stories, her war novel, *Bowen's Court* – it's clear that her sceptical and uneasy attitude to her civilisation was confirmed by the war. All her disenchantment with England and Europe in the 1930s came to a head. The war intensified her sense that the century she had grown up with was rotten and impoverished. In this she was not alone: many other writers felt that the war was our due. Evelyn Waugh repeatedly described a diseased society approaching an inevitable crisis. In *Unconditional Surrender* (1961), the section called 'The Death Wish' makes the point that the war was not only earned but desired:

> It seems to me there was a will to war, a death wish, everywhere. Even good men thought their private honour would be satisfied by war. They could assert their manhood by killing and being killed.[3]

Graham Greene, writing about the Blitz in an essay of October 1940 called 'At Home' sounded like Ezra Pound raging at the inevitability of the First World War:

> Violence comes to us more easily because it was so long expected – not only by the political sense but by the moral sense. The world we live in could not have ended any other

way . . . One feels at home in London . . . or in any of the
bombed cities . . . because life there is what it ought to be. If a
cracked cup is put in boiling water it breaks, and an old dog-
toothed civilization is breaking now.[4]

The idea of a civilisation which has earned, and deserves,
its own destruction, is central to *The Heat of the Day*, which
registers 'an impoverishment of the world' in its evocation of
wartime London, and in its pursuit of 'the meaning of
treason'. All through her writing, Bowen has presented
English middle-class life as having something very wrong
with it. With its over-protective families, its atrophied social
groups, its injured innocents, its sinister, misused, locales –
'Bowen terrain' has been a 'mined area' of dispossession and
compromise. Now, in wartime London, even the rooms and
furniture, those 'imperturbable *things*' on which Portia could
fix as guarantee of safety ('they remind us how exceedingly
seldom the unseemly or unforeseeable rears its head'),[5] are at
risk. Disinheritance is not just a metaphor any more, it is a
brutal fact. The war, to her, is the outcome of 'the dire period
of Personal Life' which in *Bowen's Court*, she said, super-
seded, disastrously, the 'healthy abstract' idea on which the
eighteenth-century bourgeoisie had flourished:

And to what did our fine feelings, our regard for the arts, our
intimacies, our inspiring conversations, our wish to be clear of
the bonds of sex and class and nationality, our wish to try to
be fair to everyone bring us? To 1939.[6]

Bowen's Court, written between 1939 and 1941, defines
the historical nature of the loss in the context of Anglo-Irish
civilisation. At the same time she was starting to write her
wartime short stories. Four of these were published in her
1941 collection, *Look at All Those Roses*. The rest came out
in magazines like the *Listener*, *Horizon* and *Cornhill* between
1941 and 1944, and were collected in *The Demon Lover*
(1945) – by which time she had written the first five chapters
of her war novel, *The Heat of the Day*.[7] The stories describe
with 'hallucinatory' clearness life lived under conditions of
violent abnormality. Bowen's obsession with diminished

places, displacement and alienation is answered by the conditions of wartime London. These stories linger with especially poignant intensity on abandoned and ruined places, and on how they affect people.

In the 1945 Preface written for the American edition of *The Demon Lover*, she calls the writing of these stories 'resistance' writing, and likens it to the way people in wartime clung to small objects and mementoes, by which they could identify themselves. What has always characterised her treatment of place is the loss of self. When places cease to function properly, their inhabitants lose their sense of themselves. In wartime this became part of the everyday lives of people whose houses were being destroyed:

> People whose homes had been blown up went to infinite lengths to assemble bits of themselves – broken ornaments, odd shoes, torn scraps of the curtains that had hung in a room – from the wreckage. In the same way, they assembled and checked themselves from stories and poems, from their memories, from one another's talk . . . Every writer during this time . . . was aware of . . . the passionate attachment of men and women to every object or image or place or love or fragment of memory with which his or her destiny seemed to be identified, and by which the destiny seemed to be assured.[8]

Bowen's wartime stories describe a dislocation between places and what is remembered or imagined. The narrator of 'Songs My Father Sang Me' (1944) remembers a lost England her father showed her as a child. The girl and her soldier in 'Mysterious Kôr' (1944), walk through a desolate, antique civilisation with no inhabitants but themselves. The woman whose house has been bombed in 'The Happy Autumn Fields' (1944) and who lies surrounded by wreckage – plaster, dust, calico tacked over the windows, sounds of hammering and someone thumping a piano – struggles back into the lost world of Victorian Ireland she's glimpsed from some old letters. Mary's relationship to the long-dead Sarah and Henrietta, whose lives she inhabits as she lies in the *débris* of her real present, is made up of an elegiac sense of their rich emotional lives and her own neurotic feeling of insubstantiality:

> 'How are we to live without natures? We only know inconvenience now, not sorrow. Everything pulverizes so easily because it is rot-dry; one can only wonder that it makes so much noise. The source, the sap must have dried up, or the pulse must have stopped, before you and I were conceived. So much flowed through people; so little flows through us. All we can do is imitate love or sorrow.'

The story's style acts out a painful contrast between the slow, melancholy Victorian world and the thin inadequateness of the present. The Victorian family is presented with decorous formality:

> Papa, astounded, let go of Arthur's hand, whereupon Arthur fell flat on the stubble.
> 'Dear me', said the affronted Constance to Robert.

> There was no end to the afternoon, whose light went on ripening now they had scythed the corn. Light filled the silence which, now Papa and the others were out of hearing, was complete.

The language for wartime London, in violent contrast, is disjointed and ugly:

> From somewhere else in the hollowness came a cascade of hammering. Close up, a voice: 'Oh, *awake*, Mary?' It came from the other side of the open door, which jutted out between herself and the speaker – he on the threshold, she lying on the uncovered mattress of a bed. The speaker added: 'I had been going away.'

The brittleness of the modern world at war, 'the anaesthetised and bewildered present', so vulnerable to the 'discharge' of feelings from the past, is presented in this story with an immense poignancy and sense of loss. In other stories, the 'desiccation' of personal life in wartime is more sinister.

In 'The Demon Lover', the most terrifying of these stories, a middle-aged woman returns to her shut-up London house, to be trapped into a spectral appointment with her dead *fiancé*, who was killed in the First World War. His parting words to her had been: 'I shall be with you . . . sooner or later . . . you need do nothing but wait.' Now she finds that the ghost's sinister threat from the past overpowers her null, dislocated present:

> The desuetude of her former bedroom, her married London home's whole air of being a cracked cup from which memory, with its reassuring power, had either evaporated or leaked away, made a crisis – and at just this crisis the letter-writer had, knowledgeably, struck. The hollowness of the house this evening cancelled years on years of voices, habits and steps.

The story makes wonderful use of charged, ominous details. As Mrs Drover arrives at her shut-up house, the language of the first paragraph at once warns the reader of the story's intentions:

> In her once familiar street, as in any unused channel, an unfamiliar queerness had silted up; a cat wove itself in and out of railings, but no human eye watched Mrs Drover's return.

This is a place at once too deserted and not deserted enough. Inside the house is a letter without a stamp: but no one can have been in. All her post is being re-directed to the country. As Mrs Drover prepares to read it, sitting in fear at the top of the silent house, Bowen lets in the weather as a 'terror-ingredient':

> The room looked over the garden and other gardens: the sun had gone in; as the clouds sharpened and lowered, the trees and rank lawns seemed already to smoke with the dark.

The histrionic touches ('rank', 'smoke') tune in with Mrs Drover's horror at being summoned to an assignation with her dead lover. The silent closed-up house and street, the sudden burst of rain, make up the suspense, as Mrs Drover remembers with fear his tyranny over her, and prepares for flight. She is consoled by the thought of a taxi: 'This evening, only one taxi – but this, although it presented its blank rump, appeared already to be alertly waiting for her.' The combination of 'blank' and 'alertly' is peculiarly alarming: it is the taxi driver who turns out to be her demon lover:

> Mrs Drover's mouth hung open for some seconds before she could issue her first scream. After that she continued to scream freely and to beat with her gloved hands on the glass all round as the taxi, accelerating without mercy, made off with her into the hinterland of deserted streets.

Every detail of this counts: the pointless formality of screaming 'freely', the lack of sound produced by the beating of 'gloved' hands, the purposefulness of 'made off with', and the concluding phrase, which returns us to what the story has already established: the sinister quietness of wartime London streets, in which Mrs Drover will never be found again. Bowen comments on her reason for using the supernatural in her Preface to *The Demon Lover* stories:

> The past, in all these cases, discharges its load of feeling into the anaesthetised and bewildered present. It is the 'I' that is sought – and retrieved at the cost of no little pain. And the ghosts . . . they are the certainties . . . hostile or not, they rally, they fill the vacuum for the uncertain 'I'.[9]

London is the most potent, but not the only setting for these stories of 'the uncertain "I"'. One of the best of the wartime stories is 'Ivy Gripped the Steps' (published in *Horizon* in September 1945), set on the South Coast. It's a long story, which looks ahead to *The Little Girls* (1964), and shares some of the feeling of her friend L. P. Hartley's novels of the past as 'another country', *The Shrimp and the Anemone* (1944) and *The Go-Between* (1953). Gavin Doddington returns to Southstone (presumably Folkestone) in September 1944, and sees again the house of his mother's friend, the romantic unhappy Mrs Violet Nicholson, whom he visited and loved as a boy, and who has left him 'with a whole stopped mechanism for feeling'. In a long flashback, the story shows the link between the harm done to Gavin's emotional life, and the loss of a whole world (not in itself all that valuable), summed up by Southstone society before the First World War, and by Violet's useless, civilised life. Gavin's holidays away from his parents' grim Midlands farm (an 'unprogressive' existence 'mortgaged to necessity'), his infatuation for and inevitable disillusionment with Violet, seem to shimmer in a lost past. Returning on a clouded evening in September 1944 he finds a moribund ghost town and a house choked with ivy. Bowen uses her favourite words for Southstone's abandonment: 'desuetude and decay', 'an etiolated slowness', 'vacuum mounted up'. We see the place as it was, in Gavin's memory, and as history has made it. Though there's obviously a contrast between the past and the present, there's also a sense that the pre-war world – complacent, hedonistic – had hung on for too long:

> That September was an extension of summer. An admirable company continued its season of light opera at the theatre, in whose gardens salvias blazed. The lawns, shorn to the roots after weeks of mowing, were faintly blond after weeks of heat. Visitors were still many; and residents, after the fastidious retreat of August, were returning – along the Promenade, all day long, parasols, boater hats and light dresses flickered against the dense blue gauze backdrop that seldom let France be seen.

> Outside the theatre a very few soldiers stood grouped about ... The theatre gardens had been cemented over to make a lorry park; and the engine of one of the lorries was being run ...
>   Crossing the Promenade obliquely, he made, between wire entanglements, for the railings; to become one more of the spaced-out people who leaned among them, willing to see a convoy or gazing with indifference towards liberated France. The path and steps up the cliff face had been destroyed; the handrail hung out rotting into the air.

All Bowen's wartime stories deal with diminished capacities for feeling and with a worldwide – not merely a personal – loss of innocence. The Victorian life of 'The Happy Autumn Fields' is dominated by images of childhood: Sarah and Henrietta, the two sisters at the centre of the family, are very young. Though old enough to be in love, they are still caught in an intense, expectant prelude to life. They sleep together, they share each other's thoughts, and their lives are defined through the family, and, as it turns out, both die young. Mary, the woman who finds their papers and foresees their tragedy, not only seems more worldly (she has a house, a lover) but much older than the Victorian girls. So, the title's reference to Tennyson's poem, 'Tears, Idle Tears', ('In looking on the happy Autumn-fields,/ And thinking of the days that are no more') is very appropriate. The story evokes a vanished age, and laments, like Tennyson's poem, for a vanished youth.

Mary is racked with despair. Like Stella, the heroine of *The Heat of the Day*, she is 'a soul astray'. In her wartime stories and her war novel, Bowen writes powerfully about despair. Gavin, in 'Ivy Gripped the Steps', feels the full desolating force of *'l'horreur de mon néant'*. This, the horror of experiencing oneself as nothing, perceiving the self as it really is, without subterfuge or consolation, is at the heart of Bowen's work. It comes to a climax in wartime, as in the story 'Summer Night' (1941):

'We're confronted by the impossibility *of* living – unless we can break through to something else. There's been a stop in our senses and in our faculties that's made everything round us so much dead matter – and dead matter we couldn't even displace. We can no longer express ourselves: what we say doesn't even approximate to reality; it only approximates to what's been said. I say, this war's an awful illumination; it's destroyed our dark; we have to see where we are. Immobilized, God help us, and each so far apart that we can't even try to signal each other. And our currency's worthless – our "ideas", so on, so on. We've got to mint a new one. We've got to break through to the new form – it needs genius. We're precipitated, this moment, between genius and death. I tell you, we must have genius to live at all.'

In *The Heat of the Day*, Bowen develops many of her familiar themes. The limbo of middle-class life becomes the breeding ground of the traitor. The sense of unreality is played out in the surreal, spectral theatre of wartime London. A secret love affair has to create its own 'habitat'. And again we find, as characters, a fearsomely repressive ageing woman, a sinister onlooker with no background, a decent, unimaginative English soldier, and a fatalistic, nervy heroine. Bowen returns, too, to the Kentish coast and to an Irish house – Mount Morris, another Danielstown.

But, though it is in some ways the culmination of her work, *The Heat of the Day* was not an easy novel to write, and it is a strained and strange performance. The first five chapters, finished in 1944, had to be rewritten when Bowen returned to the novel in 1945, and it wasn't published until 1949. In 1945 she wrote to Charles Ritchie, to whom she dedicated the novel: 'Any novel I have ever written has been difficult to write and this is being far the most difficult of all . . . It presents every possible problem in the world.'[10]

The sense of strain makes it a very mannered book. Bowen's idiosyncratic style is always very carefully controlled. But in *The Heat of the Day*, for the first time, it begins to look like affectation. Although this was her most successful novel,[11] it was after its publication that critical objections to 'the unusually evasive surface' 'the proliferation of detail that is fascinating in itself but ultimately distracting'[12] began to be heard. To get its feeling of tension and pressure, *The Heat of the Day* uses double negatives, inversions, broken-up sentences, and passive constructions: 'Up his sleeve he had something'; 'Soon now however should come King's Cross'; 'To a fault not unfeeling, she was not wholly admirable.' This can make not just for an evasive surface but for an impenetrable one: 'The seeming of this to be for ever was astonishing'; 'Mr Kelway had been to be watched seeing out.' Daniel George, Jonathan Cape's otherwise admiring reader of *The Heat of the Day*, called these mannerisms 'more Jacobean than James':

> One sentence from the book – which she did not amend – was '"Absolutely," he said with fervour, "not".' His comment was: 'Far, I diffidently suggest, fetched.'[13]

Such effects are easy to parody and they can be irritating. But they do express the oddness and dislocation of the wartime experience. In 'Mysterious Kôr', the unreal quality of London brightly lit by moonlight is given in a peculiar sentence construction:

> It was late, but not yet midnight; now the buses had stopped the polished roads and streets in this region sent for minutes together a ghostly unbroken reflection up.

Similarly, in *The Heat of the Day*, unnatural turns of phrase create unease:

> Around her the unsubstantial darkness was quicked by a not quite wind.

> Nothing more than an intimation was in the dark air; the fall's softness vicariously was to be felt on the roofs around, in the streets below.

> Not knowing who the dead were you could not know which might be the staircase somebody for the first time was not mounting this morning.

These mannerisms deliberately establish a peculiar, fraught place and state of mind. In context they read more as evidence of strong feeling than as affectations.

Strong feeling fills *The Heat of the Day*. With *The Last September*, it is the novel which most passionately evokes Bowen's own experience. There is a great deal of her life story in the character and situation of Stella Rodney. Her wartime spent in London, and her secret official work, get into the stories as well. There are two comical stories in *The Demon Lover*, 'Careless Talk' and 'Green Holly', which make fun of 'experts', the kind of people who are 'in the know'. ('Careless Talk' first appeared in the *New Yorker* with the title 'Everything's Frightfully Interesting'.) In the novel, being 'in the know' has a more sombre force, in the sinister secret activities of Harrison, Stella's unwanted pursuer, and in the treachery of her lover Robert Kelway. Bowen's own wartime allegiances also come through strongly in the novel's acute sense of Ireland's preserving itself as a place apart.

Above all, the novel dazzlingly and weirdly evokes the quality of life in wartime London. Walter Allen calls it 'the most completely detailed evocation of [the atmosphere of the place and time] that we have in fiction; it does for the period 1940–1944 what Henry Green's *Caught* does for 1939–1940.' Anthony Burgess says that it 'gives us the very feel and smell of London in the 1940s'. Angus Calder, in *The People's War*, has a long quotation from *The Heat of the Day* at the start of his chapter on the period October 1940 to December 1942.[14]

Calder is right to use the novel for that specific period, even though some of the novel's descriptions could apply to any part of the war: the ghastly, brightly lit subterranean grill-bar off Regent's Street, the darkening park, the empty shop windows of a provincial town ('the fruiterer filled a long-standing void with fans of cardboard bananas and a "Dig for Victory" placard'), the blind night-time train journey, windows muffled, 'every mainline landmark . . . blotted out'. But Bowen is particularly interested in the darkest middle period of the war, long after the fall of France and long before the Second Front. This is just at the turning point of El Alamein, when occupied Europe seemed very close ('the breath of danger and sorrow travelled over freely from shore to shore'), and the 'heady autumn' of the Blitz was recalled almost with nostalgia:

That autumn of 1940 was to appear, by two autumns later, apocryphal, more far away than peace. No planetary round was to bring again that particular conjunction of life and death; that particular psychic London was to be gone for ever; more bombs would fall, but not on the same city. War moved from the horizon to the map. And it was now, when you no longer saw, heard, smelled war, that a deadening acclimatization to it began to set in. The first generation of ruins, cleaned up, shored up, began to weather – in daylight they took their places as a norm of the scene; the dangerless nights of September two years later blotted them out. It was from this new insidious echoless propriety of ruins that you breathed in all that was most malarial. Reverses, losses, deadlocks now

160

almost unnoticed bred one another; every day the news hammered one more nail into a consciousness which no longer resounded. Everywhere hung the heaviness of the even worse you could not be told and could not desire to hear. This was the lightless middle of the tunnel.

In these melancholy, 'dangerless', 'lightless', 'echoless' London nights (many of the scenes take place in dusk or darkness), the life of the 'stayers-on' has taken on a peculiar quality:

These were the campers in rooms of draughty dismantled houses or corners of fled-from flats – it could be established, roughly, that the wicked had stayed and the good had gone. This was the new society of one kind of wealth, resilience, living how it liked – people whom the climate of danger suited, who began, even, all to look a little alike, as they might in the sun, snows and altitude of the same sports station, or browning along the same beach in the south of France. The very temper of pleasures lay in their chanciness, in the canvas-like impermanence of their settings, in their being off-time – to and fro between bars and grills, clubs and each other's places moved the little shoal through the noisy nights. Faces came and went. There was a diffused gallantry in the atmosphere, an unmarriedness: it came to be rumoured about the country, among the self-banished, the uneasy, the put-upon and the safe, that everybody in London was in love – which was true, if not in the sense the country meant. There was plenty of everything in London – attention, drink, time, taxis, most of all space.

The Heat of the Day belongs to a *genre* of wartime London literature. Evelyn Waugh was doing wartime comedy, inimitably, in *Put Out More Flags* (1942), and used the war as bitter inspiration for elegiac feeling in *Brideshead Revisited* (1945), an influence on *The Heat of the Day*: Bowen found it 'superbly and triumphantly romantic, with that sort of shimmer of the past (or rather, the shimmer one's own feeling can cast on the past) over it all.'[15]

Henry Green, like Bowen a highly mannered and evocative writer, was also making fine use of war's surreality. *Party*

Going (1939) takes a party of decadent socialites, unable to get to France because of a thick London fog, holed up inside a railway station hotel with a restless crowd outside, as an alarming metaphor for the onset of war and the end of an era. *Caught* (1943), is a vivid, bizarre account of life in the Auxiliary Fire Service during the Blitz: 'What will go on up there tonight in London, every night, is more like a film, or that's what it seems like at the time. Then afterwards when you go over it, everything seems unreal, probably because you were so tired . . . You get so frightfully tired that half the time you're in a fog'.[16] Bowen's feeling for the bombed city overlaps, too, with Graham Greene's picture of the Blitz, of 'odd devastated boarded-up London' in *The Ministry of Fear* (1943), like *The Heat of the Day* a novel about treachery and concealment between lovers. Bowen's 'icelike tinkle of broken glass being swept up among the crisping leaves' compares with Greene's 'the sound of glass being swept up, like the lazy noise of the sea on a shingled beach'. In both novels there are the nightly anxieties brought on by 'the thickening darkness', and the incongruous details which create a sense of strangeness:

> It was an empty London with only occasional bursts of noise and activity. An umbrella shop was burning at the corner of Oxford Street; in Wardour Street he walked through a cloud of grit: a man with a grey dusty face leant against a wall and laughed and a warden said sharply, 'That's enough now. It's nothing to laugh about.'[17]

Many factual accounts (there's a useful selection in *The People's War*) corroborate the mood of *The Heat of the Day*. The diplomat Harold Nicolson (who briefed Elizabeth Bowen for her 'activities')[18] kept a vivid wartime diary. Charles Ritchie's diaries, *The Siren Years*, are full of references to Bowen and also give some lively – and very Bowenesque – accounts of wartime London:

27 October 1941.
The sights – the long tree-lined avenue in Hyde Park at dusk echoing with the noise of soldiers' boots as they come strolling

. . . The whole length of the avenue is alive with desires . . . Silhouetted in the half-light soldiers with their girls sit on the deck-chairs on the grassy stretches that border the avenues . . .

In the expensive restaurants at this hour pink, well-scrubbed schoolboys masquerading in guards uniforms are drinking bad martinis with girl-friends in short fur capes and Fortnum and Mason shoes, who have spent the day driving generals to the War Office or handing cups of tea and back-chat to soldiers in canteens. Grass widows in black with diamond clips or pearls are finding the conversation of Polish officers refreshingly different from that of English husbands. Ugly, vivacious A.T.S. are ordering *vin rosé* at the Coquille . . . It is a world of hotels and bars and little pubs that have become the fashion overnight . . . In Berkeley Square the railings are down. An old man is making a bonfire in the centre of the garden.[19]

The closeness of *The Heat of the Day* to Bowen's wartime love affair is poignantly illustrated by this account, in Ritchie's diaries, of a September afternoon they spent together in 1941:

29 September 1941.
This afternoon, Elizabeth and I went to see the roses in Regent's Park. For days we had been talking of those roses, but I could never get away from the office before nightfall, and it seemed as if we should never go together to see them. Then one perfect September afternoon she telephoned to say that if we did not go today it would be too late – they were almost over. So I put away the Foreign Office boxes in the safe, locked up the files and took a taxi to Regent's Park. As we walked together I seemed to see the flowers through the lens of her sensibility. The whole scene, the misty river, the Regency villas with their walled gardens and damp lawns and the late September afternoon weather blended into a dream – a dream in which these were all symbols soaked with mysterious associative power – Regent's Park – a landscape of love. A black swan floating downstream in the evening light – the dark purplish-red roses whose petals already lay scattered – the deserted Nash house with its flaking stucco colonnade and overgrown gardens – all were symbols speaking a language which by some miracle we could understand together.[20]

The Heat of the Day begins in Regent's Park on 'the first Sunday of September 1942', when the 'great globular roses' are 'at the height of their second blooming', and it is the story of a wartime love affair. Stella Rodney and Robert Kelway, meeting 'throughout this heady autumn of the first London air-raids', have their first conversation interrupted by the 'cataracting roar' of a nearby direct hit. Their first weeks together are 'transfixed' by 'the extraordinary battle in the sky'. The nerve-racking extremes of the Blitz give their meetings an air of theatrical unreality. Stella feels as though she has crossed 'over the borderline of fiction'. As, during the next two years, they become each other's 'habitat', their intimacy thrives on the conditions of uncertainty: 'Wartime, with its makeshifts, shelvings, deferrings, could not have been kinder to romantic love.' Stella, like Bowen in her forties, belongs to the generation which was 'to be made to feel it had muffed the catch'. She identifies with her period: 'the fateful course of her fatalistic century seemed more and more her own.' This sense of identification is intensified by the relationship with Robert: 'We are friends of circumstances – war, this isolation, this atmosphere in which everything goes on and nothing's said . . . Look how all this ruin's made for our perfectness!'

This is the central theme, presented by the narrator with typical gravity:

> But they were not alone, nor had they been from the start, from the start of love. Their time sat in the third place at their table. They were the creatures of history, whose coming together was of a nature possible in no other day – the day was inherent in the nature. Which must have been always true of lovers, if it had taken till now to be seen. The relation of people to one another is subject to the relation of each to time, to what is happening. If this has not always been felt – and as to that who is to know? – it has begun to be felt, irrevocably . . . Could these two have loved each other better at a better time? At no other would they have been themselves; what had carried their world to its hour was in their bloodstreams.

The novel doesn't begin with this intense description of a

wartime love. By the time we get to it, it is already under threat. Like *The Death of the Heart*, *The Heat of the Day* opens at dusk in Regent's Park, with a concert in the open-air theatre. The first characters we meet are not Stella and Robert, but the lonely, feeble Louie Lewis, fresh from an unsatisfactory pick-up, and the mysterious Harrison, who is at once established as a threat:

> This man's excessive stillness gave the effect not of abandon but of cryptic behaviour . . . One of his eyes either was or behaved as being just perceptibly higher than the other . . . This was a face with a gate behind it.

Stella's first scene in her flat in Weymouth Street is not with Robert, but with Harrison, who has come to inform her that Robert is a spy, selling secrets from the War Office to the enemy, and to blackmail her. If Stella will give up Robert and accept Harrison instead as her lover and companion, Harrison will leave Robert 'on the loose'. Before Stella's appalled and disbelieving response to this information is developed, the novel pursues her 'impoverished' relationship with her son Roderick, home for the night on leave, and goes back four months to the funeral of Stella's Irish cousin-by-marriage, Francis Morris. At the funeral, Stella discovers that Roderick has inherited the Big House, Mount Morris, and Harrison, an interloping mourner, accosts Stella with an unlikely story of his friendship with Cousin Francis. Only when the relationship between mother and son, the Irish inheritance, Stella's reputation amongst her late ex-husband's relatives, and the first meeting with Harrison have been put into place does the novel close in on the love affair.

So *The Heat of the Day* is not allowed to be a suspense story, a thriller like *The Ministry of Fear*. We know at once what Stella has to fear from Harrison, and what Harrison knows. What is in suspense is not plot but psychology. Is Robert Kelway a traitor, and if so, what will Stella do about it?

Stella's first action is to go with Robert to Holme Dene, his horrible family home; as Harrison comments in the course of their next and more threatening meeting, 'to look at the first place where rot could start'. Then she goes away to Ireland. On her return she challenges Robert, and is answered with a passionate denial and a proposal of marriage. (Here the narrator puts in her grave comment on the lovers' subjection to history.) Roderick's pursuit of his inheritance comes between this scene and Stella's third, climactic meeting with Harrison, witnessed by Louie, in the nightmarish grill-bar. Harrison confirms his prediction that Robert would alter his habits once challenged. Stella, convinced, hopelessly offers herself to Harrison, but is unaccountably repulsed. An account of Louie's life follows, before a scene at Holme Dene, the only point at which we see Robert, now clearly guilty, without Stella. Then, at night in Stella's flat, Robert confesses and explains his treachery, and goes out on the roof to his death. This dramatic climax is undercut, however, by two low-key scenes which follow. When Harrison reappears after a long disappearance, to visit Stella, who is 'learning to be a survivor' in the air-raids of 1944, he has become almost a familiar, while the romantic Robert has dropped out of the book into non-existence. It is at this point that Harrison reveals that his first name, too, is Robert.

The organisation of this plot presents, as Elizabeth Bowen said to Ritchie, 'every possible problem in the world'.[21] One of these is the balance between Stella's two suitors; Bowen is really more interested in 'doing' Harrison than Robert:

> His vocabulary *and* his moral vocabulary keep presenting new possibilities and yet the other man, the heroine's lover, Robert, is still the problem character and the touchstone of the book.[22]

Harrison is the fitting inhabitant of the spectral city, a man from nowhere ('There are always two or three places where I can turn in'), mechanically addicted to calculation and policy, at once aggressive and self-deprecating, with no understanding of feeling. He has never been loved; he can have no relationship in which 'motives' aren't suspected; he 'makes a spy' of everyone he meets. He looks implausible. Stella at first takes him for one of the lunatics who have come to the funeral from the Home where Cousin Francis's wife is kept, and later, for a travelling salesman. And he does represent a kind of universal lunacy and exploitation. He is a man of his time, above all in his clumsy, slapdash, inert speech. When Robert talks of language as 'dead currency', we think of Harrison:

> 'War, if you come to think of it, hasn't started anything that wasn't there already – what it does is, put the other lot of us in the right. You, I mean to say, have got along on the assumption that things don't happen; I, on the other hand, have taken it that things happen rather than not. Therefore, what you see now is what I've seen all along. I wouldn't say that puts me at an advantage, but I can't help feeling "This is where I come in."'
>
> 'In other words, this is a crooks' war?'
>
> 'I shouldn't call it that. It's a war, of course; but for me the principal thing is that it's a time when I'm not a crook. For me there've been not-so-good times when I did seem to be a bit out in my calculations, so you must see how where I'm concerned things have taken a better turn: everything about adds up to what I made it.'

Stella's scenes with Harrison are more interesting than those with Robert (though one of the plot's weaknesses is that she should warm to Harrison in any degree: the peculiar intimacy that grows up between them is as hard to credit as Harrison's Scarpia-like lust.) Until his last confessional scene, Robert can only be a romantic, impenetrable figure of mystery.

In *The Last September*, the other novel which explicitly combines the personal and the political, what happens to individuals meshes perfectly with the situation in Ireland. In *The Heat of the Day* the relationship is more awkward. The violence which in her previous books arose exclusively out of private emotional warfare (Max's suicide, Emmeline and Markie's crash) now has to arise from the conditions of history. But the novel is personal and suggestive, rather than public and factual. She didn't want to write a novel about 'an international plot to sabotage the Allied War effort during the autumn of 1942'.[23] By structuring the novel as a series of claustrophobic interviews, all coloured by misunderstandings or concealment, between people whom we see only in relation to each other, not to their work, she writes a spy story without any 'action'. There are no scenes of recruitment, no government department meetings, no stories of infiltration, no details of espionage or counter-spying, no information about Intelligence, nothing about the operations of MI5 or MI6. Harrison and Robert make only the vaguest of references to their respective organisations: we see them only as Stella can. It is, deliberately, a woman's view of the male world of 'Intelligence', rendering in personal terms 'a war of dry cerebration inside windowless walls'. Hence the difference between *The Heat of the Day* and the standard male English espionage novel (now in such vogue that 'the spy ranks as one of the most potent images of mid twentieth-century life').[24] *The Heat of the Day* looks like a peculiarly unconvincing or sketchy 'spy story', if set against the work of Conrad or Kipling, Buchan or Greene, Fleming or le Carré.

Yet Bowen was in a good position to write a detailed and convincing spy story. Her own war work for the Ministry of Information would have given her some useful background – she wrote to Virginia Woolf in 1941, of the talks she'd had in Dublin: 'It is the political people I see mostly: it seems a craggy dangerous miniature world.'[25] Her long friendship with John Buchan could have been helpful. The love affair with Charles Ritchie accentuated her sense of belonging to two countries: 'We are curiously self-made creatures,' she wrote to him, 'carrying our personal worlds around with us like snails their shells, and at the same time adapting to wherever we are.'[26] He would also have given her a certain amount of diplomatic and 'Intelligence' gossip. And she knew his attitude to the war which, when he met her, he thought the Allies would probably lose 'within the next six months'.

The war offers us no ideal worth dying for – we make no sacrifice for a noble cause. We fight with no faith in the future. It is too late to pretend (though we shall pretend) that we are defending the sanctity of international obligations or the freedom of individuals. We are fighting because we cannot go on any longer paying blackmail to a gangster. Whoever wins, we who belong to what we call 'twentieth century civilization' are beaten before we start.[27]

Bowen's equally disenchanted view of 'twentieth-century civilization' may also have taken something from her friendship with Goronwy Rees. As the Burgess–Philby–Maclean scandal revealed in the 1950s, and as the 1979 exposure of Anthony Blunt re-emphasised, traitors came from the heart of the British establishment. Many of the upper-class English intellectuals who were close friends of Elizabeth Bowen (or of Charles Ritchie) – Maurice Bowra, Isaiah Berlin, Cyril Connolly, Miriam Rothschild[28] – were well acquainted also with Burgess and Maclean. Goronwy Rees first met Guy Burgess, who became his friend, at an Oxford dinner party given in the summer of 1932 by Maurice Bowra (whom Bowen had known well since 1926).[29] It was also in the early 1930s that Rees came to know Bowen, while he was at All Souls. In 1936 the house party at Bowen's Court took place at which he neglected his hostess for Rosamond Lehmann.[30] At about this time, Rees was seeing Burgess frequently in his flat in Ebury Street, and was beginning to notice Burgess's startling apparent change from Communist to Fascist sympathies. And it was soon after Rees became assistant editor on the *Spectator*, in 1936, that Burgess (by then working for the BBC) told him that he (and Blunt) were Comintern agents, and tried to recruit Rees as a Soviet spy.[31] Rees was 'so amazed' by this that he confided in Rosamond Lehmann. 'She found the information a revelation. "For the first time I understood why Guy, whose views were obviously left-wing, had been spending so much time with Fascists." '[32] Rosamond Lehmann could not believe that Burgess was really a spy until very much later, after the defection, when she made a statement to MI5. Nor could Rees, who remained sceptical until further evidence came up just before Burgess and Maclean's get-away. In the end Rees made a statement to MI6 – an act from which Anthony Blunt tried to dissuade him with the 'Cambridge liberal humanist' argument. Rees rejected the Forsterian choice between betraying one's country or one's friend:

> I said Forster's antithesis was a false one. One's country was not some abstract conception which it might be relatively easy to sacrifice for the sake of an individual; it was itself made up of a dense network of individual and social relationships in which loyalty to one particular person formed only a single strand.[33]

In a television interview in 1977, Rees described the reluctance of many people in the Foreign Office to believe that Philby and Maclean were spies, and the indication that the whole affair gave of 'something profoundly wrong with the English social structure'.[34]

These are intriguing links. The historian Andrew Boyle suggests that Rees and Lehmann may have spread rumours within a small social circle ('the gossip about Burgess did not spread beyond his intellectual friends of the left').[35] Bowen, though not 'of the left', continued to be close enough friends with Rosamond Lehmann, if not with Goronwy Rees, to have heard such gossip. It is tempting to imagine that she might have known that the model for the treacherous Eddie in *The Death of the Heart* was being asked to become a Russian spy while that novel was being written. And it's interesting that when Rosamond Lehmann commented on the character of Robert in *The Heat of the Day* (about which, like many readers, she had reservations) she thought it would have been more appropriate for him to be a Soviet spy: 'What bothers me a little is that I cannot see why he shouldn't have been a Communist and therefore pro-Russian, pro-Ally, rather than pro-enemy.'[36]

I am doing no more than suggesting that Bowen may have been aware of 'the climate of treason'. But it is, in any case, the psychological 'climate' which interests her. Robert Kelway's disaffection crystallised at Dunkirk ('an army of freedom queuing up to be taken off by pleasure boats'),[37] where he was wounded. But its roots are in his family background:

170

'I was born wounded; my father's son. Dunkirk was there waiting there in us – what a race! A class without a middle, a race without a country. Unwhole ... I could have loved a country, but to love you must have – you have been my country.'

It is another version of Forster's antithesis, or of Auden's 'There is no such thing as the State ... We must love one another or die.'[38]

Robert's home, the birthplace of his alienation, is the summation of all Bowen's Gothic home counties houses. 'Holme Dene', 'one of a monstrous hatch-out over Southern England of the 1900s ... conceived to please and appease middle-class ladies', is too large, over-furnished and perpetually for sale on the agents' books. The war has simply confirmed its discomfort. Outside, there's a notice saying 'CAUTION: CONCEALED DRIVE'; gables covered with virginia creeper; 'a tennis pavilion, a pergola, a sundial, a rock garden, a dovecote, some gnomes, a seesaw, a grouping of rusticated seats and a bird bath'. Inside, there are screens, archways, an elaborate staircase, mahogany furniture, 'cotton chenille' curtains, a bowl of orange dahlias 'like an arranged decoy'. The upper floors, planned with 'a sort of playful circumlocution' feel to Robert 'flock-packed with matter – repressions, doubts, fears, subterfuges and fibs'. In his room (kept, Stella says, 'as though you were dead') are sixty or seventy photographs of him: 'my criminal record'.

In this horrid house sits Mrs Kelway, ruling with careful, contemptuous tyranny over her hearty widowed daughter Ernestine, and the two stolid children (whose hero-worship of Robert is nicely done) of her other daughter, now in India. Until his death, she ruled also over a husband who had 'let himself be buckled into his marriage like Ernie's labrador used to let itself be buckled into its collar.' Robert and his father, whose eyes in this 'man-eating house' could never meet, were an embarrassment to each other. By the end his existence had become 'derisory'; his death was a relief.

Bowen does some excellent burlesque, Waikiki-style, in the

Holme Dene scenes (conversations about butter rationing, Ernestine's busy-ness: 'Hark, though: there goes the telephone! Someone else after me!'). But she has to make sure that her aesthetic satire on this kind of house will have enough weight to stand for a moral failure in civilisation, and to explain Robert's treachery. His father's impotence, his mother's *régime* and the imprisoning nullity of Holme Dene have to justify his loathing of English democracy:

> 'Freedom. Freedom to be what? – the muddled, mediocre, damned ... Look at your mass of "free" suckers, your democracy – kidded along from the cradle to the grave ... One in a thousand may have what to be free takes – if so, he has what it takes to be something better, and he knows it: who could want to be free when he could be strong? Freedom – what a slaves' yammer! ... We must have something to envisage, and we must act, and there must be law.'

Stella, whose two brothers were killed in the last war ('They were lucky to die before the illusion had broken down'), who has trusted and believed herself intimate with Robert, tries unsuccessfully to understand the catastrophic truth:

> 'So you are with the enemy.'
> 'Naturally they're the enemy: they're facing us with what has got to be the conclusion. They won't last, but it will.'
> 'I can't believe you.'
> 'You could.'
> 'It's not just that they're the enemy, but that they're horrible – specious, unthinkable, grotesque.'
> 'Oh, *they* – evidently! But you judge it by them. And in birth, remember, anything is grotesque.'
> 'They're afraid, too.'
> 'Of course: they have started something ... You may not like it, but it's the beginning of a day. A day on our scale.'

In explaining this kind of Nietzschean ideology through childhood trauma, Bowen, though not a Freudian, is in tune with current ideas. There's a parallel in *The Ministry of Fear*:

> 'In this war there are all sorts of ideologies ... The scrapping of all the old boundaries, the new economic ideas ... the

hugeness of the dream. It *is* attractive to men who are not tied
– to a particular village or town they don't want to see
scrapped. People with unhappy childhoods, progressive people
who learn Esperanto, vegetarians who don't like shedding
blood.'

'But Hitler seems to be shedding plenty.'

'Yes, but the idealists don't see blood like you and I do.
They aren't materialists. It's all statistics to them.'[39]

Rebecca West, in *The Meaning of Treason* (1949), her book
on the trial of William Joyce (Lord Haw Haw, who 'enjoyed
the fellowship of Nazis, whom he believed to be about to
inherit the earth because they were not meek'), makes much
of the infantile roots of anarchism and fanaticism:

> Most parents and children contrive to gentle their relationship
> by tolerance of each other's wills so that it serves them well,
> and most citizens make the claims of the state and their
> individualities balance on their books. But there are those who
> never persuade the love and hatred they feel for their parents
> to sign a truce; and these often find themselves compelled to
> spend their lives in love and hatred of the society of which they
> are a part, striving to make it more beautiful and noble, but
> insisting that the prerequisite of its reform is its destruction.

Like Bowen, West diagnoses a relationship between misan-
thropy, disdain and treachery. 'If a man does not love his
country enough to concede its right to self-government he
will end by not loving it at all, by hating it.'[40]

Bowen may well (at the same time that West was writing
The Meaning of Treason) have been influenced by Lord Haw
Haw in her creation of Robert Kelway as a pro-Nazi, not a
pro-Soviet spy. But the difference between *The Meaning of
Treason* and *The Heat of the Day* is not only that between
fact and fiction. Rebecca West makes it clear that William
Joyce was an eminently dislikable person; Bowen, though,
has tried to make us like Robert Kelway, whose disaffected-
ness to some extent resembles hers. This involves a political
and moral difficulty as well as an aesthetic one. And it makes
the novel's whole treatment of treachery peculiarly unstable
and strange. Bowen always finds betrayal, secrets, double

lives, very alluring and exciting material. Here, the whole structure, atmosphere and feeling of the novel seem to hover between an emotional affiliation with Kelway's alienation and duplicity, and a horror of it.

On technical grounds Robert has been much criticised. He is too blandly transformed from romantic lover to idealist-traitor, and is unconvincing as either.[41] But there is a problem too in the novel's Jamesian desire to render the state of civilisation through personal relationships. It takes a great deal of sleight of hand for the personal affairs of Harrison, Stella and Robert, and the family history of Holme Dene, to represent the hollowness of English civilisation, the operations of British intelligence and the threat of a Nazi victory.

Bowen strains for this meaningfulness by using a lot of loaded images. Harrison stands in Stella's drawing-room and 'looked about him like a German in Paris'. Stella arrives at Euston like a shade at Hades. Outside, in a car hired by Robert and 'parked secretly under a sweating wall', Ernestine 'bundled around invisibly inside there like a ferret'. The shadows in the underground grill-bar where Harrison takes Stella have been 'ferreted out and killed'. Robert, waiting for the same fate, looks up at the 'swastika-arms of passages leading to nothing' at Holme Dene, and then hears the telephone begin its 'demoniac ringing'. From the first scene in the Regent's Park theatre, there are references to dramatic illusions: Harrison makes his appearance like 'a ghost or an actor', the furniture at Holme Dene is like 'touring scenery . . . Reassemble it anywhere: you get the same illusion'. The underground grill has 'no air of having existed before tonight' and seems to be full of two-dimensional extras and scenery:

> A zip fastener all the way down one back made one woman seem to have a tin spine. A dye-green lettuce leaf had fallen on to the mottled rubber floor; a man in a pin-stripe suit was enough in profile to show a smudge of face powder on one shoulder . . . Wherever she turned her eyes detail took on an uncanny salience . . .

The characters have dramatic counterparts. Robert is Hamlet-like,[42] Stella's isolation and bereavement evoke the Duchess of Malfi. The sense of an inevitable tragedy is intensified by all the novel's clocks, bells and watches. Every scene has its precise time, its urgent sense of waiting ('Now the clock had struck, no step could not be his'). Both Robert and Harrison consult luminous watch dials (evidently a claustrophobic image for Bowen). Stella's suspicions of Robert are like a watch 'ticking under the pillow'. There is a sinister grandfather clock at Holme Dene (as in the story 'The Inherited Clock'). By contrast, the lovers meet in their early days in a restaurant with a 'shock-stopped' clock, and Stella escapes to the timeless world of Mount Morris, where there is no telephone, and a 'faceless' clock. In the last night-time scene between Robert and Stella, time is running out and the watcher is waiting in the street below. Robert's death is then ironically counterpointed by the nation's bells, ringing for the victory of El Alamein.

The novel strains to invest its personal relationships with historical significance. It has difficulties, too, in establishing alternatives to the traitor's position. The narrator is to an extent in sympathy with Robert's dislike of his country. So the extreme position to which this dislike has driven him has to be counterbalanced by other possibilities. After all, *The Heat of the Day* doesn't itself condone fascism and the destruction of England, though it shares the traitor's disenchanted view of his class. It provides possibilities of pride, hope, and survival.

These are embodied in the novel's two subplots, of Louie, and Roderick. Louie is associated with the Kentish coast, Roderick with Ireland, Bowen's two childhood terrains. Both belong to the next generation, who witness Stella's tragedy without fully understanding it. Both are uncorrupted. And both guarantee the survival of posterity, Louie through her haphazard fertility and Roderick by taking on his Irish inheritance.

Louie Lewis (her name balances 'Roderick Rodney') is alone in London 'like a day-tripper who has missed the last night train home'. Her elderly parents were killed during the Battle of Britain. Louie left her home in 'Seale-on-Sea' with her soldier husband, Tom, who's now away fighting. She is on her own, naïvely promiscuous, weepy and silly: 'she felt she did not make sense'. After her failed attempt to attach herself to Harrison in the park, she finds consolation in a friendship with Connie, a bossy ARP warden (no identity problem for *her*) and in discovering that newspapers can give her a sense of herself:

> Was she not a worker, a soldier's lonely wife, a war orphan, a pedestrian, a Londoner, a home and animal-lover, a thinking democrat, a movie-goer, a woman of Britain, a letter-writer, a fuel-saver and a housewife?

Louie strikes up a fleeting and unlikely intimacy with Stella (it is a bit like Yellow Hat's encounter with Karen, in *The House in Paris*) on the night Harrison convinces her that Robert is a traitor. But the romantic image which Louie cherishes from this meeting is destroyed by the newspaper report of the inquest on Robert's death. (As in her divorce, Stella conceals the unbearable truth by allowing herself to appear as worse than she is: a dubious society lady with a drunken lover.) The minor loss of faith – now Louie has no one to admire – fits in to the novel's pattern. In 1944 Louie gets pregnant and hears of Tom's death; the book ends in September, exactly two years after its beginning, with the Allies in Europe and Louie in Seale-on-Sea with her baby, Tom. On the canal path they hear the roar of homecoming bombers and see three swans overhead, 'disappearing in the direction of the West'.

The ending echoes Forster's *Howards End*, with the underclass and the next generation providing some hope and energy.[43] And Connie and Louie, simplified caricatures of lower-middle-class types, raise the same sorts of qualms about condescension as the Basts. The clichés are intentional: Bowen wanted to incorporate a 'Mass Observation' version of the ordinary Londoners' war into the novel, and these sections are packed with details about coupons and bobby-pins and life at the warden's post, in contrast to the more privileged, less material concerns of Stella and Robert. But she didn't want to do entirely naturalistic lower-class dialogue, as Henry Green did with the cockney Mrs Howells in *Caught*:

> 'Yus', she said, 'I'm in the W.A.F.S. in London, a real cockney I am, 'ardly ever been out of the old place, an' I 'ave to wear trousers, though I'm not that sort. What my 'usband would say if 'e was alive I can't imagine ... It won't never come to nothink, mark my words, I wasn't born yesterday, I've seen two of the things, this is my third war, an' the last wasn't no picnic let me tell yer.[44]

Bowen's Connie sounds less colloquial, more prophetic:

> 'I've never been so wakeful – must be something I ate: nothing's pure these days. No, I'm not in pain, nor is it fullness or wind, only the universe fevering round inside my head. – Ever got a bicarbonate? – No, I suppose not.'

Louie and Connie can't just be typical Londoners. They also have to be the factor left out of Robert's ideology – the unconscious natural will to survive and produce life.

Bowen provides a more convincing alternative to despair in the idea of inheritance and in the solid, likeable, literal-minded character of Roderick. The relationship between Stella and her son is very well done. Stella's feelings of guilt at having deprived Roderick of what he likes best, 'organic family life' and a 'high, abstract idea of society', are touchingly set against Roderick's candid, puzzled desire for clarity and order.

Roderick's Irish inheritance is not idealised. Its last inhabitants (who could be straight out of *Bowen's Court*) have failed: Cousin Francis, an eccentric old Anglo-Irish landlord to whom Irish neutrality was a final blow, and his wife Netty, driven quietly mad by the solitude of Mount Morris, who has withdrawn into the rosy, genteel retreat of 'Wisteria Lodge'. Stella's visit to Mount Morris (like Karen's to Rushbrook in *The House in Paris*), is not a complete escape. Harrison has been there before her, leading old Cousin Frankie into some conspiracy or other (presumably relating to Irish neutrality: this is discreetly obscured). Stella spends her time in Mount Morris haunted by her doubts about Robert. In the drawing-room, she finds a picture of the sinking of the *Titanic*, which was, to Bowen in Ireland in 1912, 'the first black crack across the surface of *exterior* things'.[45]

All the same, Ireland releases Stella. She feels there as though she has come into another time. Images of peace are brought in – the calm innocent face of the Irish servant girl, the three swans on the river (like those that Louie will see, flying west), the autumnal weather. It's here that Stella is given news of the turning-point in the war, Montgomery's victory in North Africa.

Roderick is felt to be the rightful heir in this place. 'He had been fitted into a destiny; better, it seemed to her, than freedom in nothing.'

> Possessorship of Mount Morris affected Roderick strongly. It established for him, and was adding to day by day, what might be called an historic future.

He is concerned to start right, making sure that Aunt Nettie doesn't want to challenge his inheritance (the young soldier's interview with her at Wisteria Lodge is trustful and unworldly, in touching contrast to the main plot), and that he has interpreted the will correctly:

> 'When he's said . . . "*In the hope that he may care in his own way to carry on the old tradition*" . . . does he mean, that I'm free to care in any way I like, so long as it's *the* tradition I carry on; or, that so long as I care in the same way he did, I'm free to mean by "tradition" anything I like?'

At his first visit to Mount Morris in 1944 he is immediately 'possessed'. For the first time he becomes aware of the possibility of his own death, and of the importance of 'continuing'. The section ends without telling us whether Roderick survives the Allied Invasion, but with a powerful sense of the will for survival in the place itself.

It is that attachment to place which forms the centre of

resistance in *The Heat of the Day*. When Robert says he has no country, Stella's response evokes the whole atmosphere of the novel, which by the end becomes the justification for patriotism:

> 'No, but you cannot say there is not a country!' she cried aloud, starting up. She had trodden every inch of a country with him ... Of that country, she did not know how much was place, how much was time. She thought of leaves of autumn crisply being swept up, that crystal ruined London morning when she had woken to his face; she saw street after street fading into evening after evening ...

An aesthetic vision provides a moral order. Stella's answer to Robert makes explicit Elizabeth Bowen's concept of wartime writing as 'resistance writing', which sets the individual's 'passionate attachment' to 'every object or image or place or love or fragment of memory with which his or her destiny seemed to be identifed, and by which the destiny seemed to be assured', against the depersonalisation of war.[46] The threat to the self which her wartime fiction describes is met with an acute, passionate feeling for particulars, for the past, and for place.

8

THE BEND BACK

'What fails in the air of our present-day that we cannot breathe it?'

THE 'AWFUL ILLUMINATION' of war confirmed, on a vast scale, Bowen's personal vision of an arid, dispossessed civilisation. 'How are we to live without natures? ... So much flowed through people; so little flows through us. All we can do is imitate love or sorrow.' The future seems to require 'genius' to be lived in at all. Her wartime feelings are summed up in the voice of a young soldier, in her radio play of 1946 about Trollope, who dreams on a railway journey that he is speaking to Trollope and explaining to him his love of the novels:

'We're homesick for anything right-and-tight ... The whole way of life that is quite, apparently, gone ... I think your novels are a support against the sort of *hopelessness* we're inclined to feel ... It's essential for us, these days, to believe in people, and in their power to live ... we long for what's ordinary.'[1]

Bowen's post-war writing deals more than ever with the failure of feeling and certainty in modern civilisation, and with the need for consolatory retreats into memory and fantasy. Her last three novels express a profound distaste for their times: 'Her time, called hers because she was required to live in it and had no other, was in bad odour, and no wonder ... too much had been going on for too long.'[2] 'Nothing's

180

real any more . . . There's a tremendous market for prefabricated feelings.'[3] 'What becomes of anyone's nature?'[4] When she writes about contemporary fiction, she finds 'an increasing discrepancy between facts, or circumstances, and feeling, or the romantic will',[5] and a compulsion to retreat from the nullity of modern life into 'the better days'. This is from an essay called, typically, 'The Bend Back':

> Now, after a second war, with its excoriations, grinding impersonality, obliteration of so many tracks and landmarks, heart and imagination once more demand to be satisfied . . . Can this demand be met only by recourse to life in the past? It at present seems so.
> . . . What fails in the air of our present-day that we cannot breathe it: or, at any rate, breathe it with any joy? Why cannot the confidence in living, the engagement with living, the prepossession with living be re-won?[6]

The three novels she wrote in the 1950s and 1960s are about displacement, alienation and the search for consolation. They 'bend back' into her own past, returning to pre-war Ireland and to schooldays in Kent, and into the characters' past, in trying, like Proust, to summon up lost time. Her last novel is set in the present, but its characters are at a loss in an alien world.

In their emphasis on dislocation, on the discrepancy between 'fact, or circumstances, and feeling, or the romantic will', the last novels confirm her long-held attitudes to existence. And they arise from the mixed fortunes of Bowen's later years. After the war, she and Alan Cameron spent more time in Ireland than in England. Alan was unwell, his eyesight was failing, and he had a severe drinking problem. They spent a good deal of time at Bowen's Court. They didn't like post-war London under a socialist government, and Clarence Terrace was given up. In 1952, Alan Cameron died in his sleep.

Bowen mourned him and missed him greatly. In her professional life, she was famous and much in demand, as a broadcaster, reviewer, literary prize judge, and lecturer for the British Council. She was given honorary degrees by Trinity College Dublin and Oxford, and had been made a CBE in 1948. She was a member of a Royal Commission on Capital Punishment. She was beginning to visit the United States regularly, lecturing and teaching in creative-writing programmes – and seeing Charles Ritchie whenever she could. She went on making new friends, notably Stephen and Ursula Vernon, whose homes in County Limerick and in Kinsale became refuges for her.

This was especially so after 1959. Bowen's Court had become, at last, financially unmanageable. *A World of Love* (her first book since the war apart from a book of essays and reviews, *Collected Impressions*, and a short, lively, evocative book on Dublin's great hotel, *The Shelbourne*) was begun in Ireland after Alan Cameron's death. The shabbiness of its Irish house reflects, as Victoria Glendinning says, her 'own predicament at Bowen's Court'.[7]

After the sale and demolition of Bowen's Court in 1959, she continued to go to Ireland, usually as the guest of the Vernons. Her life now became even more peripatetic. She went often to the States (to Vassar, Princeton, Bryn Mawr and elsewhere). But she had no long-term home after Bowen's Court. Her attempts to settle down in England took the form of journeys back into her past. She first moved to a flat in Headington, in a house belonging to Isaiah Berlin, and then, in 1965, took a house in Hythe, called Carbery. Her last years were dominated by illness – bronchitis and pneumonia. (She was a heavy smoker all her adult life.) In 1972, lung cancer was diagnosed. She died (with Charles Ritchie in attendance) on 22 February 1973.

Bowen put a brave face on her circumstances and was active, busy and sociable until the last possible moment. But her last two novels communicate a painful sense of uncertainty and disequilibrium. There were personal but also literary reasons for this. Bowen's greatest fiction, in the 1930s and 1940s, came out of a match between her historical attitudes, her literary manner and her idea of society. In the post-war years, her writing seemed less in tune with the world she was describing. The last two novels are profoundly uneasy, and their tone is uncertain. And though *A World of Love*, her only novel of the 1950s, is atmospheric and touching, it is also extremely mannered, and, unlike *The Death of the Heart* or *The House in Paris*, sentimental about youthful innocence.

After *A World of Love* she felt she needed to turn herself into a different kind of novelist. This is like Virginia Woolf's reaction against *The Waves* (1931), and her attempt to find a method which would make her next novel, *The Years* (1937) into an appropriate fictional document for the 1930s. Bowen, similarly, wanted to come to terms with the 1960s. Victoria Glendinning notes the influence of Iris Murdoch and Muriel Spark on *The Little Girls* (1964), particularly their interest in 'nightmare and fantasy'.[8] Bowen planned to write this novel 'externally', without revealing her characters' thoughts and feelings.[9] This suggests her predicament. She had begun her writing influenced by James, Forster and Virginia Woolf. She shared some qualities with novelists like L. P. Hartley, Henry Green, Rosamond Lehmann and early Graham Greene. But in the 1960s she seemed ill-at-ease with her own style. As her interest in the unconscious and the abnormal increased (the last two novels are concerned with involuntary recall, non-verbal communication, retardation, infantilism and fantasy life), her controlled analyses of motives and emotions began to come undone. And, as her environment became increasingly alien to her, so her intense evocation of place was unsettled. Her last two novels are looking for a new kind of fictional language and method. In doing so, they stir up qualms about the novel form itself.

All three of the late novels are preoccupied with time and recollection. They make similar references to *déjà vu* and to the overlap between memory and fantasy: 'Were there not those who said that everything *has* already happened, and that one's lookings-forward are really memories?'[10] 'They say – don't they? – one never is doing anything for the first time.'[11] 'Imagining oneself to be remembering, more often than not one is imagining: Proust says so. (Or is it, imagining oneself to be imagining, one is remembering?)'[12] In the last two books retrospection is confused: there's uncertainty as to what actually has happened. Memory itself, so important for Bowen's work, has fallen into disrepute.

But her only novel of the 1950s, *A World of Love* (1955), is all about memory, and makes a poignant quest for the past. It is a touching farewell to Bowen's Irish story and to many of her favourite materials. As the lyrical title implies (taken from Traherne's 'There is in us a world of Love to somewhat, though we know not what in the world that should be'), it is a romance of feelings and personal relations, in retreat from the wider political reverberations of *The Heat of the Day*. It is also as close to being a ghost story as her novels were ever allowed to come.

From the start of the novel – County Cork, the sun rising ('on the heat of the day before') for an exceptionally hot June day, an 'expectant, empty, intense' landscape, a dilapidated Irish house, Montefort, 'somewhat surprisingly' fronted by an obelisk, a beautiful girl of twenty in a 'trailing Edwardian muslin dress' coming out to read a letter – the atmosphere is so typically Bowenesque as to be almost parodic. Like 'The Happy Autumn Fields', the novel initially gives the impression of being set in the past. And, like that story, it cuts roughly and abruptly to the squalid modern litter of a woman's bedroom inside the house: 'a packet of Gold Flake, a Bible, a glass with dregs, matches, sunglasses, sleeping pills, a nail file and a candlestick caked with wax into which the finished wick had subsided'. Montefort's run-down modern condition is going to be contrasted with a more dignified past. The rapt romanticism of the girl reading the letter will be set against the disabused toughness of the woman asleep in the bedroom.

Like Henrietta and Leopold uncovering the past of the house in Paris, Jane Danby has found a bundle of letters in the trunk with the Edwardian dress which unlocks the past of Montefort. Her chance discovery not only raises ghosts but liberates her into her own future. This is (like many of Bowen's plots) the story of a sleeping princess, but in this case the heroine is not awakened for a tragic shock or disillusionment, like Lois, Emmeline, or Portia. *A World of Love* is allowed a happy ending.

But, as in *The House in Paris*, there is an unhappy past to be uncovered, which has produced the uneasy circumstances of life at Montefort. Antonia, the woman in the bedroom, has been the owner of the house since her cousin Guy (the writer of the letters) died in the war in 1918. At his death, Guy was engaged to an English girl, Lilia, then a beautiful and bewildered seventeen-year-old. But he has also been having a ruthless, rather cruel affair with Antonia. Antonia took charge of Lilia's life, to the extent of marrying her off at thirty to another cousin, the 'wild', illegitimate Fred Danby, and of installing the couple at Montefort. There, the marriage worked itself out through stages of passion and coldness, and two children were born, Jane and her eccentric younger sister, Maud. The Danbys' ill-defined status as 'caretakers', farmers and hosts to Antonia continued for twenty-one years, since they are all averse to 'sitting down and having anything out'. Lilia's brooding dislike of Montefort and of Antonia, Fred's infatuation with his elder daughter, the estrangement of Fred and Lilia, and Antonia's nervous impatience with the whole set-up, are ignited by Jane's discovery of Guy's letters. Thirty or more years on, he seems to return, as the letters fall into the hands of every member of the household. Jane falls in love with her idea of him; and the emotion translates her from a girl to a woman. Spotted at the local fête as a rising beauty by the neighbouring *châtelaine*, Lady Latterly, she goes to a dinner party at the castle – a comic setting which the ghostly presence of Guy (who often dined there with the past owners) transforms into a bridal feast. Jane moves into Lady Latterly's orbit, and is driven by the castle chauffeur to Shannon airport, to meet one of Lady Latterly's guests – and cast-off boyfriends – Richard Priam. The time is right, the letters have prepared the ground: 'They no sooner looked but they loved.'

Jane's romantic story is grotesquely counterpointed by the antic 'possession' of her little sister Maud, struggling with her 'familiar', laying curses on her family, and racing to the radio to listen to the strokes of Big Ben. Jane's innocence is also set against the disconcerting effect of the letters on the older generation, now, like Bowen, in their fifties. Antonia's painful love of Guy, Fred and Lilia's jealousy and bitterness are re-enacted. They are all haunted by the writer of the letters, who, it transpires, has been unfaithful to both women. But, unlike *The House in Paris* and *To the North*, and like *The Death of the Heart*, this is a novel of compromise, not of tragedy. Lilia and Fred move towards a more companionable relationship, Antonia belatedly accepts Guy's love for Lilia and her own necessary bond with her. Though 'one was never quite quit of what one has done', by the end of the novel the ghost has been exorcised, and 'the future was the thing'.

A World of Love is full of echoes of Bowen's earlier works. The past breaks in on the present, as in *The House in Paris* or 'The Happy Autumn Fields'. A young girl waits for something to happen in an Irish house, as in *The Last September*. And there are more specific allusions. Maud is a compound of all Bowen's horrible small girls. Guy's parting words, 'You'll never see the last of me!' recall the leave-taking of the soldier in 'The Demon Lover'. ('I shall be with you . . . sooner or later. You won't forget that. You need do nothing but wait.')[13] The cousins' tormenting love affair is like the cruel relationship between the child cousins in the story 'The Inherited Clock', which has been repressed in the grown woman's memory. Jane's visit to Lady Latterly's castle is like Marianne's excursion with Davina in 'The Disinherited'. Like Marianne, Jane moves in a rapt, ethereal trance through the 'void, stale, trite and denying drawing-room'. Lady Latterly's English guests are ghostlike: there was 'something phantasmagorical about this circle of the displaced rich'. *A World of Love* is haunted by its author's past creations, and most of all by her past treatments of Anglo-Ireland.

Compared with the Anglo-Irish novel of 1929, *A World of Love* is shadowy. *The Last September* was much more full-blooded. Lois was, after all, in love with a real soldier, and not the ghost of one. Anglo-Irish society, though diminished, was still felt to possess energy and decorum. Individual lives were inextricably related to the political situation. In *A World of Love* the girl is in love with a phantom, there is no Anglo-Irish society any more, and the lives at Montefort and at the castle, lives of demeaning poverty or demeaning wealth, exist in a vacuum. Although the novel describes a dreamy prelude to adult love, its real subject is loss. This is the last, faint, spectral chapter in Bowen's history of Anglo-Ireland.

And what *A World of Love* does best are not the romantic set-pieces, like Jane sensing Guy's presence opposite her at the castle dinner party, but the wry accounts of the disintegrated Anglo-Irish. The Dickensianly named English Lady Latterly, of dubious past, who's bought up 'an unusually banal Irish castle, long empty owing to disrepair' is part of an influx of *nouveaux riches* moving in on a landscape once 'vigilant' against intruders, and scattered with 'eyeless towers and time-stunted castles'. To one old Irish guest, who remembers County Cork as it used to be, Lady Latterly and her friends are no substitute for the real society they have replaced: 'You can buy up a lot; you can't buy the past . . . these days, one goes where the money is – with all due respect to this charming lady. Those days, we went where the people were.'

The castle's money is good enough for the local shopkeepers, however, who have been known to stop Montefort's credit. A comparison between this depressing town, and the liveliness of Mrs Fogarty's Clonmore drawing-room in *The Last September*, shows how things have declined:

There on the kerb outside Lonergan's, Lilia braced her shoulders as though facing reality – looking up then down the Clonmore straight wide main street at the alternately dun and painted houses, cars parked askew, straying ass-carts and fallen bicycles. Dung baked on the pavements since yesterday morning's fair; shop after shop had insanely similar doorways, strung with boots and kettles and stacked with calicoes – in eternal windows goods faded out. Many and sour were the pubs. Over-exposed, the town was shadeless – never a tree, never an awning. Ice cream on sale, but never a café. Clonmore not only provided no place to be, it provided no reason *to* be, at all.

Montefort (based on a deserted farmhouse near Bowen's Court but with much of the atmosphere of Bowen's Court itself)[14] has, like a house in a Somerville and Ross novel, 'the air of having gone down'. The obelisk was built by a typical Anglo-Irish landlord:

'Married the cook ... went queer in the head from drinking and thinking about himself, left no children – anyway, no legits. So this place went to his first cousin.'

Now it is isolated ('no calls to the telephone for there was not a telephone, no vans delivering, seldom a passer-by, no neighbours to speak of') and decrepit:

The green of the ivy over the window-bars and the persisting humidity of the stone-flagged floors made the kitchen look cool without being so. This was the room in Montefort which had changed least: routine abode in its air like an old spell. Generations of odours of baking and basting, stewing and skimming had been absorbed into the lime-washed walls, leaving wood ash, raked cinders, tea leaves, wrung-out cloths and lamp oil freshly predominant. The massive table, on which jigs had been danced at the harvest homes, was probably stronger than, now, the frame of the house ... The great and ravenous range, of which no one now knew how to quell the roaring, was built back into a blackened cave of its own – on its top, a perpetual kettle sent out a havering thread of steam, tea stewed in a pot all day, and the lid heaved, sank on one or another of the jostling pots, saucepans and cauldrons. Mush for the chickens, if nothing else, was never not in the course of cooking ... The sink's one tap connected with a rain-water tank which had run dry – since then, a donkey cart with a barrel rattled its way daily down to the river pool ... On the dresser, from one of the hooks for cups, hung a still handsome calendar for the year before; and shreds of another, previous to that, remained tacked to the shutter over the sink. These, with the disregarded dawdling and often stopping of the cheap scarlet clock wedged in somewhere between the bowls and dishes, spoke of the almost total irrelevance of Time, in the abstract, to this ceaseless kitchen.

This is a marvellously realised room, but also an exasperating piece of writing. 'Mush for the chickens was never not in the course of cooking' is a grotesquely, self-parodic mannerism. The paragraph is full of similar stylistic quirks: obtrusive commas, coy adjectives like the 'perpetual' kettle and the 'ceaseless' kitchen, inversions, qualifications, and double negatives. Striving for a heightened poetical mood the novel relies heavily on these familiar tricks: 'All round Montefort there was going forward an entering back again into possession'; 'Decay . . . was apparent – out it stood! Nothing now against it maintained the place.'

The manner blurs events and relationships. Fred's absorption with Jane, Antonia's brutal treatment of Lilia, Jane's attraction to Vesta Latterly, are hazily rendered, especially if compared with Thomas and Anna Quayne's marriage, or Leopold's encounter with Mme Fisher. The characterisation of Jane is soft and conventional: 'Her brows were wide, her eyes an unshadowed blue, her mouth more inclined to smile than in any other way to say very much – it was a face perfectly ready to be a woman's, but not yet so, even in its transcendancy this morning.' Maud, venomously Protestant and covered in boils, a gruesome embodiment of 'moral force', is an exception. But In her obsession with Big Ben, she also has to work as a convenient reminder of 'the absolute and fatal' stroke of time.

The novel's fascination with time and memory is its most interesting (and characteristic) quality. Jane resists 'the time she was required to live in', but dislikes the past's 'queeringness': 'this continuous tedious business of received grievances, not-to-be-settled old scores'. This is set ironically against the older generation's inability to free itself from the dead. The character most like the narrator, Antonia, poignantly contemplates the effect of the wars on our response to death, and the post-war sense of unreality. This central passage explains why *A World of Love* has to be so shadowy and 'uncertain':

Life works to dispossess the dead, to dislodge and oust them. Their places fill themselves up; later people come in; all the room is wanted . . . Their being left behind in their own time caused estrangement between them and us, who must live in ours.

But the recognition of death may remain uncertain, and while that is so nothing is signed and sealed. Our sense of finality is less hard-and-fast; two wars have raised their query to it. Something has challenged the law of nature: it is hard, for instance, to see a young death in battle as in any way the fruition of a destiny, hard not to sense the continuation of the apparently cut-off life, hard not to ask, but *was* dissolution possible so abruptly, unmeaningly and soon? . . . These years she went on living belonged to him, his lease upon them not having run out yet. The living were living in his lifetime . . . They were incomplete.

Almost ten years elapsed before the next novel. The only intervening work, written at a very low point in Bowen's life, was *A Time in Rome* (1960), too personal to be a successful guide book, too impressionistic for a historical study. But it does make some Bowenish remarks about time and memory, which point towards her last novels:

It is in nature (at least in mine) to make for the concrete and particular, to 'choose' a time and reconstitute, if one can, one or another of its moments . . . In Rome I wondered how to break down the barrier between myself and happenings outside *my* memory. I was looking for splinters of actuality in a shifting mass of experience other than my own. Time is one kind of space; it creates distance. My chafing geographical confusion was in a way a symptom of inner trouble – my mind could not be called a blank, for it tingled with avidity and anxieties: I was feeling the giddiness of unfocused vision. There came no help from reason, so I was passive . . . To talk of 'entering' the past is nonsense, but one can be entered by it, to a degree.[15]

The idea of being passively entered into by the past is derived from Proust, who has always interested her. She quotes him at the start of *The Last September*, and in 'The Mulberry Tree', her excellent 1934 essay about her English school in Kent, Downe House, which partly inspired the school in *The Little Girls*: 'Memory is, as Proust has it, so oblique and selective that no doubt I see my schooldays through a subjective haze.'[16] Eva Trout mentions Proust's idea of the overlap between imagination and memory. In Bowen's last collection, *Pictures and Conversations*, there is a long, careful and penetrating essay on Proust's novelist character, Bergotte. *The Little Girls* is the most 'Proustian' of her novels. It describes an involuntary recall of the past, and the break-down set in motion by that recall. The novel not only contains a Proustian experience, it produced one. When she began her draft of an autobiography in the 1970s she said that she had 'completely forgotten' one of her schoolgirl experiences 'till it was returned to me by *The Little Girls*'.[17]

So *The Little Girls* (1964) re-works a central preoccupation, the uncontrollable activity of memory and the disabling legacy of the past. As she has done before, she moves into the past in the middle section of the novel. This section describes schooldays at 'St Agatha's, Southstone'. It echoes the factual account of her schools in 'The Mulberry Tree', and her many characterisations of schoolgirls, like Theodora Hirdman in *Friends and Relations*, or Pauline and her friend Dorothea in *To the North*, or the girl haunted by 'the Crampton Park School Tragedy' in 'The Apple Tree'. She says in 'Pictures and Conversations' that 'St Agatha's is imaginary, in that it has no physical origin.'[18] But she admits that it runs together features from her three English schools: Lindum House, her Folkestone day-school; Harpenden Hall, a Hertfordshire boarding school (where, as one of a series of 'crazes', 'a smallish biscuit tin, sealed, containing some cryptic writings and accompanied by two or three broken knick-knacks, was immured in the hollow base of a rough stone wall dividing the kitchen garden'),[19] and Downe House, her wartime Kentish boarding school, where the girls cultivated 'foibles and mannerisms' in the interests of social success, and 'personality came out in patches, like damp through a wall'.[20]

On either side of the novel's flashback to the three girfriends at school in 1914, are two parts set in the 1960s. 'Dinah Delacroix' is a well-preserved, eccentric widow living in a Somerset villa, its garden lush with flowers and vegetables, in the company of her vain, temperamental, nosy house-boy, Francis (a faint reworking of Eddie) who waits (and spies) on Dinah while deciding what to do with his future, and her loyal simple old friend Frank Wilkins, (reminiscent of Major Brutt – and of Alan Cameron). The novel opens with Dinah embarked on her latest 'craze': burying evidence for posterity in a cave. 'Clues to reconstruct *us* from. Expressive objects. What really expresses people? The things, I'm sure, that they have obsessions about . . .' As she and Frank haphazardly go about this whimsical task, a neighbour's question ('Who's going to seal it up?') and the sight of a crooked swing in the garden suddenly ignite Dinah's memory:

> 'I've been having the most extraordinary sensation! Yes, and I still am, it's still going on! Because, to remember something all in a flash, so competely that it's not "then" but "now", surely *is* a sensation, isn't it? I do know it's far, far more than a mere memory! One's right back into it again, right in the middle . . . They say – don't they? – one never is doing anything for the first time.'

Fifty or so years before, she and two other 'little girls' – 'Dicey', 'Mumbo', and 'Sheikie' – also buried evidence for posterity in a coffer in the school garden. Ignoring Frank's sensible warning ('Can't you see, they're not there any more!') Dinah is fired with the desire to summon her two friends and to dig up the treasure: 'We are posterity, now.' Her obsession sets in motion a comedy of reappearances and recognitions. 'Sheikie', 'Southstone's wonder, the child exhibition dancer' has become the respectable Mrs Sheila Artworth, wife of a Southstone estate agent, once a much-bullied little boy whom Dinah last remembers as stuck inside a drainpipe at a picnic. 'Mumbo', the clumsy, clever child of an unhappy marriage, is now Clare Burkin-Jones, owner of

'MOPSIE PYE chain of speciality giftshops', operating 'throughout the better-class London suburbs and outward into the Home Counties'.

The first part, in which 'Dicey' brings about the reunion, is farcical, full of little fragmentary surprises and revelations, ending with 'Sheikie's' news that St Agatha's no longer exists: it was bombed in the Second World War. The flashback of the second part to 1914 has a softening, mellowing effect on the novel. The suppressed romantic feeling between Dicey's beautiful, unworldly mother (whose husband killed himself before Dicey was born) and Mumbo's father, the sad, handsome Major, is tenderly touched upon, and the school-girl comedy (poetry recitations, swimming lessons, the visit of a suffragette aunt, shopping for a chain to go round the coffer in Southstone's picturesque old High Street, the end-of-term picnic) is nostalgically idealised. It's like the pre-war South Coast scenes in 'Ivy Gripped the Steps', where Mrs Nicholson's relationship with the Admiral, and her refusal to believe in the coming war, anticipate this part of *The Little Girls*:

> Summer evening concerts began in the Pier Pavilion, which like a lit-up musical box admired itself in the glass of the darkening mauve sea; above, the chains of lamps along the Promenade etherealized strollers in evening dress, from the big hotels, bright-ghostly baskets of pink geraniums and the fretwork balconies they were slung from.

The partings on the beach at the picnic between Dicey's mother and the Major, and between Dicey and Mumbo, just before the outbreak of war, are poignantly done. This, and the chilling account of the Major's home life (his wife, another Mrs Kelway, 'successfully cauterized her loved ones'), have the haunting quality of a good short story. Bowen's potent memories of her childhood in England with her mother are once more put to good use.

The jerky, comical tone associated with the present day is resumed in the third part, for the farcical night-time scene in which the three women dig up the coffer from what is now the back garden of a typical Bowenesque villa, 'Blue Grotto'.

The coffer is empty. After this discovery, Dinah breaks down; 'Nothing's real any more.' The last part of the book, in which Sheila and Clare and Frank and Dinah's grown-up sons, (with little girls of their own) look after the invalid, becomes increasingly sombre. The unhappiness of the two other women is revealed: Sheila, her dancing come to nothing, had, before her marriage, a clandestine affair with a sick man whom she left on his deathbed. Clare, whose marriage was 'a mess', has never quite recovered from her childhood passion for Dinah's mother – but will not answer the question, 'Are you a Lesbian?' Behind their unhappy stories lies the fate of the romantic, undeclared lovers of the last generation: Clare's father fell at Mons, Dinah's mother died in the outbreak of Spanish flu at the end of the war. Until now, Dinah is the only person in the novel who has avoided pain. The others accuse her of cheating:

'All your life, I should think, you have run for cover. "There's Mother!" "Here's my nice white gate!" Some of us have no cover, nothing to run to. Some of us more than *think* we feel.

Dinah is made to pay for her self-protective infantilism by the terrible feeling of nullity which now comes over her. In the last part of the book she becomes a kind of visionary commentator on the hollowness of contemporary life:

'There's a tremendous market for prefabricated feelings . . . And I'll tell you one great centre of the prefabricated feeling racket, and that is, anything to do with anything between two people: love, or even sex . . . So many of these fanciful ways people have of keeping themselves going, at such endless expense of time and money, seem not only unnecessary but dated.'

Her breakdown, an interesting study of alienation, reveals Bowen's own current unease as a novelist. Dinah raises the question of the value of art: if the past has gone, any attempt to recapture it, like her own pursuit of the buried coffer, must be a lie. A bad water-colour of the old Southstone High Street, which has itself long since disappeared, provokes this outburst:

'Something has given the man the slip, so in place of what's given him the slip he's put something else in . . . It might be better to have no picture of places which are gone. Let them go completely.'

The remark undermines the very act of writing this novel about memory. As Clare says to Dinah while she is exposing the 'unnecessary' and 'prefabricated' feelings of the modern world: 'You'd put more than half the world out of business, including novelists.'

The Little Girls is inspired by Proust's idea of the past returning through the action of involuntary memory, working through association. And the novel is Proustian in other ways too. Bowen tries for Marcel's sense in *À la Recherche* that he lives 'surrounded by symbols'[21] by introducing some rather obvious symbolic props: a butterknife with a gnarled thumb-shaped handle bought by Dinah from 'MOPSIE PYE'; the objects placed in the original coffer, which include a revolver (to be used more melodramatically in *Eva Trout*); three grotesque masks made by a local craftwoman; and the china objects which used to clutter Dinah's mother's cottage and which are, for Clare, 'a fragile representation of a world of honour, which is to say unfailingness'.

The failure of that world reflects Proust's saying that 'the true paradises are the paradises that we have lost'.[22] The novel also pursues Proust's interest in what goes on in the mind in sleep, and in the self-forgetfulness necessary for refinding oneself. And the abortive re-encounters between the three women – particularly between 'Dicey' and 'Mumbo' – follow the pattern of disenchanting confrontations in Proust's novel, one of which Bowen describes in her essay on Bergotte: 'A relationship . . . anticlimactic, patchy, uninspirational – a relationship haunted by what it should have been.'[23]

But, as she points out, 'a magnified Bergotte exists on another plane'.[24] The disappointments of social intercourse, the inevitable failure of love (since we love only what we don't possess or have lost) are redeemed, in *À La Recherche*, by what Bowen describes as 'the notion of purgation, of self-redemption, of brought-back virtue being possible for the artist by means of art'.[25] But this concept of redemption through art – the point of Proust's novel – isn't there in *The Little Girls*. In Bowen's novel, art is seen as a lessening of experience rather than its justification: there is no escape from disappointment and dispossession. Her negation of Proust's idea is reflected in the difference of style: *The Little Girls* is not at all Proustian in its manner. Roger Shattuck says of Proust: 'As his novel tenaciously aims at assimilating the whole meaning of life, so each sentence strives to digest its whole subject.'[26] Exactly the opposite effect is produced by the style of *The Little Girls*. The 'whole meaning of life' is held at arm's length. Such 'meaning' as there is appears in fragmentary, diffused form, and is presented without depth or resonance. The novel describes an unlikely, whimsical situation, and dresses it up with awkward attempts at comedy, uneasy ventures into symbolism, and contrived literary allusions (mostly to *Macbeth*, in order that the three 'revenants' should seem like the three witches – 'Sheikie' even had a sixth toe at birth). The whole effect is dubious and disconcerting.

Bowen has decided, now, to give up the controlled, elaborate commentary and the sharp, inward presentation of character of her earlier novels. *The Little Girls* has, from the start, a provisional, indeterminate air. A man and a woman are carrying objects into a space in the ground. Everything is described uncertainly, conditionally:

> This was, if anything, on the large and deep side . . . Across the uneven rock floor, facing the steps, was either a shallow cave or a deep recess – or, possibly, unadorned grotto? . . . A woman, intent on what she was doing to the point of a trance, could be seen in back-view . . . She may not have heard the man, who was wearing espadrilles – she did not, at any rate, look round.

The dialogue these two embark on is brusque, jerky, and flatly colloquial: 'Oh, bother you,' she grumbled, 'do put your *specs* on!' – and the commentary on it is casually banal: 'This was Frank's cue for another repeat-remark.' Though a few familiar baroque mannerisms linger on ('To pot it would all be going, before long') the first chapter establishes a deliberately diminished, vapid level of prose. Although the flashback lets in a more lyrical, alluring manner ('From across the shrinking watery miles came an expiring sigh – not like the sound of wind, a sigh in itself'), all three sections are awkwardly written. An insecure search for a new method is going on. There is the naming of people by their activities, as in 'said the willing learner', or 'the maker-free then threw open the window' or 'sang out the homecomer'. There's the equivocal commentary, as in 'Yet she faltered, if for less than an instant, or just barely – how rarely? – overrode a misgiving.' And there's the thin, banal dialogue:

> 'I wondered whether you'd telephone.'
> 'Well, I didn't.'
> 'No. – Last night, when *I* rang up, you sounded so cross.'
> 'You made me jump, suddenly coming through like that.'
> 'That's the worst of telephones. What were you doing?'
> 'Well, I was in my flat.'
> 'Of course you were, else you couldn't have answered. What were you doing?'
> 'Thinking about you,' said Clare crossly.

These late techniques are not merely failures of assurance – though they partly read like that. They suggest that Bowen was now becoming increasingly concerned with the idea of a breakdown in language. That her highly charged, controlled style should have been reduced to these techniques has to do with more than personal reasons – uncertainty, dissatisfaction with out-dated formulae. More challengingly, the last two novels try to imagine a future without any verbal 'style' at all. When the three schoolgirls bury their most precious possessions in the coffer with a proclamation written in Mumbo's invented 'Unknown Language', they ask each other whether it matters that posterity won't understand them: 'And it may all be the same, by then? They may have no language.'

A future without language has become the present, in Bowen's last novel, *Eva Trout* (1968), an intriguing but bizarre conclusion to her work. The heroine, who is twenty-four at the start of the novel, is a recognisable 'displaced person'. She recalls Annabelle in 'The Last Night in the Old Home' ('Inside the big, bustling form of a woman she was a girl of ten')[27] or Valeria in 'Her Table Spread', 'abnormal – at twenty-five, of statuesque development, still detained in childhood'.[28] Like those unmanageable innocents, Eva Trout, an orphaned heiress, has peculiar habits. She stammers, is incapable of weeping, cannot behave with normal indifference or self-protectiveness, takes obsessional delight in mechanical objects (her car, her audio-visual machines), is large and ungainly, and has 'a passion for the fictitious for its own sake'. Her distraction goes with 'the patient, abiding encircling will of a monster, a will set on the idea of belonging and of being loved'. 'I remain gone. Where am I? I do not know – I was cast out from where I believed I was,' Eva complains. Her need to compensate for these feelings makes her dangerous: 'You plunge people's ideas into deep confusion . . .' she is told. 'You roll round like some blind indestructible planet.'

Though she first appears in rural, homely circumstances – driving the vicar's wife and children in her Jaguar to look at a castle which used to be her school – it becomes apparent that she is out of touch with reality and attracts violence. Her family history is squalid and dramatic. Her father was a rich, popular businessman who 'deviated', running off with the 'wicked' 'Constantine Ormeau'. (This is Bowen's first explicitly homosexual character, but he has all the chilly fastidiousness of St Quentin in *The Death of the Heart*.) Her mother was killed in a plane crash with her lover, just after Eva's birth. Twenty-three years later, her father committed suicide. Eva, left on Constantine's hands, considers that he has murdered both her parents.

Her oddness is mainly attributed to this macabre history, but also to her disjointed education. For a time she attended the dubious experimental school at the castle (a 'Bavarian fantasy' on the Welsh border) bought by her father as a means of getting rid of Constantine's other friend, Kenneth, whose authority over the school's rich little delinquents (wittily sketched) came to an abrupt end. At this school Eva has a passion for a wraith-like child called Elsinore. After being dumped at various temporary international homes, Eva asked to go to an 'ordinary' girls' school, where she fell in love with the brilliant young English teacher, Iseult Smith. At the start of the novel Eva is living with Iseult and her husband Eric Arble, whose shaky marriage, which has involved the end of her career and the compromise of his (from fruit farming to a garage) is weakening under Eva's destructive presence.

The random history of Eva's temporary homes and thwarted affections emerges patchily, not through Eva's thoughts but through information provided by other characters, and through an equivocal, obscuring narrative. The fragmentary effect is helped by a plot which jumps with deliberate waywardness through a series of unlikely journeys and settings: the novel's sub-title is 'Changing Scenes'.

Feeling betrayed by Iseult, Eva moves away from the Arbles and the neighbouring vicarage to a huge, gloomy, baroque villa ('Cathay') on the South Coast at Broadstairs. (This is Bowen's last return to her Kentish childhood scenes.) Eric visits her, and Eva leads Iseult to suspect them of an affair. Then Eva suddenly disappears to America (where she accidentally encounters Elsinore). Her journey there is recorded in the letter of a comical American professor who becomes infatuated with her on the plane, but who never reappears. Eight years later she returns to England with an adopted eight-year-old deaf mute, Jeremy, to find that the Arbles have separated, one of the vicarage daughters, Louise, has died, Constantine is as bland and shady as ever, and the vicar's son Henry has grown up into an elegant Cambridge undergraduate, who becomes the last of Eva's grand, impractical passions. Her time is erratically divided between stays in London hotels, outings to Cambridge and the castle with Henry, and a journey to France in search of a cure for Jeremy, whom she leaves with the Bonnards, two married 'environmentalist' doctors at Fontainebleau.

The preposterously haphazard plot culminates in a farcical melodrama on Victoria Station. Eva and Henry are embarking on a mock wedding journey (a scene staged, at her request, in payment for all her 'longing in vain' for him), witnessed by all the novel's protagonists, when Jeremy comes running up with a revolver he's found in Eva's luggage (which in fact – it's a clumsy piece of plotting – belongs to the Arbles) and shoots his 'mother' dead. The violent ending has been anticipated not only by Eva's family history but also by a succession of drastic events: Louise's death; the abduction of Jeremy in London from a sinister sculptress who is supposed to be minding him, by a 'mystery' woman who turns out to be Iseult; a reckless car drive with Henry (reminiscent of the 'last ride together' in *To the North*) and Jeremy's fits of temper.

The methods of this novel are new, but the themes are familiar, especially the havoc wreaked by innocence. Eva's (and Jeremy's) destructive influence is a grotesque version of the violent extremism of Emmeline or Portia, desperately intent on having their affections returned, as dangerous to the adult world as it is to them. The worldly corrupters are recurrent characters too, though Bowen is more outspoken in these last two novels about her characters' sexuality. In the usual conflict between the innocent girl and the worldly woman, there is now an explicit suggestion of a potential or a thwarted love affair. Though Bowen deals very unsympathetically with homosexuals in *Eva Trout*, there's a clear expression of understanding for lesbian feelings in the last two novels.

The women's unrealistic names suggest their roles: Eva, 'cast out from where I believed I was' (the first section is called 'Genesis'); Iseult the temptress, who 'betrayed' Eva's hopes, 'having led them on'. As well as being victim and seductress, however, the two women share the same malaise. Eva, who cannot weep and would prefer not to be able to speak ('What is the object? What is the good?') asks the question: 'What becomes of anyone's nature?' The more articulate, literary Iseult speaks of her deadened feelings ('I've undergone an emotional hysterotomy') and describes life as an 'anti-Novel': no importance, no sensation, attaches to events. She has been trying to write a novel which was 'still-born', and she arranges to meet Eva in Dickens's house at Broadstairs, a scene which provides an excuse for Iseult to meditate enviously on his rich literature of 'longing'. The theme of dispossession, particularly in contrast with the Victorians, continues to the last.

But the novel's haphazard plot and sketchy relationships make it startlingly different from Bowen's other work. There are patchy attempts at depth of character, like Henry's sardonic combativeness with his father, or Iseult's standing up to Constantine. But, clearly, this isn't what interests Bowen now. *Eva Trout* presents itself as a fairy tale, with Eva as its spellbound princess. Its settings (the castle, 'Cathay'), its names (Eva, Iseult), and its arrangement of characters, all suggest this, quite apart from Eva's propensity for strange journeys, sudden appearances and fantastical inventions. It is the most schematic, as well as being the most disorganised, of her novels. The conflict between good and evil angels is no longer suppressed beneath a realistic narrative. The novel is full of guardians. At the start there's a contest of wills over Eva between Iseult and Constantine. Towards the end there's a struggle for authority over Jeremy between Eva, Iseult, the sinister sculptress, and the wise Bonnards. There are even two men of God, Henry's father, stern but incapacitated by hay fever, and Constantine's latest friend, a suspect Anglican East End priest who 'specialized in iniquity'.

Of all these figures of authority, the French doctors, who reject 'the horrible doctrine of Predestination' and speak wisely for happiness ('a matter of genius') and for love ('We are at its mercy, but not altogether') are the most convincing. But their belief in choice and self-improvement in the end can't affect the fated outcome of the relationship between Eva and Jeremy. This final act is presumably meant to be, to an extent, triumphant. Jeremy, the only character with the true authority of pure innocence, liberates Eva through his violent act from the world to which she is so ill-adapted. This point is obscured, but what comes over strong and clear is the wordless relationship between Eva and Jeremy.

Eva's alienation is a form of instability. Her inability to articulate, her fantasies, her dislocated sense of her own past ('Time, inside Eva's mind, lay about like various pieces of a fragmented picture') handicap her to the point of insanity. But the deaf-mute child, whose physical condition provides an image of Eva's alienation, seems somehow to compensate for her abnormality, to make her seem normal. Like Eva, Jeremy doesn't want to speak. But unlike her, he feels no lack: 'He would like to stay happy the way he is.' Jeremy's inward contentment provides a queer, mirror-image of Eva's desolation.

> The effect was not so much of more intelligence as of a somehow unearthly perspicacity. The boy, handicapped, one was at pains to remember, imposed on others a sense that *they* were, that it was *they* who were lacking in some faculty.

When Jeremy and Eva are alone together in America they inhabit an 'Eden' which is entirely innocent of words. Her attempts to have him cured are a betrayal of that state (like Iseult's seduction of Eva through education). Jeremy's shooting of Eva may be an involuntary revenge for her betrayal of their intimacy in 'the inaudible years':

> His and her cinematographic existence, with no sound-track, in successive American cities made still more similar by their continuous manner of being in them, had had a sufficiency which was perfect. Sublimated monotony had cocooned the two of them, making them as near as twins in a womb. Their repetitive doings became rites ... They had lorded it in a visual universe. They came to distinguish little between what went on inside and what went on outside the diurnal movies, or what was or was not contained in the television flickering them to sleep. From large or small screens, illusion overspilled on to all beheld. Society revolved at a distance from them like a ferris wheel dangling buckets of people. They were their own. Wasted, civilization extended round them as might acres of cannibalized cars. Only they moved. They were within a story to which they imparted the only sense.

After these references to the cinema, the end of the novel is made to seem like a scene in a film, with Jeremy as the 'child star'. This – not fiction – is going to be the art form of a posterity without language. As long as Jeremy and Eva are undivided, they have found the perfect means of entering the still innocent, still inheritable, speechless future. So it's no accident that this is the only one of her novels to be set partly in America, where the conditions of the future, such as the ascendancy of film and television over the novel, are already in place. The prospect of an entirely 'visual universe' is not offered as entirely consolatory. But our present conditions, the novel suggests, can no longer be mastered or even registered by our language:

> '*Feel*? – I refuse to; that would be the last straw! There's too much of everything, yet nothing. Is it the world, or what? Everything's hanging over one. The expectations one's bound to disappoint. The dread of misfiring. The knowing there's something one can't stave off. The Bomb is the least. Look what's got to happen to us if we do live, look at the results! Living is brutalizing: just look at everybody!'

This last fiction, in its uneasy struggle with its own language and structure, and in its distressing account of alienation, describes an almost unbearable present, with which the traditional novel of order and feeling can no longer deal.

9

A FORM OF EXPERIENCE

> A novel which survives . . . does not stand still. It accumulates
> round itself the understanding of all these persons who bring
> to it something of their own. It acquires associations, it
> becomes a form of experience in itself.

EVA TROUT WAS not Bowen's last work. *Pictures and
Conversations*, published posthumously in 1975, two years
after her death, included a substantial draft of a 'writer's
autobiography', an essay on Proust's character 'Bergotte', a
script of a Nativity Play which had been performed in the
Protestant Cathedral in Londonderry in 1970, the first
chapter of a novel called 'The Move-In', and 'Notes on
Writing a Novel', which had originally appeared in *Orion* in
1945. It's an attractive conclusion to her non-fictional work,
of which there was a good deal. There were two other
collections of non-fiction, *Collected Impressions* (1950) and
Afterthought (1962), and many interesting uncollected
pieces.[1] Bowen wrote essays, reviews and introductions all
through her writing life, and her work as a critic reflects back
on what she was doing in her fiction.

Some of the uncollected journalism was routine. Bowen
contributed to magazines as diverse as the *Listener* and
Vogue, the *New Statesman* and *Mademoiselle*, the *New York
Times Book Review* and *House and Garden*, with easy-going
facility. She was happy to write pieces like 'For the Feminine
Shopper',[2] 'How to be Yourself, But Not Eccentric',[3] or 'The
Teakettle'.[4] She could be relied on to answer questionnaires

about the writer's place in society and how much he needed
to live on ('I should like to have £3,500 a year net', she wrote
in 1946),[5] or about her own writing habits: 'I work up to a
table, and straight on to a typewriter . . . Conversation,
which I enjoy writing, always goes fairly fast.'[6] She took part
in wartime radio discussions on subjects like 'Do women
think like men?' and 'Do conventions matter?' – in which she
said that women's special gifts were 'flexibility, quickness in
the uptake, sensitiveness and a sympathetic attitude towards
the other person's point of view',[7] and that the destruction of
conventions would lead to 'an appalling waste of social
energy'.[8]

She turned her hand to theatre criticism, too, including a
stint from 1937 to 1938 as theatre critic for Graham Greene's
short-lived weekly, *Night and Day*.[9] Her 1970 nativity play is
a gently contemplative and atmospheric piece. *Castle Anna*,
the play she wrote with John Parry, seems to have been an
uncomfortable cross between Ibsen and Somerville and Ross.
It was performed at the Lyric Hammersmith in 1948, but
never published.

But although she left no major critical work, a coherent
pattern of literary attitudes and an impressive sense of a
writer who knew what she was doing comes out of her essays,
prefaces and reviews. *Bowen's Court*, *Seven Winters*, 'The
Big House' and 'The Mulberry Tree' show her gift for
autobiography and social history. And the autobiographical
pieces always illuminate the fiction. Bowen is very interested
in the thin dividing line between what one remembers and
what one invents.

> Almost no experience, however much simplified by the
> distance of time, is to be vouched for as being wholly my own
> – did I live through that, or was I told that it happened, or did
> I read it?[10]

A novelist writing an autobiography will, she says, inevitably
touch things up or, virtually, 'invent' himself. 'The novelist
arrives at seeing himself by seeing himself as a character in
one more novel.'[11] Having lived perhaps more consciously

than most, having shaped his experiences even before he makes use of them, 'he can write of himself with a cold familiarity'.[12] (Or 'she', but like all writers of her time, Bowen always uses 'he'.)

That 'cold familiarity' — as of the spy in the camp, the secret onlooker — is the hallmark of all her writing. It comes through strongly in the way she remembers herself, as in the amused schoolgirl recollections of 'The Mulberry Tree'. Her childhood reminiscences are bound up with her sense of herself as a novelist. This is particularly true, as for many writers, when she looks back on her early reading. Bowen warns us against any sentimental delusions that we can read our way back into childhood: 'It is not only our fate but our business to lose innocence, and once we have lost that it is futile to attempt a picnic in Eden.' Yet her own fictions turn out to be inextricably linked to her imaginative needs as a child:

> The expectation, the search, was geographic. I was and I am still on the look out for places where something happened . . . My identity, so far as I can pin it down at all, resides among these implacable likes or dislikes, these subjections to magnetism spaced out between ever-widening lacunae of indifference. I feel certain that if I *could* read my way back, analytically, through the books of my childhood, the clues to everything could be found.[13]

There's a witty example of 'reading back' in the radio talk she gave on Rider Haggard's *She*, first read when she was twelve. Like Graham Greene's account of his childhood fascination for Marjorie Bowen's *The Viper of Milan*[14] ('From that moment I began to write') or V. S. Naipaul's recall of the first taste of Conrad,[15] this talk records a turning-point in the child's imaginative life (which she made good use of in the story 'Mysterious Kôr'). She looks back amusedly at herself as a bored twelve-year-old longing for primary colours, for an undiscovered country, for 'an accession to full power'. *She* answered to the need. 'The narrator's style, with its blend of the jocular and the blood-curdling was to have on me the effect of well-sugared cocoa laced with some raw and subtle intoxicant.' It was the moonblanched ruined city in Rider Haggard's novel which affected her most, as she already had a feeling for ruins from her Irish scenery. *She* forever conditioned her sense of London:

> I saw Kôr before I saw London: I was a provincial child. Inevitably, the Thames Embankment was a disappointment, being far, far less wide than Horace Holly had led me to expect. I was inclined to see London as Kôr with the roofs still on. The idea that life in any capital city must be ephemeral, and with a doom ahead, remained with me – a curious obsession for an Edwardian child.

More profoundly, *She* answered to an idea she already had as a child of 'obstination'.

> Want one thing hard enough, long enough, and it must come your way. This did strike deep: it came up like reinforcement, because in my day, my childhood, all polite education was against the will – which was something to be subdued, or put out of sight as though it did not exist.[16]

Bowen doesn't say so here, but this conflict was to be the subject of her fictions. *She* gave her a lead, and it also taught her about the power of style: 'Writing – that creaking, pedantic, obtrusive, arch, prudish, opaque overworded *writing* – what it could do!'

In the autobiographical sketch, 'Pictures and Conversations', she explores the link between her childhood and her writing. She describes the effect of the transition from Ireland to England, her father's illness, the Kentish villas (so 'heady' a contrast to severe Irish Georgian) where she lived with her mother, the English rectory where, like Eva Trout, she felt ill at ease with a specimen of 'genuine idyllic family life', and the 'voluptuous' sense of history which England gave her. Her childish characteristics – 'over-impatience, self-importance', typically Anglo-Irish 'belligerence' – and the uprooted circumstances of her early life are presented as clues to the work:

Possibly, it was England made me a novelist. At an early though conscious age, I was transplanted. I arrived, young, into a different mythology – in fact, into one totally alien to that of my forefathers . . . From now on there was to be (as for any immigrant) a cleft between my heredity and my environment – the former remaining, in my case, the more powerful. Submerged, the mythology of this 'other' land could be felt at work in the ways, manners and views of its people, round me: those, because I disliked being at a disadvantage, it became necessary to probe. It cannot be said that a child of seven was analytic; more, with a blend of characteristic guile and uncharacteristic patience I took note – which, though I had at that time no thought of my future art, is, after all, one of the main activities of the novelist.[17]

This is what explains her voluptuous sense of place, her interest in the spy or note-taking child, her precise eye for manners. She always said that early landscapes are an ineradicable part of the writer's terrain: 'Impressions and feelings formed there and then underly language, dictate choices of imagery.'[18] And 'Pictures and Conversations' quickly turns from being an autobiography into a critique of her own art: 'If anybody *must* write a book about Elizabeth Bowen, why should not Elizabeth Bowen?' She puts herself in context with 'cold familiarity', accounting for the influence of 'Anglo-Irish peculiarities', laying most weight on the visual effect of places ('Am I not manifestly a writer for whom places loom large?'),[19] and pointing out that her imagination thrives on the 'unfamiliar', on changes and dislocations. Like her, her characters are travellers, 'sensationalists'.

'Pictures and Conversations' includes a sustained analysis of two passages from *The House in Paris*, one (Mme Fisher's bedroom) to display her employment of 'staticness: the all-out of the dead weight', the other (the ship drawing in to Cobh harbour) to show the creation of 'the illusion of movement'. Like her accounts of her behaviour as a child, these critical passages are formidably self-aware:

Mme Fisher's hand does *not* stir on the sheet – though it could have. The one thing in action here is the incense cone consuming itself by its slow burning (and *it* is a sickness symbol). The room, felt by the child as 'so full and still', is a case not of mere immobility but of immobilisation. In a terrible way, it is a *bois dormant*. What has brought this about? Mme Fisher: on the bed in the centre.[20]

The 'cold familiarity' with which Bowen analyses her own techniques here is applied to a disturbing and sensational passage of writing. That's a typical mixture. In her temperament, severe, satirical self-awareness is crossed with a 'farouche', impulsive romanticism. In the novels' plots, the knowing world of manners and conventions constricts the unworldly, fanatical innocents. And in the writing, self-conscious artistry controls the melodramatic, haunting or grotesque subject. The books on Ireland, *Bowen's Court* and *The Shelbourne*, have another version of this conflict in their admiration for good behaviour, their nostalgia for mannered societies (in which 'one might be free to *be*, but not bound to exhibit, oneself')[21] and yet their sympathy for the hubris and obsession which gave birth to the Big House. And the same pattern is found in her belief that the short story is more liberated than the novel – a 'free zone' – yet requires even more discipline.

Her retrospective prefaces to her short stories and to *The Last September* all show this pull between dispassion and involvement.[22] She's fond of her early work ('the *Encounters* stories have build, style, and occasional felicities of expression which I must say I like')[23] but coolly aware of its faults: the 'blend of precocity and naivety', the 'harshness' of the characters in *Encounters*, the 'odious superiority' and 'prettiness' of *Ann Lee's*. As usual she gives a clear account of her states of mind at the time: *Encounters* was related to her youthful attempts to become a poet or a painter, *Ann Lee's* was dogged by the sense that she ought to be writing a novel.[24] All the prefaces authoritatively describe the nature and function of the short story.

Her critical firmness, rational and precise, is always there in the longer theoretical pieces about fiction and the fiction-writer. Even when she is really talking about her own methods, these pieces are of general interest, like the exchange of letters with Graham Greene and V. S. Pritchett, *Why Do I Write?* (1948). Here, she describes her own motives for writing – 'the need to work off, out of the system, the sense of being solitary and farouche' – but she is not being merely personal. Like Pritchett, who believes that 'the obligation of the state towards writers ... is to let them alone', and like Greene, who believes that the writer has an imperative duty to be 'disloyal', Bowen feels that the artist needs to be in some sort of conflict with the State:

> I am convinced, too, that the more outwardly regulated, planned, organised, and equitable the world becomes, the stronger will be the unholy (possibly) domination of the artist ... the writer ... will take on the status of a Resistance leader.

This is like her images of the novelist as spy, of wartime writing as 'resistance writing'. The writer should keep off platforms, and should not be asked to have any relation to the community other than his writing: 'My books *are* my relation to society.'[25] But then there's the usual conflict between individualism and discipline. She ends by saying that the writer must be seen to behave with a respectable amount of 'demeanour', and that he is to be praised for 'not contributing to anarchy'. These ideas are developed in an article called 'The Writer's Peculiar World' (renamed 'Disloyalties' in *Afterthought*), where she pursues Graham Greene's belief in 'the danger to the writer of anything which may exercise a restrictive and ultimately a blinding hold'. She agrees with this, and it leads her to an interesting distinction between two kinds of writers. There is the 'intellectual novelist', whose disloyalties will take the form of conscious disengagements from publicly held faiths or theories. And there is the 'intuitive writer' (by which she means herself), 'the product of an intensive environment – racial, local, or social', whose loyalties are 'involuntary and inborn' and whose disloyalty will be the gradual struggle to 'strike out' from the shelter of 'the particular enclave which has given him birth'.[26]

In 'Notes on Writing a Novel' (1945), her first and most interesting collection of remarks about fiction, she uses her own methods as the basis of an analytical approach to the novel. But analysis, as usual, comes up against what's involuntary and temperamental. The writer is moved to action by things not fully under his control. Plot is not 'a matter of choice', but what the novelist is 'driven to' after the accumulation of 'a mass of subjective matter . . . impressions received, feelings about experience, distorted results of ordinary observation'. Characters are not made but *found*: 'They reveal themselves slowly to the novelist's perception', she says, echoing Virginia Woolf, 'as might fellow-travellers seated opposite one in a very dimly-lit railway carriage.' Settings, too, are 'assembled – out of memories which, in the first place, may have had no rational connection with one another'. Nevertheless, what the writer does with this often inexplicable material can always be interrogated. For instance, she says there must always be a 'magnetic' character in every novel, 'capable of keying the reader up, as though he . . . were in the presence of someone he is in love with'. 'The unfortunate case is', she adds drily, 'where the character has, obviously, acted magnetically upon the author, but fails to do so upon the reader.'

Bowen's account of how novels should work is indebted to Flaubert and to James. Flaubert's 'Il faut intéresser' and James's 'The Art of Fiction' (1884) – 'What is character but the determination of incident? What is incident but the illustration of character?' – inspire the 'Notes' in their treatment of plot ('must not cease to move forward'), of characters in action ('the play and pull of alternatives must be felt'), of settings ('nothing can happen nowhere') and of dialogue, on which she writes particularly well:

> During dialogue, the characters confront one another. The confrontation is in itself an occasion. Each one of these occasions, throughout the novel, is unique. Since the last confrontation, something has changed, advanced. What is

being said is the effect of something that has happened; at the same time, what is being said *is in itself something happening*, which will in turn, leave its effect . . . Dialogue . . . crystallizes relationships . . . Speech is what the characters *do to each other*.[27]

Her interest in 'angles' (which, in 1945, long before *Eva Trout*, acknowledges the influence of the cinema), in movement (especially in techniques for changes of pace) and in 'relevance' (nothing must be redundant, the novelist must 'whittle down his meaning to the exactest and finest possible point') are in James's tradition of literary criticism. And they are well illustrated by the work of Flaubert, whom (in 1941) she calls the 'master of poetic objectivity':

> The plot [of *L'Éducation sentimentale*] is elliptic, with scenes moved on and transitions made in a phrase. The method is visual; thought is not analysed, and no consciousness is examined from the inside. Each scene is made to take its peculiar emotional colour from its setting, from the objects surrounding it . . . One may say that his characters have been sacrificed to his perception. But it is perception that is the force of the book.

A few years later she returns to *L'Éducation Sentimentale*, in a masterful analysis which again concentrates on the inextricable relationship between technique, intelligence, and a fictional attitude:

> To examine the structure and motivation of *L'Éducation Sentimentale* is like opening the back of a clock. Here is an interrelation of coils and tensions, springs and weights, cogs and hammers. In the plot, nothing does not act upon something else. This is the longest, the most complex and, in its action, deliberately the slowest of Flaubert's novels . . .
>
> It has been said by some that *L'Éducation Sentimentale* fails because of a dullness or insipidity or lack of emotional range in its central figure. Actually, what may be disconcerting is the detachment of Flaubert's own attitude – a detachment which, even, subdues irony. The reader's demand to be engaged emotionally is not met – nor, even, with Frédéric does one

become, as one did with Emma Bovary, a reluctant confeder-
ate. To admire, as it deserves, and to enjoy to the degree due
to oneself *L'Éducation Sentimentale*, one has to release oneself
from the idea that character is the real subject of any novel –
the subject of this one is not the nature of Frédéric, but the
nature of feeling.[28]

Her own fiction validates her theories. The 'magnetism' of
character is displayed by Emmeline, or Leopold; the dramatic
use of setting, by the icy lake in Regent's Park or by Mme
Fisher's *bois dormant*; the functionality of dialogue by Stella's
conversations with Harrison, or Portia's with Eddie; the
manipulation of time (which the novelist, she says elsewhere,
must be able to open and shut 'like a fan')[29] by the whole
structure of *The House in Paris*. In a much later article, she
talks too about the novelist's need for 'a heightening power',
a 'dramatic element' in language.[30] Language must be kept
flexible and used subtly: 'Why do we react more to "the thin
gate clanged" than to "the iron gate shut noisily"?' The
example shows up the dangers as well as the effectiveness of
her own style.

All Bowen's writing on the novel centres around a moral
idea of fiction as 'the non-poetic statement of a poetic
truth'.[31] She puts herself firmly here in the tradition of a belief
in the novel as 'the one bright book of life': 'There is . . . no
more . . . suggestive truth . . . than that of the perfect
dependence of the 'moral' sense of a work of art on the
amount of felt life concerned in producing it.[32]

Like Henry James there, Bowen identifies a moral with an
aesthetic approach to the novel. So she calls her radio talks of
the 1950s on the novel 'Truth and Fiction'. Here she talks
more simply and with more examples than in 'Notes on
Writing a Novel' about the ways in which the novel must
'stand up to the adult tests of reality'. Her main ideas are the
same. The plot comes out of the novelist's pre-existent inner
subject. Then come the characters, who, having begun to
exist, 'take into themselves a most extraordinary and imperative reality', and who must be 'kept in play' through 'analysis
or dialogue'. Time and movement and setting are vital

elements. What's interesting here is her use of examples. Though she begins with a rather simplistic division of novels into the 'social' novel, the 'novel of action', and the 'character novel', this is made vivid by the three books whose openings she chooses as illustrations. These are *Vanity Fair*, the social novel ('What writing for the eye . . .'), *Brighton Rock*, the novel of action, both internal and actual ('quick technique . . . sense of imminent danger') and *Jane Eyre*, the character novel, which provides 'immediate drama'. Starting with 'immediate drama', she says, is one of her own preoccupations:

> As a reader, I must say that I myself am tremendously influenced for or against a book by the manner of the opening, and that as a novelist myself I have put great stress and interest into the openings of my own books. And though they are open to every criticism, I still would stand by the first two pages of most of the novels I ever wrote.[33]

She is right: think of the Montmorencys driving up to Danielstown, of Henrietta in the taxi, of the swinging doors of the station restaurant in Milan, of the girl in Edwardian dress trailing out at dawn to the obelisk, of the icy walk or the concert at dusk in Regent's Park.

Bowen goes on in 'Truth and Fiction' to give a fine example of the introduction of character: the Touchetts, father and son, on the lawn at Gardencourt in *The Portrait of a Lady*. Lady Bertram's dilemma over the carriage for Fanny, and the row in the car about running over a cat in *Howards End*, are her examples of characters being 'kept in play'. Other examples are drawn from less familiar sources. She admires a passage from Dorothy Richardson's *Pilgrimage* (Miriam deciding whether or not to go alone into a restaurant) for its subjective fusion of extraordinary perception and ordinary circumstance. She uses Ivy Compton-Burnett and Henry Green as examples of a new, 'masked', symbolic dialogue. The flower-shop scene in *Mrs Dalloway* is used for the manipulation of time and place, and the description of Chesney Wold in the rain, in *Bleak House*, as a 'wonderfully actual, clean-cut' emotional setting. *Ulysses* is given as the greatest modern example of the 'psychological story', and Proust as an instance of what she means by 'situation' (as opposed to 'plot' or 'theme'):

> Throughout Proust's long masterpiece there is his absorption in his own romantic conceptions of person after person who come his way. I would call that situation.[34]

The examples in 'Truth and Fiction' reveal some of the major influences on her writing (Proust, Dickens, Jane Austen, Forster, Woolf) and introduce the writers, like Green and Compton-Burnett, with whom she felt some affinity. She gives this information simply, appropriately for a general radio audience. And, for a complex writer, she has a great belief in simplicity: simplicity of plot, and, deeper down, the simplicity of the writer's source, his 'pre-existent' material:

> Concentration on any one writer's work almost always ends by exposing a core of naivety – a core which, once it has been laid bare, seems either infantile or august. There is little inner complexity, after all: the apparent outer complexity of the art has been little more than the effort towards expression. Somewhere within the pattern, somewhere behind the words, a responsive, querying innocence stays intact.[35]

This is a very important idea in Bowen's fiction-writing. She expresses a few strong consistent preoccupations (innocence, dispossession, betrayal, the action of time) through a highly patterned and elaborate surface. And she believes in the childhood sources of all writing. The Bowen innocent who disrupts a regulated society with the force of a fanatical, romantic will, is a version of the novelist.

The critic's job, Bowen says, is to analyse style and structure, to work out the novelist's pattern. But, ultimately, he will come up against the 'core', and there only intuition will serve. By this she seems to mean an inbuilt moral touchstone: 'the vital test is the sense of truth in the vision'.[36] This formulation underlies her own practice as a critic. In a late preface to a collection called *Critics Who Influenced Taste*, she distinguishes between criticism as 'a by-product of creative energy' (that of, for instance, Ben Jonson, Dryden, Coleridge, Shelley, Virginia Woolf) and the writer who has found his *mêtier* as a critic: Hazlitt, Sainte-Beuve, Macaulay, A. C. Bradley, Desmond MacCarthy. Though she belongs to the first group, she has a writer's qualified admiration for the professional critic who 'respects taste, but does not attempt to "form it"'.[37]

Her own criticism of other writers was courteous and urbane; she was a 'notoriously kind reviewer of novels',[38] and wrote generously about contemporaries such as Rosamond Lehmann, Henry Green, or V. S. Pritchett.[39] But she was not particularly kind to the political writers of the 1930s in John Lehmann's *New Writing in Europe*. Their 'professional youthfulness' made them, she said, 'isolated, special, intensive, charged with personal feeling and, in the long run, as claustrophobic as any middle-class home'.[40] Not much sympathy there for a major literary movement of her time. But her criticism is good because it is self-revelatory. 'He perceives in another man's work what he himself knows,' she says of Forster's essays.[41]

Her finest critical essay, the preface to Le Fanu's *Uncle Silas*, brilliantly displays her talent for diagnosing the atmosphere and quality of a book for which she feels a close affinity. She understands the novel's 'sublimated infantilism', its 'voluptuousness', its 'overheated psychic air', its 'claustrophobia'. Her feeling for Le Fanu's 'oblique suggestive art', and 'the negligent virtuosity in which [he] shows his race' are as suggestive about her own writing as about his.[42] It's that sympathy which inspires her best criticism. She has a sensitive introduction to Elizabeth Gaskell's *North and South*, which feelingly describes Margaret Hale as 'a displaced person', and praises Gaskell as a novelist who is 'visually minded, quick to convey sensation, aware of the greatness of small things'. The passage she quotes about Margaret's disappointing return to Helstone might be from one of her own novels:

A sense of change, of individual nothingness, of perplexity and disappointment, overpowered Margaret. Nothing had been the same; and this slight, all-pervading instability had given her greater pain than if all had been too entirely changed for her to recognise it.[43]

There's the same lucky correspondence between writer and subject in her 1948 introduction to Antonia White's *Frost in May* (1933), a 'minor classic' about a rebellious girl in a convent school, whose 'hermetic' atmosphere is completely 'shown and felt'. 'In the biting crystal air of the book the children and the nuns stand out like early morning mountains. In this frigid, authoritarian anti-Romantic Catholic climate every romantic vibration from "character" is, in effect, trebled.'[44] Bowen's interest is characteristically in the clash between personality and social discipline.

The essay in *Pictures and Conversations* on Proust's character 'Bergotte', is also deeply in sympathy with the way *À la Recherche* works: it's a moving, if mannered, piece of impressionistic criticism.

She can be disappointing, though, on the writers she admires. Her articles on Virginia Woolf, for example – reviews of *Between the Acts* and *The Death of the Moth*, and of Bernard Blackstone's early critical work – are indulgent and flowery ('In *The Waves* what is gradual truth in the other books is ejaculated in a succession of cries'),[45] and disconcertingly hostile to 'this obsession of hers that women were being martyrised humanly, inhibited creatively, by the stupidities of a man-made world'. She has no time for 'what must inevitably' be called Virginia Woolf's feminism: 'It was a bleak quality, an aggressive streak, which can but irritate, disconcert, the adorer of Virginia Woolf the artist.'[46] That distinction between 'artistry' and 'feminism' reads imperceptively. And, surprisingly, she isn't very interesting on Forster. The tone, again, is over-effusive:

> The world of the novels opens a vast light landscape, in which every feature is dramatic, in which every object is not only sentient, living, but sends a current direct to the human nerves. This is a world of beauty which is intimidating. Its creatures, Mr Forster's characters, dread, and rightly dread, the forces behind each other: chasms may open for them – and often do.

217

> But . . . they stand up to what is dreadful . . . they oppose the
> mass of darkness.[47]

She is better at placing a novelist's value at a particular point
in time. Her most interesting comments on Woolf are in a
1960 preface to *Orlando*, where she compares her generation's feelings for the book on its first appearance in 1928 –
when it seemed élitist and whimsical – with its standing in
1960, when it could be seen as a necessary 'rebellion' against
solemnity, and a precursor to *The Waves*.[48] Writing on D. H.
Lawrence, she says that he has come into his own in the
1940s, answering to what she calls 'the new raw personal
social consciousness'. 'During the war in London Lawrence
was the one artist whom I, for one, constantly had in mind.'[49]
She places Ivy Compton-Burnett as an Edwardian who is
carrying on (with a vengeance) the Victorian 'account of the
battle for power that goes on in every unit of English middle-
class life'.[50] Trollope, on whom she always writes feelingly,
interests her because he has been rediscovered in wartime by
younger readers wanting consolation: 'Your people are
stronger than circumstances . . . It's essential for us, these
days, to believe in people, and in their power to live.'[51] She
has a long and sympathetic essay on Katherine Mansfield,
first published in 1956.[52] She clearly feels an affinity with her,
both as an uprooted writer whose New Zealand stories show
a greater depth of feeling than her London stories, and as a
writer primarily influenced by visual scenes. (In her preface to
Encounters, she says that she first read *Bliss* after writing her
early stories, and thought: 'If I ever *am* published, they'll say I
copied her.')[53] Bowen admires Mansfield for her keen eye, for
the balance held between 'factual firmness' and 'hallucinatory
floatingness' in the stories, but most of all because it's
impossible, in 1956, not to 'feel' her as a contemporary. The
title of the shorter version of the article was 'A Living Writer':

> Of love for experiment for its own sake, Katherine Mansfield
> shows not a sign. Conscious artist, she carries none of the
> marks of the self-consciously 'experimental' writer . . . She
> uses no literary shock tactics. The singular beauty of her

language consists, partly, in its hardly seeming to *be* language at all, so glass-transparent is it to her meaning. Words had but one appeal for her, that of speakingness. (In her journal we find noted: 'The *panting* of a saw.') . . . It is a style generated by subject and tuned to mood . . . There are no eccentricities.[54]

In 1945, Bowen wrote an illustrated guide to *English Novelists* (one of the Collins 'Britain in Pictures' series). In this clear, stylish, but necessarily superficial survey, it's interesting to see where she lays the emphasis. The English novel, she says, comes of a 'new kind of English self-consciousness' born in the Civil War. After praising Defoe ('*Moll Flanders* – a great fascinating acute short book on no account to be missed by anybody'), she lays the weight firmly on Fielding and Richardson as representing 'two opposed, but equally real, aspects of the English temperament – in a sense, all succeeding English novelists descend from one or other of them.' Her account of what happens to the novel after the eighteenth century is like her description in *Bowen's Court* of 'personal life' overtaking a social ideal. After 'the first great English impulse towards the novel, the social impulse', comes the 'revolt against Reason'. 'Fancy, so long kept down, violently reasserted itself.' From the time of the Gothic novel, English fiction had to hold a balance between 'that shadowy, deep underneath of the English nature' (fundamentally Richardsonian) and its 'daylit, ordered top'. Naturally Bowen gives a good deal of space to Jane Austen as a key figure in this balancing act:

Her people . . . seek, with degrees of determination, ideal circumstances, ideal relationships inside that world they already know. They locate, and never far from themselves, possible darkness, chaos; they feel the constant threat of the wrong – be this only a mean act, a callous or designing remark, a subtly deceiving proposition, a lie. The world Jane Austen creates remains an absolute world because of its trueness to its own scale.[55]

She places the nineteenth-century novel as following either Jane Austen's grown-up control, or Scott's romantic 'loosening' effect. Thackeray is handicapped by being 'preyed upon by nostalgia for the eighteenth century', Dickens (who inherits the characteristics of both Fielding and Richardson) is energised by his 'childish' emotional vision, which produced 'the most mobile kind of English romantic prose'. She praises Trollope, Wilkie Collins and Gaskell, and writes enthusiastically about *Wuthering Heights* and *Jane Eyre*. She is distinctly unenthusiastic about George Eliot, mentions the importance of *The Egoist* and *The Way of All Flesh*, is respectful to Hardy and profoundly admiring of James (especially as a social analyst). In the Edwardian period she singles out Kipling, Wells, Bennett and Galsworthy (whom she dislikes), ignores Gissing, Moore, Stevenson, Ford, Conrad and Lawrence; and ends with Forster and, last, Virginia Woolf: 'Imagination of this pure power has not been brought to narrative style before.' Her partial views show who her models are.

The see-saw which she describes throughout *English Novelists* between the social and the personal, the decorous and the romantic, has reached, in 1945, another point of change. The English novel, she suggests, is becoming 'less exclusively interested in character', more 'poetic', and 'self-conscious', and less spontaneous. 'Is this because we live in an age . . . in which individual destinies count for less?'[56] It's the question which recurs throughout her writing. It is difficult, she insists repeatedly, to write at a time of dislocation: 'These years rebuff the imagination as much as by being fragmentary as by being violent.' 'Our century, as it takes its frantic course, seems barely habitable by humans: we have to learn to survive while we learn to write.' What in *Bowen's Court* is called 'the dire period of Personal Life' has left its imprint both on history ('Today [1942] the mutilated frontiers of Europe show the outcome of the romantic obsession'),[57] and on the novel.

Throughout the war years, Bowen insists that the English novel must break away from subjectivism:

Personal relationships, colour-coded by sex and not placed or framed by any clear sense of economic realities have been, too much, the English preoccupation . . . To an extent, the world of the English novel has remained the provincial, if lively, world of the 'I'.[58]

And this has got to change.

> If personal experience is to survive and have any value, and continue to be communicated by art, it must be cleared of the twilight of vague romanticised feeling and of the received idea.[59]

These sorts of remark are dotted about her reviews: 'Romantic individualism is at a discount now';[60] 'We have exhausted the merits of the subjective landscape.'[61] It isn't sexual freedom she wants for the novel (which she regards as a symptom of inadequacy: 'What is the matter with us: are we under-sexed?'),[62] but a freedom from the enfeebling effects of romanticism, and, by the 1950s, from the 'cult of nostalgia', the 'bend back'.

> I should like to see a whole generation keep the power of taking moments 'straight' – not half overcast by fantasy, not thinned down by yearning.[63]

This severe resistance to romanticism is the keynote of Bowen's writing about contemporary fiction.

> We want ... writers more normal and disengaged ... Freedom – from self-interest, from obsession, from nostalgia, from arbitrary loyalties ... We want more emotion implied (not merely written up), more relevant fact stated, more vital relations shown.[64]

Bowen's magisterial attacks on subjectivity and romanticism in fiction are paradoxical. Her best novels and stories, after all, are full of passionate longings, narcissistic characters, obsessions, fantasies and personal dramas. Yet, at the same time, they are highly controlled, and refuse to be autobiographical or sentimental. These contradictions proved difficult for the critics who tried to sum up her work, from the 1940s onwards. She was often read simply as a subjective writer, and praised or blamed for exactly the qualities she most disliked in the twentieth-century novel. There's a good example of the kind of attack which damned her for her sensibilities in Raymond Williams's 1959 essay, 'Realism and the Contemporary Novel'. Williams invented a category which he called 'the novel of special pleading'. One of his examples was *The Heat of the Day*:

> The persons exist primarily as elements in the central character's emotional landscape, and are never seen or valued in any other terms, though there is no first person narrative, and there is even some careful descriptive realism, to make the special pleading less stark.[65]

This kind of novel 'ends by denying the majority of persons. The reality of society is excluded, and this leads, inevitably, in the end, to the exclusion of all but a very few individual people.' This is why, he concludes, so much of this 'personal' experience is the experience of 'breakdowns'.

That sort of social attack on her work (very similar to the critiques of Virginia Woolf from the 1930s on) was often linked to a masculine impatience with feminine sensibilities. Bowen would be accused of being self-parodyingly 'hypersensitive', of presenting 'a dream world of half-felt feelings and half-precise words, draped in a mist of self-induced poesy',[66] a world 'overly feminine and gossipy, in a final view, shadowy'. Henry James (not masculine enough) is seen as a bad influence here. John McCormick, criticising Bowen's late novels as examples of 'feminine preoccupation with technique', remarked that Henry James has often served the English novelist badly.[67]

The most rumbustious of these attacks was Anthony Burgess's 1964 *Spectator* review of *The Little Girl* – 'Moral profundities whirl about, among the aubergine jerseys and the coloured scenery-motifs in cups and bowls' – where Bowen was dismissively characterised as a 'Female Novelist':

> Forget the big Tolstoyan or Joycean architectonic gift, and you will find that women have a better natural fictional equipment than men. They notice surfaces, which is what novels are made of; they have a phenomenal semantic range when it

comes to dealing with texture, colour and nuance of speech; being the primal order of creation, they enclose men and see through them. Their faults are the faults a man finds in a woman: they chatter, they are deficient in moral values, they are too empirical, they fall in love with the accident and miss the essence, they are distracted by a golden apple. Naturally, there is a way of looking at these vices which turns them into virtues.[68]

Burgess included James as a Female Novelist – 'those endlessly qualified sentences with their spinsterish scruples' – who bequeathed to writers 'like' Elizabeth Bowen a fanciful poetic prose style, an attention to atmosphere, a lack of strong characters ('the real protagonist is the sensibility of the author') and – in short – a lot of fussiness about nothing. 'Behind the whirl of phenomena, there doesn't seem to be much of a thing-in-itself.'

It wasn't only male critics who attacked Bowen for being too 'female'. The American novelist and critic Elizabeth Hardwick, in a scathing piece in 1949 in the *Partisan Review*, complained that Bowen's readers fell under the spell of a complex evasive style ('these are obviously womens' books') and found themselves swallowing 'the oppressive tidiness of the values'. Hardwick greatly disliked Bowen's nostalgic conservatism, which she called 'the moral intransigence of the interior decorator'. She found the narrators' weighty generalisations quite unjustified by the heroines' actual behaviour: 'With fanatical doggedness they deceive their parents and friends, have illegitimate children, open affairs with men they know little about, and even commit murder . . .'[69]

Critiques of Bowen's sensibility and conservatism often described her as a snob. Without taking note of her bleakly acute analyses of middle-class bad faith, they looked no further than the fact that her fiction mostly confined itself to a narrow social range. Angus Wilson's witty 1950s lectures on the sense of evil in English fiction described Bowen, unfairly but provocatively, as a *déclassée* Virginia Woolf, perpetuating a watered-down version of the novel of sensibility. It's a wicked passage, worth quoting in full:

I should like to ask you to accompany me now to the country, into the home of some middle-aged, upper middle-class woman – the wife of an army officer or a business director with intellectual interests, a don's wife, or the wife of a clever Principal or Assistant Secretary in a Government office, who yet has time amid the cares of office to cultivate taste. Note please the splendid herbaceous borders glowing with every shade of blue delphinium ... look inside, please, at the unexceptionable furniture ... Now please look at Mrs Green – for so we will call her – her good tweeds, her untidy grey hair, her interesting beauty – for to her friends and indeed to herself she has always 'interesting beauty'. She is thinking – for we may transgress so much as to probe her thoughts – of the changing seasons, of the funny hat that her father used to wear at the seaside so many years ago, of the pleasure it gives to her to hear her daughter so happy at the flute – Scarlatti is it? or Mozart? she can never quite remember – and of Mr Green who is enjoying a mathematical problem – the square root of π – she can't quite help visualising it as the strange square-shaped root of the oak that fell last autumn – and then she watches with pleasure Ada, dear, loyal, beloved Ada emptying the ashes, only Ada's niece wears terrible shiny flesh-coloured stockings – and no! it is no good, whatever they say she cannot forgive people who have the wireless on at full blast all day and prefer pilchards and canned beans – but now the square root of π is not doing its part and Mr Green is frowning, pray Heaven the risotto will be perfect ...

I am afraid all this is a little crude, but it is, I hope, a recognisable picture of the cultured, upper-middle-class woman. It is also, how imperfectly I am well aware, Mrs Ambrose and Mrs Ramsay and Rhoda in *The Waves*, and *mutatis mutandis* Clarissa Dalloway ... But note something more interesting. Mrs Green and her unresolved moments of significance belong not only to Virginia Woolf, they permeate the works of Miss Elizabeth Bowen, they can perhaps be seen more archly in the pages of Mrs Thirkell. Was it not, with extra emphasis on courage and nostalgia, the same Mrs Green that emerges so opportunely as Mrs Miniver? Her values and her doubts now suffuse the high-class women's magazines, but more crudely and with more self-satisfaction, until Mrs Green herself, turning over their glassy pages, does not know

> whether to shudder with participation or disgust. We have
> travelled in fact from the heart of Virginia Woolf's austere,
> proud creed of highbrowism to the land of the middle-
> brow . . .[70]

This is wildly unfair, both to Woolf and Bowen, but it's an
interesting example of how women's writing in the post-war
years could be condescended to for domestic concerns and
emotionalism. Wilson's own snobbery about 'the land of the
middlebrow' makes him get Bowen quite wrong. (He later
changed his mind about her, writing in his introduction to her
Collected Stories of 1980 of 'perceptions which range from
marvellous realistic observations of daily life to the innermost
recess of the human soul'.) Perhaps the comparison with
Angela Thirkell, with her endless stream of compulsively
readable novels about English village life, is the most
damning thing here. Unlike Thirkell, Bowen is not compla-
cently or cosily describing the provincial English upper-
middle classes. She is the spy inside the gates.

Some of the critics who praised her in the 1940s and 1950s
also tended to do so reductively, paying attention only to her
'exquisitely sensitive' mind, her resemblance to Rosamond
Lehmann, her 'small and perfect universe'.[71] And when her
detractors found good things to say about her, it was only in
terms of her creation of atmosphere: Burgess, for instance,
liked the icy lake in *The Death of the Heart* and the 'very feel
and smell of London in the Nineteen-Forties' in *The Heat of
the Day*.[72] But there is more to Bowen than elegant craftsmanship and exclusive sensibilities. That line of approach
doesn't allow for her hardness, her acerbity, her disenchanted
precision, by which personal dramas are related to the state
of a civilisation. A. S. Byatt made this point well when she
described, in her 1975 Penguin introduction to *The House in
Paris*, her change of attitude towards Bowen. As a child *The
House in Paris* was a revelation to her: 'I learned that "the
modern novel" was difficult . . . and I learned that Elizabeth
Bowen had *got Henrietta right*. Later, no longer 'shocked or
confused' by modernism, she 'saw merits in the heavy, broad,
open-ended Victorian novels, admired by Dr Leavis and Iris

Murdoch', which made 'Elizabeth Bowen's precise distinctions, her craftsmanship, appear minor virtues, and her world, so economically, so selectively presented, appear shadowy'. But in time the novel proved itself as something which grew in her mind, and hung together. Its debts to James and Woolf came to seem not 'narrowing, or claustrophobic', but energising. In the end she valued it not as a novel of 'sensibility and fine discrimination', but for its 'harshness', or what Bowen praised in Ivy Compton-Burnett – hardness, 'implacability'.[73]

Such accurate praise of Bowen was hard to come by until the 1980s. Elizabeth Hardwick said in 1949 that her reputation was difficult to track down, consisting in a 'quick smile from Connolly, Pritchett, or E. Sackville-West'.[74] In 1968, one Bowen critic was still complaining that 'unfortunately the work of Elizabeth Bowen has received scant attention'.[75] Between the 1950s and the 1980s there were two books on Bowen published in the United States – an intelligent account of the early novels by William Heath in 1961, and a far-fetched interpretation of the novels as Christian allegories, by Harriet Blodgett, in 1975. There were three short surveys – Jocelyn Brooke's British Council pamphlet of 1952 (which Bowen liked), and two 'Readers' Guides', Allan Austin's in the Twayne's English Authors Series for 1971, and Edwin Kenney's for the Irish Writers Series for 1975. Victoria Glendinning's invaluable biography makes a bold case for Elizabeth Bowen as 'the link which connects Virginia Woolf with Iris Murdoch and Muriel Spark',[76] but was not primarily concerned with literary criticism. A few thematic analyses of Bowen's work have dealt with the 'lunatic giant' battling against the world, or the breaking of the romantic innocents, or pastoral traditions threatened by cities.[77] Not much attention was paid to her use of language.[78]

The best early responses to Bowen's work came from critics who tried to make sense of her subject-matter, and to understand her 'manner'. These included Walter Allen, who called *The Death of the Heart* 'one of the best novels of the century' in 1964; Raymond Mortimer, who recognised the classless, universal quality of that novel's 'distress' when he first reviewed it; John Strachey, who called her early novels 'classic descriptions of the banality and despair of the English middle-class', and her friend L. P. Hartley, who saw the value of James's influence on her, especially in her novels' 'quasi-supernatural' elements.[79]

Her most sympathetic early critics were her collaborators on *Why Do I Write?*, Graham Greene and V. S. Pritchett. Greene wrote brilliantly on the structure of *The House in Paris*:

> She has made of her omissions a completely individual method, she has dramatised ignorance . . . The darkness which hides [the characters'] past makes the cerebrations which are to follow the more vivid . . . it is exquisite sleight of hand . . . We must fill in for ourselves what happened between . . . She has made capital out of the gap in the records: how can we doubt the existence of a past which these characters can so easily convey to each other?[80]

Pritchett's acuteness about Anglo-Irish literature made him see the relation, so often overlooked by her early critics, between the personal and the historical in her writing:

> Without knowing it, often by responding with his private sensibility only, the novelist has slipped into the role of unofficial historian. He has become the historian of the crisis in a civilisation, whether he writes politically (as Koestler has done), as a religious man like Graham Greene, or with the obliquity of those dispossessed poets, Henry Green and Miss Elizabeth Bowen.[81]

It was her close friend, the Irish writer Sean O'Faolain, who made the most perceptive reading, in Bowen's lifetime, of her value and quality. He saw that her novels (which he calls 'exquisitely composed of logs of disaster') present a tragic-comic clash – between 'innocence and knowledge? Youth and maturity? The dream and the actuality? Romance and that ordinary which we tend to call reality? The wish to be heroic

227

and the nature of things which defeats heroism?' He recognised the 'fabulous atmosphere as of people under a spell' in *The Last September*, or the 'lengths to which Miss Bowen will go' (as in the plotting of *Friends and Relations*) 'to deprive her characters of autonomy'. And he noted well the clash between the 'early influence of Flaubert' and her Anglo-Irishness. Pointing to 'the Flaubertian coldness imposed on Irish feeling', he explained the tension in Bowen's work very convincingly:

> She ... exposes the brittleness of romance by soliciting it ruthlessly ... She must state coldly that heroism ... does not stand a chance in modern society, even while she insists passionately that it is always worthwhile to try.[82]

Yet, apart from those few understanding accounts, Elizabeth Bowen has been neglected, at least in Britain. (She is paid more attention in America and in Ireland.) Perhaps the conservatism which separated her from the political writers of the 1930s has been to her disadvantage. Perhaps she has been overshadowed by her immediate predecessors, Woolf, Forster and Mansfield. Possibly, too, the changes in her late work, and the length of time which her whole writing career spanned, from 1923 to the posthumous collection of 1975, has made it hard to see her in focus.

But Bowen's marginality is undeserved. She demands attention not just because of her interesting connections with her fictional ancestors (from Jane Austen to Henry James, from the Anglo-Irish to the French novel). Much more than that, it's for her formal mastery of an idiosyncratic style, for her sense of place, for her brilliance as a short-story writer, for her creation of troubled, complicated, modern characters, and for her compelling obsessions: with betrayal, with the supernatural, with life lived in war, with the perceptions of children. Her strange, dramatic, extraordinary writing tells the story not only of private lives, but of the dislocation and dispossession of a whole society.

NOTES

Notes to pp. 1–8

Page references to Bowen's works are to the Jonathan Cape Uniform Edition of the novels and stories or to the editions specified.

Chapter 1 Re-reading Bowen

'Easy to be wise . . .': 'Foreword', *A*, p. 9.

1 John Hayward to Frank Morley, September 1939, quoted in Heather Bryant Jordan, *How Will the Heart Endure* (University of Michigan Press, 1992), p. 114.

2 Seamus Deane, *The Field Day Anthology of Irish Writing* (Field Day Publications, 1991), Vol. II, p. xix.

3 Roy Foster, *Paddy & Mr Punch* (Allen Lane, 1993), p. xiii.

4 Declan Kiberd, *Inventing Ireland* (Cape, 1995), p. 5.

5 Eibhear Walshe, ed., *Sex, Nation and Dissent in Irish Writing* (Cork University Press, 1997), pp. 2–3.

6 W. J. McCormack, *Dissolute Characters* (Manchester University Press, 1993), p. ix.

7 Hubert Butler, *Escape from the Anthill* (Lilliput Press, 1987), p. 147.

8 *Ibid*, p. 201.

9 *Ibid*, p. 151.

10 Foster, *op. cit.*, p. 122; note 52 to Ch. 6, p. 331.

11 Sean O'Faolain, 'A Reading and Remembrance of Elizabeth Bowen', *London Review of Books*, 4–17 March 1982, pp. 15–16, quoted Foster, *op. cit.*, p. 122.

12 Patricia Craig, *Elizabeth Bowen* (Penguin, 1986), p. 39.

13 Deane, *op. cit.*, p. 1167.

14 Foster, *op. cit.*, p. 103.

15 John Hildebidle, *Five Irish Writers* (Harvard University Press, 1985), p. 217.

16 McCormack, *op. cit.*, pp. 229, 250.

17 Kiberd, *op. cit.*, p. 368.

18 Robert Fisk, *In Time of War* (University of Pennsylvania Press, 1983), pp. 352–8, 371, 378.

19 Jordan, *op. cit.*, pp. 13, 99, 163, 190. cf. Antoinette Quinn, 'Elizabeth Bowen's Irish stories – 1939–1945', in *Studies in Anglo-Irish Literature*, ed. Heinz Kosok (Bouvier, 1982), pp. 314–20, who also concludes that Bowen's divided loyalties, especially in time of war, were 'peculiarly congenial to the obliquity of her talent'.

20 McCormack, *op. cit.*, p. 215.

21 Foster, *op. cit.*, pp. 117–18.

22 Kiberd, *op. cit.*, pp. 365, 368.

23 Katie Donovan, *Irish Women Writers* (Raven Arts, 1988), p. 16.

24 Bridget O'Toole, 'Three Writers of the Big House: Elizabeth Bowen, Molly Keane and Jennifer Johnston', in *Across a Roaring Hill*, ed. Gerald Dawe and Edna Longley (Blackstaff Press, 1985), p. 85.

25 Walshe, *op. cit.*, pp. 6, 10.

26 Quoted Jordan, *op. cit.*, p. xvi, note 36.

27 See Ch. 9, note 46.

28 Renée Hoogland, *From Marginality to Ex-centricity: Feminist Critical Theory and the Case of Elizabeth Bowen* (thesis, 1991), pp. 29, 52, 94, 143; *Elizabeth Bowen: A Reputation in Writing* (New York University Press, 1994), pp. 19, 21, 301, 303.

29 Patricia Coughlan, 'Women and Desire in the Work of Elizabeth Bowen', in Walshe, *op. cit.*, pp. 104–5, 112, 131.

30 Diane Swanson, 'Subverting Closure', in *Sexual Practice, Textual Theory: Lesbian Cultural Criticism*, ed. Susan Wolfe and Julia Penelope (Blackwell, 1993), p. 160.

31 Harriet Chessman, 'Women and Language in the Fiction of Elizabeth Bowen', *Twentieth-Century Literature*, 29, Spring 1983, pp. 69–85; reprinted in Harold Bloom, ed., *Elizabeth Bowen: Modern Critical Views* (Chelsea House Publishers, 1987), p. 124.

32 Phyllis Lassner, *Elizabeth Bowen* (Macmillan, 1990), pp. 15, 71, 72, 153, 163.

33 Andrew Bennett and Nicholas Royle, *Elizabeth Bowen and the*

Dissolution of the Novel: Still Lives (Macmillan, 1994), pp. xiii, xv, 2, 73, 135, 115.

Chapter 2 Only Children

'Each of these houses . . .': *BC*, Ch. 1.
  1 *SW* (Longmans, 1943), p. 15.
  2 *SW*, p. 44.
  3 *SW*, p. 32.
  4 'Two Cities', *New Statesman*, XII (25 July 1936), 128. *CI* (entitled 'Dublin') p. 176. *MT*.
  5 *SW*, p. 30.
  6 *PC*, p. 28.
  7 *PC*, p. 30.
  8 *PC*, p. 23.
  9 *PC*, p. 47.
10 *BC* (Longmans, 1942), p. 323.
11 Glendinning, p. 40.
12 *Ibid*, p. 44.
13 Preface to *The Last September* (1952), *A*, p. 97.
14 *PC*, p. 23.
15 'Portrait of a City', *New Statesman*, XII (31 October 1936), 516. *CI* (entitled 'Dublin'), p. 180. *MT*.
16 Preface to *A Day in the Dark* (1965), p. 9. 'The locale of the Victorian family house in "The Happy Autumn Fields" is, though not stated, to me unshakeably County Cork.'
17 *Journal of the Butler Society*, ed. Hubert Butler, Vol I, No. 8 (1978 and 1979), 596.
18 *BC*, p. 138.
19 *PC*, p. 62.
20 *BC*, p. 293.
21 George Dangerfield, *The Damnable Question* (Constable, 1977), pp.34–5.
22 J. C. Beckett, *The Anglo-Irish Tradition* (Faber, 1976), p. 132.
23 *Ibid*, p. 81, 134.
24 *Ibid*, p. 141.
25 George Birmingham, *An Irishman Looks at his World* (Hodder & Stoughton, 1919), p. 187.
26 Arthur Young, *A Tour in Ireland* (1780), ed. C. Maxwell (Cambridge, 1925), p. 169.

27 *BC*, p. 194.
28 *HP*, p. 94.
29 Jonah Barrington, *Personal Sketches of His Own Time* (Colburn, 1827), I, pp. 137–8; II, p. 124.
30 *The Anglo-Irish Tradition*, pp. 74–5.
31 Dorothea Herbert, *Retrospections 1770–1789* (Gerald Howe, 1929), pp. 156–7.
32 *BC*, pp. 161, 153, 295.
33 J. D. Herbert, *Irish Varieties* (William Joy, 1836), p. 54.
34 *BC*, pp. 92–3.
35 *BC*, p. 205.
36 Barrington, I, pp. 5–6.
37 Aubrey de Vere, *Recollections* (Edward Arnold, 1897), p. 79.
38 *SW*, pp. 21, 44.
39 'One Ireland', *New Statesman*, XIII (26 June 1937), 1050, *CI*, p. 172.
40 Maria Edgeworth, *The Absentee* (1812), Ch. 6.
41 Edmund Burke, *Letters, Speeches and Tracts on Irish Affairs*, ed. Matthew Arnold (1881), 'Tracts on the Popery Laws, 1750–1765', p. 60.
42 *BC*, p. 338.
43 *The Shelbourne* (1951), pp. 16, 128, 43.
44 *BC*, p. 23.
45 *The Anglo-Irish Tradition*, p. 70.
46 *BC*, p. 15.
47 *BC*, p. 19.
48 'The Big House', *The Bell* I (October 1940), 71–7. *CI*, pp. 196–7. *MT*.
49 *BC*, p. 190.
50 *BC*, p. 92.
51 'The Moores', *New Statesman*, XVIII (25 November 1939), 759–60. *CI*, p. 161. *MT*.
52 *BC*, p. 76.
53 *BC*, pp. 205, 339.
54 *BC*, pp. 204, 153, 203, 175, 209.
55 *BC*, p. 74.
56 *BC*, p. 73.
57 *BC*, p. 226.
58 *BC*, p. 240.
59 *BC*, p. 278.
60 *The Sickle Side of the Moon: The Letters of Virginia Woolf*,

1932–1935, ed. Nigel Nicolson (Hogarth Press, 1979), pp. 299–300.

61 'The Big House', *CI*, pp. 197–8, 198–9.
62 Dorothea Herbert, *op. cit.*, p. 21.
63 Lady Augusta Gregory, *Journals 1916–1930*, ed. Lennox Robinson (Putnam & Co., 1946), 1 August 1921.
64 'The Moores', *CI*, p. 161.
65 *BC*, pp. 174, 150, 207.
66 Somerville and Ross, *The Big House of Inver* (1925; Quartet Books, 1978), p.8.
67 *BC*, p. 182.
68 *The Big House of Inver*, pp. 79–80.
69 *BC*, p. 105.
70 Review of Lord Dunsany's *Memoirs*, 'One Ireland', *New Statesman*, XIII (26 June 1937). *CI*, p. 172.
71 *BC*, pp. 324, 58, 10.
72 Lady Gregory, *op. cit.*, 8 October 1924.
73 *The Absentee*, Ch. 12.
74 *BC*, pp. 11, 22, 97, 297.
75 George Birmingham, *op. cit.*, p. 108.
76 *Ibid*, pp. 189, 194.
77 Sean O'Faolain, *The Irish* (Pelican Books, 1947), p. 87.
78 *The Anglo-Irish Tradition*, p. 103.
79 Dangerfield, *op. cit.*, p. 31.
80 Glendinning, p. 121.
81 *BC*, pp. 335, 117.
82 Preface to *The Last September*, *A*, pp. 96, 98–9. *MT*.
83 *BC*, p. 326.
84 Preface to *The Last September*, *A*, p. 100.
85 *Ibid*, p. 96.
86 *Ibid*, pp. 96–7.
87 'Sunday Afternoon', *DL*.
88 *BC*, p. 116.

Chapter 3 The Disinherited

'She saw that events . . .': 'The Disinherited', *CJ*.
 1 *The Voyage Out* (1915), Ch. 9.
 2 'Post-Victorian', *Cornhill*, CLXI (October 1944), 92–6. *CI* (entitled 'Ivy Compton-Burnett'), p. 86. *MT*.

3 *Ibid*, p. 89.
4 Glendinning, p. 82.
5 'Notes on Writing a Novel', *Orion*, II (Autumn 1945), 18–29. *CI*, p. 253, *PC*, p. 176. *MT*.
6 'Pictures and Conversations', *PC*, p. 35. *MT*.
7 'The Disinherited', *CJ*.

Chapter 4 The Fatal House

'The fatal house . . .': *HP*, Ch. 12.
1 Glendinning, p. 95.
2 Charlotte Brontë, *Villette*, Ch. 8.
3 Virginia Woolf, *The Waves* (Hogarth Press, 1931), p. 186.
4 *PC*, pp. 41–4.
5 A. S. Byatt, Introduction to *The House in Paris* (Penguin, 1976), p. 8.
6 *PC*, p. 39.

Chapter 5 The Death of the Heart

'Happy that few of us . . .': Part 3, Ch. 5. *DH*.
1 See Glendinning, p. 122, for the detail of the house telephone at 2 Clarence Terrace.
2 'Sunday Evening', *E*.
3 Henry James, *The Portrait of a Lady*, Ch. 19.
4 Like Elizabeth Bowen on her arrival in Rome. *A Time in Rome*, p. 1.
5 By Edwin J. Kenney, *Elizabeth Bowen* (Bucknell University Press, 1975), p. 61, and by Harriet Blodgett, *Patterns of Reality: Elizabeth Bowen's Novels* (Mouton: The Hague, 1975), p. 143.
6 Glendinning, pp. 114–16, 122, 122–3. See further, Ch. 7, pp. 168–9.
7 Goronwy Rees, interviewed by John Morgan, ATV, 5 September 1977.
8 See Ch. 7, pp. 168–9.
9 Jane Austen, *Mansfield Park*, Ch. 38.
10 Cf. Maud Ruthyn in *Uncle Silas*, whom Elizabeth Bowen describes as 'by nature, a bride of death'. *CI*, p. 5.

Chapter 6 The Life Room

'Wandering . . .': 'Her Table Spread', *CJ*.
1 Preface to *A Day in the Dark* (1965), p. 7.
2 *PC*, p. 60.
3 Introduction (1936) to *The Faber Book of Modern Stories*, ed. Elizabeth Bowen (Faber, 1937), p. 14. *CI*, p. 43.
4 *Ibid*, p. 11.
5 Preface to *Stories by Elizabeth Bowen* (New York, 1959), *A*, p. 77. *MT*.
6 *Ibid*, *A*, p. 80.
7 *Ibid*, *A*, pp. 78–9.
8 E.g. 'The Cassowary', *JC*; 'The Cheery Soul, *DL*; 'The Inherited Clock', *DL*; 'Green Holly', *DL*.
9 Sean O'Faolain, *The Short Story* (Dublin, Mercier Press, 1972), p. 240.
10 Introduction, *Uncle Silas: A Tale of Bartram-Haugh* by J. S. Le Fanu (The Cresset Press, 1947), *CI*, p. 16. *MT*.
11 *Ibid*, *CI*, p. 4.
12 *Ibid*, *CI*, p. 5.
13 Introduction, *Uncle Silas*, *CI*, p. 17.
14 Sean O'Faolain, *op. cit.*, p. 236.
15 In 'Gone Away', *DD*, Elizabeth Bowen's only science-fiction story, a village like West Wallows is kept up as a tourist spot in a mechanised England of the future.

Chapter 7 An Awful Illumination

'I say, this war . . .': 'Summer Night', *LAR*.
1 Charles Ritchie, *The Siren Years: Undiplomatic Diaries 1937–1945* (Macmillan, 1974), pp. 121–22.
2 Glendinning, p. 161–2.
3 Evelyn Waugh, *Unconditional Surrender* (1961), Bk 3, Ch. 5.
4 Graham Greene, *Collected Essays* (Bodley Head, 1969), pp. 447, 450.
5 *DH*, p. 251.
6 *BC*, p. 92.
7 Glendinning, p. 149.
8 Preface to the American edition of *The Demon Lover* (published in America in 1946 as *Ivy Gripped the Steps*). Preface dated

October 1945. *MT*. See Sellery and Harris, *Elizabeth Bowen* (University of Texas at Austin), pp. 59–61.

9 *Ibid.*

10 Glendinning, pp. 149–50.

11 Michael Howard, *Jonathan Cape, Publisher* (Cape, 1971), p. 240: 'It sold 45 thousand copies almost at once'.

12 Elizabeth Hardwick, 'Elizabeth Bowen's Fiction', *Partisan Review*, XVI (November 1949), pp. 114–21: John McCormick, *Catastrophe and Imagination* (Longman, 1952), p. 93.

13 Glendinning, p. 153; Michael Howard, *op. cit.*, pp. 181–3. For a parody, see Peter De Vries, 'Touch and Go (with a low bow to Elizabeth Bowen,)' *New Yorker*, 4, 26 January 1952, pp. 30–2. A house-guest is shown some photographs: '"But these are negatives", he said. "I did so not want to be too obvious."'

14 Also described in the essay 'London, 1940', *CI*, pp. 217–20, *MT*; Walter Allen, *Tradition and Dream* (Phoenix House, 1964), p. 195; Anthony Burgess, *The Novel Now* (Faber, 1967), p. 120; Angus Calder, *The People's War: Britain 1939–1945* (Cape, 1969), p. 228.

15 Letter to Charles Ritchie, in Glendinning, p. 169.

16 Henry Green, *Caught* (1943; New York, Viking Press, 1952), pp. 174–5.

17 Graham Greene, *The Ministry of Fear* (1943; Penguin, 1963), pp. 166, 11, 210, 63.

18 Glendinning, p. 166.

19 Charles Ritchie, *op. cit.*, pp. 121–2.

20 *Ibid*, p. 118.

21 Glendinning, p. 150.

22 Letter to Charles Ritchie, in Glendinning, p. 151.

23 Edward Sackville-West, *Inclinations* (Secker & Warburg, 1949), p. 96.

24 Bruce Page, David Leitch and Philip Knightley, *Philby: the Spy Who Betrayed a Generation* (Deutsch, 1968; Sphere, 1977), p. 134.

25 Glendinning, p. 161.

26 *Ibid*, p. 139.

27 Charles Ritchie, *op. cit.*, 28 September 1938, pp. 26–7. See Glendinning, p. 152.

28 Miriam Rothschild was a close friend of Charles Ritchie and she also knew Burgess well. See Ritchie, *op. cit.*, p. 118; Andrew Boyle, *The Climate of Treason* (Hutchinson, 1979), pp. 337–8.

29 Andrew Boyle, *op. cit.*, p. 76.

30 Glendinning, p. 114. See Ch. 5, p. 116.

31 Andrew Boyle, *op. cit.*, pp. 154–5.

32 Page, Leitch, et al, *op. cit.*, pp. 96–7.

33 Goronwy Rees, *A Chapter of Accidents* (Chatto & Windus, 1972), p. 208.

34 Goronwy Rees, interview with John Morgan, ATV, 5 September 1977.

35 Andrew Boyle, *op. cit.*, p. 156.

36 Glendinning, p. 151.

37 There is factual evidence of this feeling amongst the troops after Dunkirk in Angus Calder's book. He quotes Basil Dean, director of ENSA, who witnessed 'dismayed men, savagely wounded in their pride'. Calder, *op. cit.*, p. 109.

38 W. H. Auden, '1 September 1939'.

39 Graham Greene, *The Ministry of Fear*, p. 128.

40 Rebecca West, *The Meaning of Treason* (Macmillan, 1949), pp. 127–8, 174.

41 Kelway's character was criticised as being unconvincing by Alan Cameron (Glendinning, p. 151), by Edward Sackville-West (*Inclinations*, p. 97), by Anthony Burgess (*The Novel Now*, p. 120), by P. H. Newby (*The Novel: 1945–1950* [Longman, 1951], p. 20) and others.

42 Harriet Blodgett, in *Patterns of Reality: Elizabeth Bowen's Novels* (Mouton, The Hague, 1975), pp. 160–3, suggests that 'Holme Dene' stands for 'Home of the Dane'.

43 A point made by A. E. Austin in *Elizabeth Bowen* (Twayne Publishers, New York, 1971), p. 70.

44 Henry Green, *Caught* (1943; Viking Press, New York, 1952), p. 115.

45 BC, p. 314. One of her mother's brothers went down in the *Titanic*.

46 Preface to *The Demon Lover* (1945). MT.

Chapter 8 The Bend Back

'What fails in the air . . .': 'The Bend Back', *Cornhill*, No CLXV (Summer 1951), 221–7, MT.

  1 *Anthony Trollope, A New Judgement* (OUP, 1946), CI, pp. 241–2. MT.

2 *WL*, p. 48.
3 *LG*, p. 193.
4 *ET*, p. 86.
5 'Books in General', *New Statesman*, XLII (20 October 1951), 438–9.
6 'The Bend Back.'
7 Glendinning, p. 200.
8 *Ibid*, p. 218.
9 Spencer Curtis Brown, Foreword, *PC*, p. xxxviii, suggests Waugh as an influence on this change of style.
10 *WL*, p. 221.
11 *LG*, p. 19.
12 *ET*, pp. 108–9.
13 'The Demon Lover', *DL*.
14 Glendinning, p. 197.
15 *A Time in Rome* (1960), p. 6.
16 'The Mulberry Tree', in *The Old School: Essays by Divers Hands*, ed. Graham Greene (Cape, 1934), pp. 45–9. *CI* (dated 1935), p. 196. *MT*.
17 *PC*, p. 57.
18 *PC*, p. 46.
19 *Ibid*, p. 57.
20 'The Mulberry Tree', *CI*, p. 186.
21 Marcel Proust, *À La Recherche du Temps Perdu*, trs. Andreas Mayor, *Time Regained* (Chatto & Windus, 1970), Vol. XII, p. 265.
22 *Ibid*, p. 228.
23 'The Art of Bergotte', *Marcel Proust*, ed. Peter Quennell (Weidenfeld, 1971). *PC*, p. 81.
24 *PC*, p. 82.
25 *PC*, p. 99.
26 Roger Shattuck, *Proust's Binoculars* (Chatto & Windus, 1964), p. 122.
27 'The Last Night in the Old Home', *CJ*.
28 'Her Table Spread', *CJ*.

Chapter 9 A Form of Experience

'A novel which survives . . .': 'Truth and Fiction', 1956, *A*, p. 142.
1 E.g.: Introduction, *Frost in May*, by Antonia White (1948;

reprinted in the Virago edition, 1978); 'Flaubert Translated', *Spectator*, CLXVII (15 August 1941), 161; *Why Do I Write? An Exchange of Views Between Elizabeth Bowen, Graham Greene, and V. S. Pritchett* (Percival Marshall, 1948). All in *MT*.

2 *Holiday*, XIX (April 1956), 90–1, 129, 131–2.

3 *Vogue*, XCCVIII (July 1956), 54–5.

4 *House and Garden*, CXXIII (January 1963), 70–1.

5 'Questionnaire: The Cost of Letters', ed. Cyril Connolly, *Horizon*, XIV (August 1946), 141–2.

6 'Elizabeth Bowen at Her Typewriter', *Listener*, XLII (24 November 1949), 890.

7 'Do Women Think Like Men?', *Listener*, XXVI (30 October 1941), 593–4.

8 'Do Conventions Matter?', *Listener*, XXVI (18 December 1941), 823–4.

9 Glendinning, p. 118. Published in *Night and Day*, ed. C. Hawtree (Chatto & Windus, 1985).

10 'Out of a Book', *Orion*, III (August 1946), 10–14. *CI*, p. 269. *MT*.

11 'The Evolution of a Novelist', *TLS*, XLVII (17 July 1948), 395. Review of *Myself When Young* by Henry Handel Richardson. *CI*, p. 102.

12 'Grace', *New Statesman*, XVI (17 September 1938), 424, 426. Review of *Unforgotten Years* by Logan Pearsall Smith. *CI*, p. 130.

13 'Out of a Book', *CI*, p. 267.

14 Graham Greene, 'The Lost Childhood', 1947, *Collected Essays* (Bodley Head, 1969), pp. 17–18.

15 V. S. Naipaul, *The Return of Eva Peron* (Deutsch, 1980), pp. 207–8.

16 'The Power in the Cave', *Listener*, XXXVII (20 March 1947), 431–48. *A* (entitled 'She'), pp. 107–13. *MT*.

17 *PC*, pp. 23–4.

18 'Sources of Influence', *A*, p. 208.

19 *PC*, pp. 62, 34.

20 *PC*, p. 39.

21 'Manners', *New Statesman*, XIV (6 November 1937), 727–8. Review of *Can I Help You?* by Viola Tree. *CI*, p. 69.

22 EB wrote Prefaces to *Encounters* (date of Preface: April 1949) *MT*, to *Ann Lee's* (1951), to *The Last September* (1952) *MT*, and to *Stories by Elizabeth Bowen* (1959) *MT*, all collected in

A. The Preface to the 1946 American edition of *The Demon Lover* is in *CI* and *MT*. There is also a Preface to the 1965 collection of stories, *A Day in the Dark*.

23 Preface to *Encounters* (1949), *A*, p. 87. *MT*.

24 Preface to *Ann Lee's* (1951), *A*, p. 93.

25 *Why Do I Write?* pp. 37, 31, 56, 23.

26 'The Writer's Peculiar World', *NYTBR*, LV, pt 2 (24 September 1950), 3, 40. *A*, (entitled 'Disloyalties'), pp. 195–8. *MT*.

27 'Notes on Writing a Novel', *Orion*, II (Autumn 1945), 18–29. *CI*, pp. 249–63. *PC*, pp. 167–93. *MT*.

28 'Flaubert Translated', *Spectator*, CLXVII (15 August 1941), 161 *MT*; Preface to *The Flaubert Omnibus* (1947), *CI*, pp. 32–3.

29 'Truth and Fiction', *Listener*, LVI (25 October, 1 November, 8 November 1956), 651–2; 704–6; 751–2. 1: 'Story, Theme and Situation'; 2: 'People: the Creation of Character'; 3: 'Time, Period – Reality'. Originally a series of BBC radio talks. *A*, p. 139.

30 'Elizabeth Bowen Talks about Writing', *Mademoiselle*, LI (July 1960), 89, 29, 21. *A* (entitled 'Advice'), pp. 210–15.

31 'Notes on Writing a Novel', *CI*, p. 250. *MT*.

32 Henry James, Preface to *The Portrait of a Lady* (1881), *The Art of the Novel*, p. 45.

33 'Truth and Fiction', *A*, pp. 115–16.

34 *Ibid*, p. 122.

35 'The Search for a Story to Tell', *NYTBR*, LVII (14 December 1952), I. *A*, (entitled 'The Roving Eye'), p. 193. *MT*.

36 'The Roving Eye, *A*, p. 194.

37 Introduction to *Critics Who Have Influenced Taste*, ed. A. P. Ryan (Geoffrey Bles, 1965), p. ix.

38 Glendinning, p. 117.

39 E.g.: Review of *The Weather in the Streets* by Rosamond Lehmann, *New Statesman*, XII (11 July 1936), 54 ('The most remarkable, the most natural of her qualities is the power to give emotion its full value and play'). *MT*. 'Books in General', Review of *Mr Beluncle* by V. S. Pritchett, *New Statesman*, XLII (20 October 1951), 438–9 ('Mr Pritchett gives us a preposterous, major man').

40 'Advance in Formation', *Spectator*, CLXVI (17 January 1941), 65. *MT*. Review of *New Writing in Europe*, ed. John Lehmann.

41 'Abinger Harvest', *Spectator*, CLVI (20 March 1936), 521.

Review of *Abinger Harvest* by E. M. Forster. *CI*, (entitled 'E. M. Forster I'), p. 121.

42 'An Introduction', in *Uncle Silas: A Tale of Bartram-Haugh* by J. S. Le Fanu (Cresset Press, 1947), pp. 7–23. *CI*, pp. 3–17. *MT*.

43 Introduction to *North and South* by Mrs Gaskell (John Lehmann, 1951), pp. v–viii. *A*, p. 52.

44 Introduction to *Frost in May* (1948; Virago, 1978). *MT*.

45 'Between the Acts', *New Statesman*, XXII (19 July 1941), 63. *CI* (entitled 'Virginia Woolf'), p. 75.

46 'The Achievement of Virginia Woolf', *NYTBR*, LIV, Pt 1 (26 June 1949), 1, 21. Review of *Virginia Woolf* by Bernard Blackstone. *CI*, p. 81.

47 'Mr Forster', *New Statesman*, XV (2 April 1938), 572, 574. Review of *The Writings of E. M. Forster* by Rose Macaulay. *CI*, p. 125.

48 'Afterword' to *Orlando* by Virginia Woolf (New York, Signet Classics, 1960), pp. 216–22. *A* (entitled '*Orlando*'), pp. 40–6. *MT*.

49 'D. H. Lawrence: Reappraising His Literary Influence', *NYTBR*, LII (9 February 1947), 4. Review of *The Portable D. H. Lawrence*, ed. Diana Trilling. *CI*, p. 158.

50 'Post-Victorian', *Cornhill*, CLXI (October 1944), 92–6. Review of *Elders and Betters* by Ivy Compton-Burnett. *CI* (entitled 'Ivy Compton-Burnett', II), p. 86. *MT*.

51 *Anthony Trollope: A New Judgement* (OUP, 1946). First broadcast June 1945. *CI*, p. 242. *MT*.

52 'A Living Writer', *Cornhill*, CLXIX (Winter 1956–7), 120–34. Expanded as Introduction to *Stories* by Katherine Mansfield (New York, Knopf, 1956), pp. v–xxiv, and to *Thirty-Four Short Stories* (Collins, 1957). *A* (entitled 'Stories by Katherine Mansfield'), pp. 53–74. *MT*.

53 Preface to *Encounters*. *A*, p. 84. *MT*.

54 *A*, p. 60.

55 *English Novelists* (Collins, 1945), pp. 25–26. Cf. 'Jane Austen: Artist on Ivory', *Saturday Review of Literature*, XIV (15 August 1936), 3–4, 13–14.

56 *English Novelists*, pp. 28, 31, 48, 46.

57 'Contemporary', *New Statesman*, XXIII (23 May 1942), 340. Review of *In My Good Books* by V. S. Pritchett; 'Sources of Influence', *A*, p. 209. *MT*.

58 'Contemporary'.

59 Foreword to *The Blaze of Noon* by Rayner Heppenstall (New York, 1939), pp. v–xi. *CI*, p. 55.

60 'Joseph Conrad', *Spectator*, CLVI (24 April 1936), 758. Review of *Some Aspects of the Art of the Novel* by Edward Crankshaw. *CI*, p. 152.

61 'Books in General', *New Statesman*, XLII (20 October 1951), 433–9.

62 *Critics Who Have Influenced Taste*, p. x.

63 'The Cult of Nostalgia', *Listener*, XLVI (9 August 1951), 225–6.

64 'What We Need in Writing', *Spectator*, CLVII (20 November 1936), 901–2.

65 Raymond Williams, 'Realism and the Contemporary Novel', *Partisan Review*, XXVI (Spring 1959), 200–13.

66 Geoffrey Wagner, 'Elizabeth Bowen and the Artificial Novel', *Essays in Criticism*, XIII (April 1963), 155–63; Herbert Gold, 'Random Dreams, True and False', *Hudson Review*, VIII (Spring 1955), 150–5. Review of *A World of Love*; Frederick R. Karl, *A Reader's Guide to the Contemporary English Novel* (Thames and Hudson, 1963), Ch. VI, p. 129.

67 John McCormick, *Catastrophe and Imagination* (Longman, 1952), p. 93.

68 Anthony Burgess, 'Treasures and Fetters', *Spectator*, CCXII (21 February 1964), 254. See also Anthony Burgess, *The Novel Now: A Guide to Contemporary Fiction* (Faber, 1967), p. 120.

69 Elizabeth Hardwick, 'Elizabeth Bowen's Fiction', *Partisan Review*, XVI (November 1949), 1114–21.

70 Angus Wilson, 'Evil in the English Novel', *Listener*, XLIV (24 August 1950), 279–80.

71 P. H. Newby, *The Novel: 1945–1950* (Longman, 1951), p. 19; R. A. Scott-James, *Fifty Years of English Literature: 1900–1950* (Longman, 1951), p. 182; Jocelyn Brooke, *Elizabeth Bowen* (Longman, 1952) (Supplement to *British Book News*, No. 28), p. 30.

72 Burgess, *The Novel Now*, pp. 126–7.

73 A. S. Byatt, Introduction to *The House in Paris* (Penguin, 1976), p. 8.

74 Elizabeth Hardwick, *op. cit.*

75 Angela G. Dorenkamp, '"Fall or Leap": Bowen's *The Heat of the Day*', *Critique* (Spring 1968), X, No. 3, 13–21.

76 Glendinning, p. 1.

77 James Hall, *The Lunatic Giant in the Drawing Room: The*

British and American Novel Since 1930 (Bloomington and London, Indiana UP, 1968), Ch. II; Barbara Seward, 'Elizabeth Bowen's World of Impoverished Love', *College English*, XVIII No. 1 (October 1956), 30–7; Geoffrey Wagner, *op. cit.*

78 But see Alison Heinemann, 'The Indoor Landscape in Elizabeth Bowen's *The Death of the Heart*', *Critique*, X, No. 3 (1968), 5–12; Dorenkamp, *op. cit.*

79 Walter Allen, Review of *The Heat of the Day*, *New Statesman* (26 February 1949), 208–9; *Tradition and Dream: The English and American Novel from the Twenties to our Time* (Phoenix House, 1964); Raymond Mortimer, Review of *The Death of the Heart*, *New Statesman*, XVI (8 October 1939), 534; John Strachey, 'The Golden Age of English Detection', *Saturday Review of Literature*, XIX (7 January 1939), 12–14; L. P. Hartley, Review of *A World of Love*, *Spectator*, CXCIV (11 March 1965), 293–94.

80 Graham Greene, 'The Dark Backward : A Footnote', 1935, *Collected Essays* (Bodley Head, 1969), pp. 71–2.

81 V. S. Pritchett, 'The Future of Fiction', *New Writing and Daylight*, ed. John Lehmann, VII, 1946, 77.

82 Sean O'Faolain, *The Vanishing Hero: Studies in Novelists of the Twenties* (Eyre & Spottiswoode, 1956), pp. 169–70.

BIBLIOGRAPHY AND ABBREVIATIONS

Works by Elizabeth Bowen

E: *Encounters* (Sidgwick and Jackson, 1923).
   Contents: Breakfast; Daffodils; The Return; The Confidante; Requiescat; All Saints; The New House; Lunch; The Lover; Mrs Windermere; The Shadowy Third; The Evil that Men Do; Sunday Evening; Coming Home.
AL: *Ann Lee's and Other Stories* (Sidgwick and Jackson, 1926).
   Contents: Ann Lee's; The Parrot; The Visitor; The Contessina; Human Habitation; The Secession: Making Arrangements; The Storm; Charity; The Back Drawing-Room; Recent Photograph.
H: *The Hotel* (Constable, 1927; Uniform Edition: Cape, 1950).
JC: *Joining Charles and Other Stories* (Constable, 1929; Cape, 1952).
   Contents: Joining Charles; The Jungle; Shoes; An International Episode; The Dancing-Mistress; Aunt Tatty; Dead Mabelle; The Working Party; Foothold; The Cassowary; Telling; Mrs Moysey.
LS: *The Last September* (Constable, 1929; Cape, 1948).
FR: *Friends and Relations* (Constable, 1931; Cape, 1951).
TN: *To the North* (Victor Gollancz, 1932; Cape, 1950).
CJ: *The Cat Jumps and Other Stories* (Victor Gollancz, 1934; Cape, 1949).
   Contents: The Tommy Crans; The Good Girl; The Cat Jumps; The Last Night in the Old Home; The Disinherited; Maria; Her Table Spread; The Little Girl's Room; Firelight in the Flat; The Man of the Family; The Needlecase; The Apple.
HP: *The House in Paris* (Victor Gollancz, 1935; Cape, 1949).
DH: *The Death of the Heart* (Victor Gollancz, 1938; Cape, 1948).

245

LAR: *Look at All Those Roses* (Victor Gollancz, 1941; Cape, 1951).

Contents: Reduced; Tears, Idle Tears; A Walk in the Woods; A Love Story; Look at All Those Roses; Attractive Modern Homes; The Easter Egg Party; Love; No. 16; A Queer Heart; The Girl with the Stoop; Unwelcome Idea; Oh, Madam . . .; Summer Night.

BC: *Bowen's Court* (Longman, Green, 1942).

EN: *English Novelists* (Collins, 1942).

SW: *Seven Winters: Memoirs of a Dublin Childhood* (Dublin, Cuala Press, 1942; Longman, Green, 1943).

DL: *The Demon Lover and Other Stories* (Cape, 1945, 1952). Published as *Ivy Gripped the Steps* (New York, Knopf, 1946).

Contents: In the Square; Sunday Afternoon; The Inherited Clock; The Cheery Soul; Songs My Father Sang Me; The Demon Lover; Careless Talk, The Happy Autumn Fields; Ivy Gripped the Steps; Pink May; Green Holly; Mysterious Kôr. Postscript by the Author.

Anthony Trollope: A New Judgement (Oxford University Press, 1946).

Selected Stories (Maurice Fridberg, 1946).

Why Do I Write? An Exchange of Views Between Elizabeth Bowen, Graham Greene, and V. S. Pritchett (Percival Marshall, 1948).

HD: *The Heat of the Day* (Cape, 1949, 1954).

CI: *Collected Impressions* (Longman, Green, 1950).

Early Stories (New York, Knopf, 1951).

The Shelbourne: A Centre in Dublin Life for More than a Century (George Harrap, 1951).

WL: *A World of Love* (Cape, 1955).

Stories by Elizabeth Bowen (New York, Knopf, 1959).

A Time in Rome (Longman, Green, 1960).

A: *Afterthought: Pieces about Writing* (Longman, Green, 1962). Published as *Seven Winters: Memories of a Dublin Childhood and Afterthoughts: Pieces on Writing* (New York, Knopf, 1962).

LG: *The Little Girls* (Cape, 1964).

DD: *A Day in the Dark and Other Stories* (Cape, 1965).

Contents: Preface; A Day in the Dark; The Disinherited; Breakfast; Reduced; Her Table Spread; I Hear You Say So; Summer Night; Gone Away; Mysterious Kôr; A Love Story; The Dancing-Mistress; Look At All Those Roses; Hand in Glove; The Demon

Lover; No. 16; The Cheery Soul; The Happy Autumn Fields; The Dolt's Tale; The Cat Jumps; Ivy Gripped The Steps.

The Good Tiger (New York, Knopf, 1965).

ET: *Eva Trout or Changing Scenes* (Cape, 1969).

PC: *Pictures and Conversations* (Allen Lane, 1975). Edited and with a foreword by Spencer Curtis Brown.

Elizabeth Bowen's Irish Stories (Dublin, Poolbeg Press, 1978). With an introduction by Victoria Glendinning.

Collected Stories (Cape, 1981). With an introduction by Angus Wilson.

MT: *The Mulberry Tree: Writings of Elizabeth Bowen*, edited by Hermione Lee (Virago and Harcourt Brace Jovanovich, 1986).

Prefaces, Introductions, Reviews, Broadcasts, Essays

'Abinger Harvest', *Spectator*, CLVI (20 March 1936), 521. Review of *Abinger Harvest* by E. M. Forster. *CI* (entitled 'E. M. Forster I'), pp. 119–22.

'Advance in Formation', *Spectator*, CLXVI (17 January 1941), 65. Review of *New Writing in Europe*, ed. John Lehmann.

Ann Lee's, Preface to. In *Early Stories* (Knopf, 1951). *A*, pp. 89–94.

'The Art of Bergotte' in *Marcel Proust*, ed. Peter Quennell (Weidenfeld & Nicolson, 1971). *PC*, pp. 77–110.

'Autobiography as an Art', *Saturday Review of Literature*, XXXIV (17 March 1951), 9–10. *A* (entitled 'Autobiography'), pp. 199–204.

'The Bend Back', *Cornhill*, CLXV (Summer 1951), 221–7.

'Between the Acts', *New Statesman*, XXII (19 July 1941), 63–4. Review of *Between the Acts* by Virginia Woolf. *CI* (Entitled 'Virginia Woolf I'), pp. 71–5.

'The Big House', *The Bell*, I (October 1940), 71–7. *CI* (dated 1942), 195–200.

'Books in General', *New Statesman*, XLII (20 October 1951), 438–9). Review of *Mr Beluncle* by V. S. Pritchett.

'Coming to London', *London Magazine*, III, pt 1 (March 1956), 49–53. Reprinted in *Coming to London*, ed. John Lehmann (Phoenix House, 1957), pp. 74–81.

'Contemporary', *New Statesman*, XXIII (23 May 1942), 340. Review of *In My Good Books* by V. S. Pritchett.

Critics Who Have Influenced Taste, Introduction to. Ed. A. P. Ryan (Geoffrey Bles, 1965).

'The Cult of Nostalgia', *Listener*, XLVI (9 August 1951), 225–6.

A Day in the Dark, Preface to (Cape, 1965).

The Demon Lover, Preface to (New York, Knopf, 1946) (volume entitled *Ivy Gripped the Steps*). Postscript in Cape Collected Edition (1952).

'D. H. Lawrence: Reappraising His Literary Influence', *NYTBR*, LII (9 February 1947), 4. Review of *The Portable D. H. Lawrence*, ed. Diana Trilling. *CI* (entitled 'D. H. Lawrence'), pp. 156–9.

Doctor Thorne by Anthony Trollope, Introduction to (Boston, Houghton Mifflin, 1959), pp. v–xxv. *A*, pp. 13–39.

'Elizabeth Bowen Talks About Writing', *Mademoiselle*, LI (July 1960), 89, 6, 20, 21. *A* (entitled 'Advice'), 210–15.

Encounters, Preface to. In second English edition (Sidgwick & Jackson, 1949), pp. 82–94. Dated 1949.

'The Evolution of a Novelist', *TLS*, XLVII (17 July 1948), 395. Review of *Myself When Young* by Henry Handel Richardson. *CI* (entitled 'Myself When Young'), pp. 100–5.

'Exclusion', *A*, pp. 216–20.

The Faber Book of Modern Stories, Preface to. 'The Short Story' (Faber, 1937), pp. 7–21. *CI* (entitled 'The Faber Book of Modern Short Stories'), pp. 38–46.

The Flaubert Omnibus, Preface to (1947). *CI*, pp. 18–37.

'Flaubert Translated', *Spectator*, CLXVII (15 August 1941), 161.

'Mr Forster', *New Statesman*, XV (2 April 1938), 572, 574. Review of *The Writings of E. M. Forster* by Rose Macaulay. *CI* (entitled 'E. M. Forster II'), pp. 122–6.

Frost in May by Antonia White, Preface to (Eyre & Spottiswoode, 1957), pp. v–x. Reprinted in Virago edition (1978). Dated 1948.

'The Golden Apples', *A*, pp. 152–4. Review of *The Golden Apples* by Eudora Welty.

'Grace', *New Statesman*, XVI (17 September 1938), 424, 426. Review of *Unforgotten Years* by Logan Pearsall Smith, *CI*, pp. 129–31.

The House by the Churchyard by Sheridan Le Fanu. Introduction to (Anthony Blond, 1968), pp. vii–xi.

'Jane Austen: Artist on Ivory', *Saturday Review of Literature*, XIV (15 August 1936), 3–4, 13–14. Reprinted in *The English Novelists: A Survey of the Novel by Twenty Contemporary*

Novelists, ed. Derek Verschoyle (Chatto & Windus, 1936), pp. 97–110.

'Joseph Conrad', *Spectator*, CLVI (24 April 1936), 758. Review of *Some Aspects of the Novel* by Edward Crankshaw. *CI* (entitled 'Conrad'), pp. 151–2.

The Last September, Preface to. In Second American edition (New York, Knopf, 1952). *A*, pp. 95–100.

'A Living Writer', *Cornhill*, CLXIX (Winter 1956–7), 120–34. Expanded as Introduction to *Stories* by Katherine Mansfield (New York, Knopf, 1956) pp. v–xxiv, and *Thirty-Four Short Stories* (Collins, 1957), pp. 9–26. *A* (entitled 'Stories by Katherine Mansfield'), pp. 53–74.

'London 1940', *CI*, pp. 217–20.

'Manners', *New Statesman*, XIV (6 November 1937), 727–8. Review of *Can I Help You?* by Viola Tree. *CI*, pp. 67–70.

'The Modern Novel and the Theme of Love', *New Republic*, CXXVIII (11 May 1953), 18–19. Review of *The Echoing Grove* by Rosamond Lehmann. *A* (entitled 'The Echoing Grove') pp. 155–8.

'The Moores', *New Statesman*, XVIII (25 November 1939), 759–60. *CI*, pp. 160–3.

'The Mulberry Tree' in *The Old School: Essays by Divers Hands* ed. Graham Greene (Cape, 1934), pp. 45–59. *CI*, pp. 185–94. Dated 1935.

Night and Day, edited by C. Hawtree, with an introduction by Graham Greene (Chatto & Windus, 1985). Includes Bowen's theatre reviews.

North and South by Elizabeth Gaskell, Introduction (John Lehmann, 1951), pp. v–viii. *A*, pp. 47–52.

'One Ireland', *New Statesman*, XIII (26 June 1937), 1050. *CI*, pp. 170–2.

Orlando by Virginia Woolf, Afterword to (New York, Signet Classics, 1960), pp. 216–22. *A* (entitled 'Orlando'), pp. 40–6.

'Out of a Book', *Orion*, III (Autumn 1946), 10–14. *CI*, pp. 264–9.

'Pictures and Conversations', *PC*, pp. 1–64.

'Portrait of a City', *New Statesman*, XII (31 October 1936), 516. *CI* (entitled 'Dublin II'), pp. 177–80.

'Post-Victorian', *Cornhill*, CLXI (October 1944), 92–6. Review of *Elders and Betters* by Ivy Compton-Burnett. *CI* (entitled 'Ivy Compton-Burnett II'), pp. 85–91.

'The Power in the Cave', *Listener*, XXVII (20 March 1947), 431–2. *A* (entitled '*She*'), pp. 107–13.

Pride and Prejudice by Jane Austen, Introduction to (Williams & Norgate, 1948), pp. vii–xv. Reprinted as 'Elizabeth Bowen on Jane Austen' in *Novelists on Novelists*, ed. Louis Kronenberger (New York, Doubleday, 1963), pp. 9–18.

'Ride Through the Deep South', *Holiday,* XXVII (February 1960), 72–3, 105, 107, 110–11, 113. *A* (entitled 'A Ride South'), 165–90.

'The Search for a Story to Tell', *NYTBR*, LVII (14 December 1952), 1. *A* (entitled 'The Roving Eye'), pp. 191–5.

The Second Ghost Book, Introduction to. Ed. Cynthia Asquith (James Barrie, 1952), vii–x. *A*, pp. 101–6.

'Sources of Influence', *A*, pp. 205–9.

Stories by Elizabeth Bowen, Preface to (New York, Knopf, 1959). *A*, pp. 75–81.

'Truth and Fiction', *Listener*, LVI (25 October, 1 November, 8 November 1956), 651–2; 704–6; 751–2. 1: 'Story, Theme and Situation'; 2: 'People: The Creation of Character'; 3: 'Time, Period – Reality'. Originally a series of BBC Radio talks. *A*, pp. 114–46.

'Two Cities', *New Statesman*, XII (25 July 1936), 128. *CI* (entitled 'Dublin I'), pp. 175–7.

Uncle Silas: A Tale of Bartram-Haugh by Sheridan Le Fanu, Introduction to (Cresset Press, 1947), pp. 7–23. *CI*, pp. 3–17.

'Virginia Woolf, The Achievement of', *NYTBR*, LIV, pt 1 (26 June 1949), 21. Review of *Virginia Woolf* by Bernard Blackstone. *CI*, pp. 78–82.

'What We Need in Writing', *Spectator*, CLVII (20 November 1936), 901–2.

'The Writer's Peculiar World', *NYTBR*, LV, pt 2 (24 September 1950) 3, 40. *A* (entitled 'Disloyalties'), pp. 195–8.

Other works consulted

Other sources cited in the Notes are given in full in the first reference in each relevant chapter, and thereafter referred to by short title or author's name.

Allen, Walter, review of *The Heat of the Day*, *New Statesman* (26

February 1949), pp. 208–9. *Tradition and Dream: The English and American Novel from the Twenties to Our Time* (London, Phoenix House, 1964).

Austin, A. E., *Elizabeth Bowen*, Twayne's English Authors Series (New York, Twayne Publishers, 1971).

Bayley, John, *The Short Story: Henry James to Elizabeth Bowen* (Sussex, Harvester Press, 1988).

Beachcroft, T. O., *The Modest Art: A Survey of the Short Story in English* (Oxford, Oxford University Press, 1968).

Beckett, J. C., *The Anglo-Irish Tradition* (London, Faber, 1976).

Beckett, J. C., *The Making of Modern Ireland, 1603–1923* (London, Faber, 1966).

Bennett, Andrew and Royle, Nicholas, *Elizabeth Bowen and the Dissolution of the Novel: Still Lives* (Basingstoke and London, Macmillan, 1994).

Bennett, Andrew and Royle, Nicholas, ed., *The Bowen Newsletter*, Winter 1992 – . Departments of English, Universities of Bristol and Stirling.

Blodgett, Harriet, *Patterns of Reality: Elizabeth Bowen's Novels* (Mouton, Le Hague, 1975).

Bloom, Harold, ed., *Elizabeth Bowen: Modern Critical Views* (New York, Chelsea House Publishers, 1987).

Brooke, Jocelyn, *Elizabeth Bowen* (Longman, 1952). (Supplement to *British Book News*, No. 28.)

Burgess, Anthony, *99 Novels: The Best in English since 1969* (London, Allison & Busby, 1984).

Burgess, Anthony, *The Novel Now: A Guide to Contemporary Fiction* (New York and London, Faber, 1967).

Burgess, Anthony, 'Treasures and Fetters', *Spectator*, CCXII (21 February 1964), p. 254.

Butler, Hubert, *Escape from the Anthill* (Mullingar, Lilliput Press, 1985).

Byatt, A. S., Introduction to *The House in Paris* (Harmondsworth, Penguin, 1976), pp. 7–16.

Chessman, Harriet, 'Women and Language in the Fiction of Elizabeth Bowen', *Twentieth Century Literature*, 29 (Spring 1983), pp. 69–85. In Bloom, *Elizabeth Bowen*.

Coughlan, Patricia, 'Women and Desire in the Work of Elizabeth Bowen', in Walshe, *Sex, Nation and Dissent*, pp. 103–34.

Dangerfield, George, *The Damnable Question: A Study in Anglo-Irish Relations* (London, Constable, 1977).

Deane, Seamus, *A Short History of Irish Literature* (London, Hutchinson, 1986).

Deane, Seamus, ed., *The Field Day Anthology of Irish Writing* (Derry, Field Day Publications, 1991).

Donovan, Katie, *Irish Women Writers* (Dublin, Raven Arts, 1988).

Dorenkamp, A. G., ' "Fall or Leap": Elizabeth Bowen's *The Heat of the Day*', *Critique*, X, No. 3 (1968), 13–21.

Fisk, Robert, *In Time of War: Ireland, Ulster and the Price of Neutrality* (Philadelphia, University of Pennsylvania Press, 1983).

Fraser, G. K., *The Modern Writer and His World* (Verschoyle, 1953; London, Deutsch, 1964).

Frierson, W. C., *The English Novel in Transition 1885–1940* (Oklahoma, Oklahoma University Press, 1942).

Gauthier, Dominique, *L'Image du Reel dans les Romans d'Elizabeth Bowen* (Paris, Didier Erudidian, 1985).

Gill, Richard, *Happy Rural Seat: The English Country House and the Literary Imagination* (New Haven, Yale University Press, 1972).

Glendinning, Victoria, *Elizabeth Bowen: Portrait of a Writer* (London, Weidenfeld & Nicolson, 1977; Harmondsworth, Penguin, 1985).

Gold, Herbert, 'Random Dreams, True and False', *Hudson Review*, VIII (Spring 1955), 150–5.

Greene, Graham, 'The Dark Backward: A Footnote', 1935, *Collected Essays* (London, Bodley Head, 1969), pp. 71–2.

Greene, Graham, Review of *The Death of the Heart*, *Spectator*, CLXI (7 October 1936), 578.

Hall, James, *The Lunatic Giant in the Drawing Room: The British and American Novel Since 1930* (Bloomington and London, Indiana University Press, 1968), Ch. 2.

Hardwick, Elizabeth, 'Elizabeth Bowen's Fiction', *Partisan Review*, XVI (November 1949), 1114–2.

Hartley, L. P., Review of *A World of Love*, *Spectator*, CXCIV (11 March 1965), 293–4.

Heath, William, *Elizabeth Bowen: An Introduction to Her Novels* (Madison, University of Wisconsin Press, 1961).

Heinemann, A., 'The Indoor Landscape in Elizabeth Bowen's *The Death of the Heart*, *Critique*, X, No. 3 (1968), 5–12.

Hildebidle, John, *Five Irish Writers* (Cambridge, Mass.: Harvard University Press, 1989).

Hoogland, Renée, *From Marginality to Ex-centricity: Feminist*

Critical Theories and the Case of Elizabeth Bowen (Amsterdam, doctoral thesis, 1991), published as *Elizabeth Bowen: A Reputation in Writing* (New York, New York University Press, 1994).

James, Henry, *The Art of the Novel: Critical Prefaces by Henry James*, introduced by R. P. Blackmur (1934, New York, Scribner's, 1965).

Jordan, Heather Bryant, *How Will the Heart Endure: Elizabeth Bowen and the Landscape of War* (Ann Arbor, University of Michigan Press, 1992).

Karl, Frederick R., *A Reader's Guide to the Contemporary English Novel* (London, Thames & Hudson, 1963), Ch. 6.

Kenney, Edwin, J., *Elizabeth Bowen*, Irish Writers Series (Bucknell, Bucknell University Press, 1975).

Kiberd, Declan, *Inventing Ireland: the Literature of the Modern Nation* (London, Cape, 1995, Vintage, 1996).

Laski, Marghanita, 'The 'X' Factor in Beholding', *Saturday Review*, XXXXV (28 July 1962), 42–3.

Lassner, Phyllis, *Elizabeth Bowen* (Basingstoke and London, Macmillan, 1990).

Lee, Hermione, 'The Placing of Loss: Elizabeth Bowen's *To the North*'. *Essays in Criticism*, XXVIII, No. 2 (April 1978), 129–42.

Lehmann, John, ed., *The Craft of Letters in England* (London, Cresset Press, 1956).

Lehmann, John, *I am My Brother* (London, Longman, 1960).

Liddell, Robert, *A Treatise on the Novel* (London, Cape, 1947).

Lindsay, Jack, *After the Thirties* (London, Lawrence and Wishart, 1956).

Lyons, F. S. L., 'The Twilight of the Big House', *Ariel*, ed. A. N. Jeffares, Vol I, No. 3 (July 1970), 110–22.

McCormack, W. J., *Sheridan Lefanu and Victorian Ireland* (Oxford, Clarendon Press, 1980).

McCormack, W. J., *Ascendancy and Tradition in Anglo-Irish Literary History from 1789 to 1939* (Oxford, Clarendon Press, 1985).

McCormack, W. J., *Dissolute Characters: Irish Literary History Through Balzac, Sheridan Le Fanu, Yeats and Bowen* (Manchester, Manchester University Press, 1993).

McCormick, John, *Catastrophe and Imagination* (London, Longman, 1952), p. 93.

Manning, Olivia, Review of *The Heat of the Day*, *Spectator*, CLXXXII (25 February 1949), 206–7.

Mortimer, Raymond, Review of *The Death of the Heart*, *New Statesman*, XVI (8 October 1939), 534.

Newby, P. H., *The Novel: 1945–1950* (London, Longman, 1951).

O'Faolain, Sean, *The Short Story* (London, Collins, 1948).

O'Faolain, Sean, *The Vanishing Hero: Studies in Novelists of the Twenties* (London, Eyre & Spottiswoode, 1956).

O'Toole, Bridget, 'Three Writers of the Big House: Elizabeth Bowen, Molly Keane and Jennifer Johnston', in *Across a Roaring Hill: The Protestant Imagination in Modern Ireland*, ed. Gerald Dawe and Edna Longley (Belfast, Blackstaff Press, 1985).

Plomer, William, Review of *The House in Paris*, *Spectator*, CLV (30 August 1935), 334.

Pritchett, V. S., 'The Future of Fiction', *New Writing and Daylight*, ed. John Lehmann, VII, 1946.

Quinn, Antoinette, 'Elizabeth Bowen's Irish Stories: 1939–1945', in *Studies in Anglo-Irish Fiction*, ed. Heinz Kosok (Bonn, Bouvier, 1982), 314–21.

Reed, Henry, *The Novel Since 1939* (London, Longman, Green, 1946).

Rowse, A. L., *The English Spirit: Essays in History and Literature* (London, Macmillan, 1946).

Sackville-West, E., *Inclinations* (London, Secker & Warburg, 1949).

Scott-James, R. A., *Fifty Years of English Literature: 1900–1950* (London, Longman, 1956).

Sellery, Jonathan, 'Elizabeth Bowen: A Check List [up to 1969]', *Bulletin of the New York Public Library*, LXXIV (April 1970), 219–74.

Sellery, Jonathan and Harris, William O., *Elizabeth Bowen: A Descriptive Bibliography* (Austin, The University of Texas at Austin Press, 1977, 1981).

Seward, Barbara, 'Elizabeth Bowen's World of Impoverished Love', *College English*, XVII, No. 1 (October 1956), 30–7.

Stevenson, Randall, *The British Novel Since the Thirties* (London, Batsford, 1986).

Strachey, John, 'The Golden Age of English Detection'. *Saturday Review of Literature*, XIX (7 January 1939), 12–14.

Swanson, Diana L., 'Subverting Closure: Compulsory Heterosexuality and Compulsory Endings in Middle-Class British Women's Novels', in *Sexual Practice, Textual Theory: Lesbian Cultural Criticism*, ed. Julia Penelope and Susan Wolfe (Oxford, Blackwell, 1993), pp. 150–63.

Tindall, W. Y., *Forces in Modern British Literature, 1885–1956* (New York, Knopf, 1947).

Wagner, Geoffrey, 'Elizabeth Bowen and the Artificial Novel', *Essays in Criticism*, XIII (April 1963), 155–63.

Walshe, Eibhear, ed., *Sex, Nation and Dissent in Irish Writing* (Cork, Cork University Press, 1997).

Walshe, Eibhear, 'State Secrets/Secret States: Elizabeth Bowen's *The Heat of the Day* and Kate O'Brien's *That Lady*', unpublished paper given at the 1997 Elizabeth Bowen Conference, University College, Cork.

West, Paul, *The Modern Novel* (London, Hutchinson, 1963).

White, Terence de Vere, *The Anglo-Irish* (London, Gollancz, 1972).

Williams, Raymond, 'Realism and the Contemporary Novel', *Partisan Review*, XXVI (Spring 1955), 200–13.

Wilson, Angus, 'Evil in the English Novel', *Listener*, XLIV (24 August 1950), 279–80.

Wyndham, Francis, 'Twenty-Five Years of the Novel', *The Craft of Letters in England*, ed. John Lehmann (London, Cresset Press, 1956).

ACKNOWLEDGEMENTS

I am grateful to the following for help and advice: John Barnard; Andrew Boyle; the late Hubert Butler; Carmen Callil; Patricia Craig; Maura Dooley; Roy Foster; Victoria Glendinning; Nicholas Grene; Ernest Hofer; Heather Bryant Jordan; Pat Kavanagh; Josephine Lee; Mark Lefanu; W. J. McCormack; Caroline Michel; Arzu Tahsin; Jenny Uglow; Stephen Wall; Eibhear Walshe.

Chapter 2 incorporates a revised version of an article published in *Essays in Criticism* in April 1978. I am grateful to the editors for allowing me to reproduce it.

The author and publisher would like to thank the following for permission to quote extracts from the works cited: Jonathan Cape Ltd and Alfred A. Knopf, Inc for the Uniform Edition of Elizabeth Bowen's works; Jonathan Cape Ltd for *Jonathan Cape, Publisher* by Michael Howard; Jonathan Cape Ltd and Peters, Fraser & Dunlop Ltd for *The People's War* by Angus Calder; Chatto & Windus Ltd for *The Working Novelist* by V. S. Pritchett; William Collins & Sons Ltd for *English Novelists* by Elizabeth Bowen (published in the 'Britain in Pictures' series); Constable & Co Ltd for *The Damnable Question* by George Dangerfield; Curtis Brown Ltd, London, Literary Executors of the Estate of Elizabeth Bowen and Alfred A. Knopf, Inc for *Afterthought, Bowen's Court, Collected Impressions, A Day in the Dark*, Introduction to *Frost in May* by Antonia White, *Pictures and Conversations, Seven Winters, The Shelbourne* and *A Time in Rome* by Elizabeth Bowen; André Deutsch Ltd for *Philby* by Bruce Page, David Leitch and Philip Knightley; Faber & Faber Ltd for *The Anglo-Irish Tradition* and *The Making of Modern Ireland* by J. C. Beckett, and for *The Novel Now* by Anthony Burgess; William Heinemann Ltd for *The Big House of Inver* by Somerville and Ross; David Higham Associates Ltd for *A Chapter of Accidents* by Goronwy Rees; Mrs Henry Yorke and The Hogarth Press Ltd for *Caught* by Henry Green; The Author's Literary Estate and The Hogarth Press Ltd for *The Sickle Side of the Moon* (edited by Nigel Nicolson) and *The Waves* by Virginia Woolf; Hutchinson Ltd for *The Climate of Treason* by Andrew Boyle; Longman Group Ltd for *Catastrophe and Imagination* by John McCormick; Macmillan & Co Ltd for *The Siren Years* by Charles Ritchie; Mercier Press Ltd for *The Short Story* by Sean O'Faolain; Oxford University Press for *Anthony Trollope: A New Judgement* by Elizabeth Bowen and for *Sheridan Le Fanu and Victorian Ireland* by W. J. McCormack; Peters, Fraser & Dunlop Ltd for *The Meaning of Treason* by Rebecca West; Laurence Pollinger Ltd and Viking-Penguin Inc for *Collected Essays* and *The Ministry of Fear* by Graham Greene; Secker & Warburg Ltd for *Inclinations* by Edward Sackville-West; A. P. Watt Ltd for *The Irish* and *The Vanishing Hero* by Sean O'Faolain; George Weidenfeld & Nicholson Ltd for *Elizabeth Bowen: Portrait of a Writer*, by Victoria Glendinning.

INDEX